MILLER'S

COLLECTING
SCIENCE &
TECHNOLOGY

A
Geometricall
Extraction for all affected
to the Mathematickes.

With sundry strange conclusions both
by instrument and without and also by
Perspectiue glasses, to set forth the true
discription or exact plat of a Whole Region
plesant and full of delight in practis
Also, most profitable to all Surueighers, or
others that are desirous to make
any Inclosure.

With a treaty of Fortifications as well regularly as
Irregularly
by
Iohn Darker
1648

Jacob Cvinfor 1667 8/12 3

LEVINGTON THIS FIM. OF MARCY. MDCLVIII.

MILLER'S

COLLECTING
SCIENCE &
TECHNOLOGY

Lindsay Stirling
Consultant Editor: George Glastris

Miller's Collecting Science and Technology

Lindsay Stirling
Consultant Editor: George Glastris

First published in Great Britain in 2001 by Miller's,
an imprint of Octopus Publishing Group Ltd,
2–4 Heron Quays, London, E14 4JP

Miller's is a registered trademark of Octopus Publishing Group Ltd

Commissioning Editor **Anna Sanderson**
Executive Art Editor **Rhonda Fisher**
Project Editor **Emily Anderson**
Editor **Claire Musters**
Designer **John Round, Lovelock & Co.**
Illustrator **Amanda Patton**
Proofreader **Laura Hicks**
Indexer **Hilary Bird**
Production **Nancy Roberts**
Contributor **Phil Ellis**

The publishers will be grateful for any information that will assist them in
keeping future editions up to date. While every care has been taken in the
preparation of this book, neither the author and consultant editor nor the publisher
can accept any liability for any consequence arising from the
use thereof, or the information contained therein.

ISBN 1 84000 079 1

A CIP catalogue record for this book is available from the British Library

Set in Helvetica Neue and Granjon
Produced by Color Gallery Sdn Bhd, Malaysia
Printed and bound by Mladinska knjiga tiskarna d.d., Slovenia

Half title: A Heywood-Wakefield Perfektone brown wicker-bodied
cabinet phonograph, American, early 1920s
Full title: Book frontispiece

Contents

Introduction   6

Some Basic Principles   10

14   Timekeeping

22   Surveying

36   Navigation

44   Geography and Meteorology

54   Telescopes

60   Microscopes

70   Weights and Measures

78   Communication

92   Photography and Optical Toys

106   Mechanical Music

118   Calculating and Computing

126   Medicine

132   Everyday Technology

146   Fakes and Reproductions

147   Collectables of the Future

148   Care and Restoration

149   Display

Glossary   150

Further Reading   152

Useful Addresses   153

Index   155

Acknowledgments   160

Introduction

▲ **Mahogany and brass vacuum-pump outfit**
By Cary of London, *c.*1800. This outfit was used to demonstrate the physics of air and air pressure. After using the crank to evacuate the air from the glass vessels, the demonstrator could show that a coin and a feather fall at the same rate in a vacuum, or that a live bird needs air to breathe. The vessels rarely survive today. **£2,000–2,500/$3,000–4,000**

We live in an age dominated by science and technology. News programming includes updates on technical stocks and often has a section devoted to new scientific discoveries. Newsagents' shelves contain more magazines devoted to hi-tech gadgets than to news analysis.

Our fascination with science and technology is by no means a recent development. In the 19th century our ancestors read periodicals filled with glowing reports of famous inventors and scientists. Edison, inventor of the light bulb, and Marconi, inventor of radio telegraphy, were as well known then as Steve Jobs of Apple and Bill Gates of Microsoft are today. Any invention, no matter how far-fetched, was given the kind of coverage that a new technology system receives today. Expositions and World Fairs were started to introduce the public to the all the latest discoveries and gadgets. Middle-class families in London would have an evening out at the Royal Society to hear men such as Faraday lecture on subjects like electricity. Science was as much an amateur hobby as it was a specialist pursuit in those days.

As a result, many of the major breakthroughs of the 19th century were made by gentleman amateurs, who studied and experimented and then presented their findings to the world without expectation of fame or fortune. They happily shared their ideas with other scientists for the common advancement of knowledge. The public flocked to scientific lectures not just because it was fashionable to do so, but because they were thirsty for learning. The urban middle classes born of the Industrial Revolution had struggled their way up out of the poverty that had gripped most of the Western world for centuries. They owed their prosperity to science and had no intention of falling back.

At the same time, the world was expanding. Settlers and explorers were mapping the vast, unknown continents of America and Africa, and they needed accurate instruments to aid them in this. Science and technology were the tools of progress.

This book aims to explore our fascination with science and technology through the artefacts it has produced. It traces the course of our search for knowledge and finds roots going back to thousands of years before Christ. It explores how the inventions we take for granted today were arrived at, often over centuries, through the work of some of the best scientific minds of the times.

Scientific instruments and technical devices

A scientific instrument informs you of something – it may measure the height of a mountain, weigh a dose of medicine or magnify the organisms in a drop of water. It is a tool of study and research with many applications. A technical device, on the other hand, is a tool designed to perform a specific task. It cores apples, sews shirts or reproduces music incised on a wax cylinder.

Both types of instrument are discussed in this book. You will also find toys: novelties and gadgets that are not of great use, like those mentioned above, but which use scientific principles and are simply lots of fun.

Why collect science and technology?

There is an old saying to the effect that you cannot know yourself without knowing your past. The same holds true of science and technology. None of us can fully understand and appreciate today's advances without understanding the history behind them. However, you do not have to have an intimate knowledge of physics, chemistry or biology to perceive how radically our lives have been transformed by science.

Before the Industrial Revolution people's lives had continued more or less unchanged for hundreds of years. Samuel Pepys wrote his famous *Diary* in the 1660s. If he had been sent back to 1066, six centuries earlier, he wouldn't have had much trouble recognizing everyday objects and knowing how to get around. But if he had been taken forwards into 1966, just three centuries later, he wouldn't have believed it was the same world. In just six or seven generations it has utterly changed.

The artefacts of science and technology show us this extraordinary transformation in a way that no other area of collecting can. Take coin collecting, for example. A 21st-century coin, both structurally and functionally, differs hardly at all from one minted in the Roman Empire two thousand years earlier. Or consider paintings – another lively and popular field of collecting. Styles in art have changed a great deal since the Renaissance, but not everyone would agree that there's been an improvement. However, now try comparing your bedside lamp with a piece of cotton thread in a puddle of whale oil. Isn't it nice to be able to read your book clearly and easily without being overwhelmed by the smell of fish, and without the risk of setting your house on fire?

Once you have discovered some of the history behind the way we live today, your appreciation of the astonishing work that underpins almost every action we take will increase immeasurably. A simple cup of coffee will taste all the better once you've discovered the labour required to grind the beans by hand. The traffic report on the radio will become a thing of wonder when you realize what a godsend the first wireless messages were, transmitting warnings of ice to ships' captains at the turn of the century. You may even appreciate your dentist more when you realize what his or her predecessors had to do to your ancestors' teeth …

Where to look and how to buy

The umbrella of science and technology covers a very wide range of items, and interesting pieces can turn up anywhere. However, there are specialist dealers who handle certain items, such as optical instruments, and some auction houses have departments entirely devoted to science and technology. Specialist dealers tend not to have ordinary shops, or even to follow ordinary hours. They do most of their business with known clients or through antiques fairs and, increasingly, online. The best way to find such specialist dealers and auctions is through collectors' clubs and societies. Your local auctioneers or dealers may also be able to point you in the right direction.

Collectors' clubs are a good way to learn more about your subject and will also help you to make contacts within the field. Most clubs publish periodicals that carry advertisements from specialist dealers and auction houses. They also list events of interest and fairs in your area, and are an invaluable source of technical advice for repair and restoration. The clubs vary from small local groups to international bodies.

They often offer specialist books for sale, and nearly all of them hold regular meetings for members. Through them you'll get to meet other collectors, attend workshops, visit collections and attend specialist markets. It is one of the best ways to pursue collecting, and you'll meet people with a shared interest who are very friendly and welcoming to those entering the field for the first time.

Buying at auction

The difference between buying at auction and buying from a dealer is that at auction you will be in direct and open competition with other buyers. The big specialist auctions attract the most items, but of course they also attract the most collectors. However, attending an auction is an educational experience even if you don't buy anything the first few times you go. You will be able to see items you have only ever read about, and they will all be available for inspection at previews. Take advantage of these – you will be able to learn what to look for and how to judge quality if you pay close attention to what various pieces look like. There is also always a specialist on hand to answer questions and give advice. Specialist auctions turn into mini-club meetings too, which adds further interest to the experience.

Always buy the catalogue, even if you don't intend to bid for anything. Catalogues are expensive to produce so auction houses have to charge for them, but they are well worth having. Not only do they list every lot in a sale, so that you can pick out anything you are particularly interested in seeing, but it makes a valuable reference guide for the future. Don't throw a catalogue out after a sale – you will undoubtedly need it again one day to trace the provenance of a particular piece or to keep track of values. If you want to buy something but can't attend the sale, someone at the auction house will be happy to give you an objective condition report on the item that interests you and can also bid on your behalf.

If you're thinking of buying something at auction, bear in mind that the final decision on condition is yours alone. Most good auctioneers will state major faults in their catalogues, such as missing parts or serious damage. However, they cannot list every blemish, and you shouldn't expect them to guarantee condition. The items they sell are often what is known as "fresh to the market", which means that they have usually come from the general public and may not have been used for decades. But remember that a specialist is available to answer any questions, so you should take advantage of the service. You can always telephone before the sale, too, if you want more details.

Buying from dealers

Specialist dealers are a good source for buying items when there are no auctions going on or you can't attend one. It is always a good idea to make friends with at least one dealer in your local area. Not only will this give you a contact in the business, but you will also have someone to go to with your questions. One particular advantage is that, if you become a good client, your dealer may well offer you something before putting it on general sale. Many dealers sell their best pieces this way, before they even get placed in the shop, and you should be on the receiving end of such an arrangement. Dealers will also often take orders and keep an eye out for something you particularly want. This is very helpful if you are after something rare or obscure as they will let you know as soon as it appears.

However, don't forget that dealers buy at auction too and have to cover their costs. So dealer prices are likely to be higher than you would pay for doing the work yourself. In return, though, you get the benefit of their contacts and expert knowledge. Quite often they will also have worked on the piece to clean or repair it, which saves you some work once you have bought it.

Buying online

Buying over the Internet has become very popular, though some items inevitably fetch better prices online than others. Musical boxes, for example, don't do well. Much of their value lies in the quality of their sound, so obviously people don't like buying them when they cannot listen to them first. Pieces such as sewing machines are a safer buy.

Something you should always bear in mind when buying online is that the blind are leading the blind. The vast majority of sellers are private individuals or generalist dealers with no specialist knowledge of their items. Therefore you should take their descriptions with a healthy pinch of salt. The piece is very unlikely to be "rare", "hard to find" or "near mint", even if the description claims it is. When they say it is the best they've ever seen, ask yourself how many have they ever seen …

Values

The values given in the book are average auction prices for comparable pieces, assuming the goods are being sold in their country of origin. (Location will affect value, as American pieces will generally fetch more in the USA than they would in Britain, for example.) They reflect the value of pieces in average condition and also take the buyer's premium into consideration. (This is the charge you pay the auction house when making a purchase. It is usually 15–20% of the hammer price.) The prices are an estimate of those you would pay at a specialist auction, where both buyers and sellers know what the pieces are; they may be lower at general auctions.

Finally, remember that any price guide is a guide only. A piece is worth exactly what someone is prepared to pay for it. If two or more people are interested in the same item, its price will rise as they bid against each other. Auctioneers may tend to put a low estimate on a piece for the catalogue in order to attract attention to it, as an overestimated piece is likely to go unsold.

There is also an enormous unknown factor, particularly for unique items. The pre-sale estimate for the ENIAC part on page 125 was $8,000–12,000 (£5,335–8,000). This was thought by some to be rather high, although others realized that it's impossible to put an estimate on such a piece. It actually sold for $80,000 (£53,300), ten times its lower estimate.

Building a collection

You may begin collecting through a single, chance acquisition. If you decide you would like a similar type of piece and eventually acquire another, you have become a collector. However, the first piece of advice for a new collector is to wait before you buy. Your first piece almost always isn't as good as it could be. So do some homework: visit dealers, read catalogues and find good reference books.

Go for quality rather than quantity. It's better to have two or three really good pieces than a dozen average ones. It's also a good idea to keep your collection focused. If you find that you are interested in widely

differing items, such as musical boxes and sewing machines, try to link the two, perhaps by area, maker or period. If you're on a limited budget, upgrading is a good way to keep your collection tight. Fund a big buy by selling two lesser pieces. You'll preserve your space at home, and once you've got the better piece you won't miss the inferior ones.

Learn from other collectors. Most people enjoy showing off their pieces and discussing them with like-minded people. Seeing what other people collect and how they display and care for them can be very helpful (see pages 148–9 for hints on looking after your pieces). However, never offer to buy something from a fellow collector outright unless you know him or her very well. It's better to say that if a piece is ever for sale, you'd be interested in the first refusal, and leave it at that.

Networking with other collectors is one of the most enjoyable aspects of collecting. You will meet some fascinating people who will be delighted to share their knowledge and discoveries with you – just like those 19th-century amateur scientists who contributed so much to the field.

▼ **Allwin gaming machine**
English, c.1930. These classic gambling machines were popular in amusement arcades, pubs and piers around Britain for decades. Today they are popular with collectors of coin-operated machines of all kinds. **£100–200/$200–300**

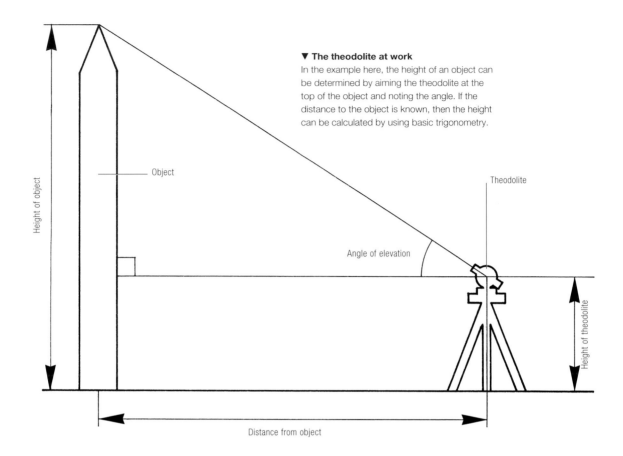

▼ The theodolite at work
In the example here, the height of an object can be determined by aiming the theodolite at the top of the object and noting the angle. If the distance to the object is known, then the height can be calculated by using basic trigonometry.

Object

Theodolite

Height of object

Angle of elevation

Height of theodolite

Distance from object

Some basic principles

Many of the instruments included in this book were the products of the greatest minds of the 19th century, yet they harnessed basic scientific principles, some of which were known to ancient civilizations. While it is not essential to be an expert on science to appreciate scientific instruments, an understanding of some of the simple principles involved will certainly enhance your enjoyment of these fascinating antiques.

As will be explained later, in the surveying chapter, mathematical principles lie behind the theodolite, a tool whose impact on history has been considerable. The theodolite is basically a sighting level with graduated horizontal and vertical movements, and is designed for use on a tripod. It can be used to calculate the height of an object, as shown in the diagram above. The theodolite is aimed at the top of the object, and the user notes the angle of elevation. If the distance to the object is measured, then this effectively gives two angles and one side of a right-angled triangle.

If the user has this information then the third side, which is the height of the object, can easily be calculated.

Map-making was one of the key applications of this instrument. Repeated measurements resulted in the creation of a network of points whose co-ordinates and elevations were known and marked on the ground. This provided extensive data on the landscape, which could be translated into map form, and the network of surveyed land could be expanded. The more data available, the more that could be measured and calculated.

As well as using mathematical principles, theodolites demonstrate the use of optics. Knowledge of lenses, the basic components of all photographic and projection equipment, goes back much further than is often supposed. In *The Clouds* the Greek comic writer Aristophanes, writing almost 2,500 years ago, refers to a glass for burning holes in parchment and also indicates that this was used for erasing writing from wax tablets. Therefore,

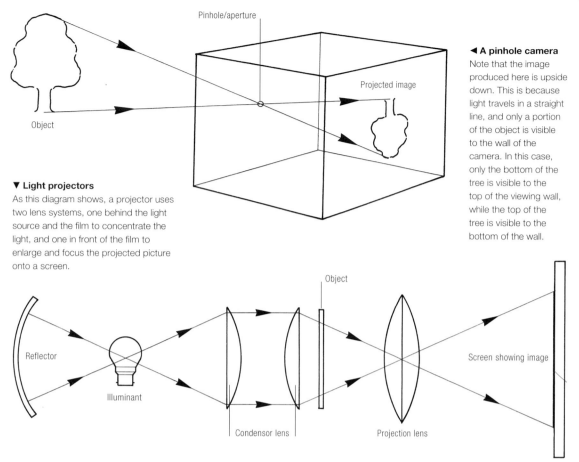

Pinhole/aperture

Projected image

Object

◄ A pinhole camera
Note that the image produced here is upside down. This is because light travels in a straight line, and only a portion of the object is visible to the wall of the camera. In this case, only the bottom of the tree is visible to the top of the viewing wall, while the top of the tree is visible to the bottom of the wall.

▼ Light projectors
As this diagram shows, a projector uses two lens systems, one behind the light source and the film to concentrate the light, and one in front of the film to enlarge and focus the projected picture onto a screen.

Object

Reflector

Illuminant

Condensor lens

Projection lens

Screen showing image

although it took many centuries for them to be applied in the ways seen in this book, lenses were certainly known to the ancients.

Lenses are of course also used by the human eye, and this is one of the things that the eye has in common with the camera. In the eye, images are created by light falling onto the retina rather than onto film, but the principle is the same. However, the pinhole camera, the simplest form of camera, does not need lenses at all. Its principles, based on the simple phenomenon of light passing through a restricted opening, can be easily observed. The ancient Chinese were aware of the principles, as were the Arabs. The camera obscura, discussed later, made use of this technique, but it wasn't until the 19th century that pinhole photography became a practical proposition (*see* pp.92–7).

A pinhole in the box of a pinhole camera lets in the light and because the hole is small, only a little light is admitted. This creates a sharp image, but it requires a long exposure time. The addition of a lens solved this problem. A box camera incorporates a convex lens to allow the use of larger holes (apertures) while providing a sharp, focused image. Without the use of a lens, larger holes would let in more light, but then this light would be scattered and the image would therefore appear blurred. The lens bends or refracts light because light travels more slowly through glass than air. When the lens is convex or curved outwards, more light is focused in one spot and the focal length is reduced.

The simplest of pinhole cameras can produce an image, but storing those images depended on the emergence of yet another branch of science. Photochemistry is the name given to the process by which light causes changes to the chemicals on film. Silver salts were used, and exposure to light created deposits of silver. More silver was deposited on areas exposed to greater amounts of light, which appeared darker on the negative. A fixing agent removed unexposed silver salt and stabilized the silver that had been deposited. A true image could

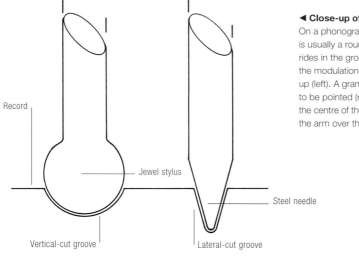

◄ **Close-up of two styluses**
On a phonograph recording, the stylus is usually a rounded jewel so that it rides in the groove and can go over the modulations without cutting them up (left). A gramophone needle needs to be pointed (right) so that it rides in the centre of the groove and can drive the arm over the record.

► **Basic differences between the phonograph and gramophone**
As shown above, the stylus is a different shape within each instrument. The gramophone's stylus needs to be straight so that it can hit the modulations on the side of the groove exactly and vibrate properly (left). In the case of the gramophone the modulations are recorded on the walls of the groove, which is of uniform depth. With the phonograph (right) the groove is of varying depth, and the stylus rides over the modulations to produce the sound.

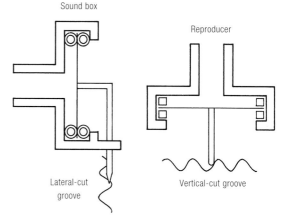

Sound box

Reproducer

Lateral-cut groove

Vertical-cut groove

then be produced by placing the negative between a light source and light-sensitive paper. Darker areas of the negative blocked more light, while lighter areas transmitted more to the receiving paper.

The projector, used to recreate and magnify images on film, shares many of the concepts and components of the camera but uses them in a rather more elaborate fashion. Projectors also need a constant and stable light source which, in the case of traditional projector lamps, was supplied by arcing carbon anodes and cathodes. These burned brightly but had to be changed frequently. Later they were replaced with xenon lamps, which lasted longer and gave truer colours to the projected image.

All projectors use a similar arrangement of lenses, including movie projectors, although these are a little more complex in operation. A shutter operates to flash each successive image onto the screen, while the film is passed through a lens system. If the pictures are shown in rapid succession, our brains interpret the succession of individual images as continuous movement. Every Hollywood star owes his or her success to this simple application of optical principles, just as the recording industry owes its very existence to the science behind those two pioneering inventions, the phonograph and the gramophone.

The phonograph and the gramophone work in different ways. Edison invented the phonograph, which was patented in 1877. In his vertical-cut system, sound vibrations are transmitted from the source through a recording horn and vibrate a diaphragm that has a stylus connected to it. This cuts a groove into the medium (usually, but not always, a cylinder), thus leaving modulations that represent sounds. The reproduction of these recordings occurs through the stylus, which is usually made from a rounded jewel such as a polished sapphire or diamond chip. The stylus rides in the groove, moving up and down over the modulations, therefore pulling and pushing the diaphragm.

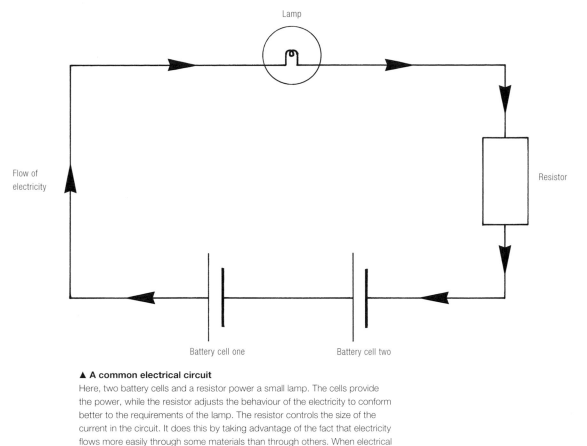

Lamp

Flow of
electricity

Resistor

Battery cell one

Battery cell two

▲ A common electrical circuit
Here, two battery cells and a resistor power a small lamp. The cells provide
the power, while the resistor adjusts the behaviour of the electricity to conform
better to the requirements of the lamp. The resistor controls the size of the
current in the circuit. It does this by taking advantage of the fact that electricity
flows more easily through some materials than through others. When electrical
circuits resist a current the energy usually turns into heat, but in the case of light
bulbs the special materials making up the filaments turn their excess energy into
light as well as heat. So a light bulb is itself essentially a large resistor.

Emile Berliner's gramophone, with its lateral-cut
method, uses a needle to reproduce the modulations.
In this case, the groove depth remains constant, and
the modulations are recorded on the wall of the
groove. The needle, sharp at its point in order to stay
in the centre of the groove, vibrates the diaphragm,
producing sound. As on the phonograph, this sound
is then amplified from the reproducer or sound box
(the part of the machine that contains the
diaphragm). From the reproducer it flows through
the arm and/or horn of the machine and is amplified.
One major difference between the two is the way in
which the stylus is moved across the record. In a
phonograph a mechanical feed is used, but on a
gramophone the grooves lead the needle over the disc.

Both machines were powered by a hand crank –
Edison's first efforts operated at a speed of about
70rpm, whereas Berliner's was initially much
slower at 30rpm, later increased to 60rpm.

The hand crank, utilizing the energy of human
effort, is a simple (not to mention environmentally
friendly) form of power, but it is by no means as
convenient as the electrical power we now take for
granted at the flick of a switch.

Lightning is an obvious, and certainly a dramatic,
natural manifestation of electricity. Lightning
was the subject of one of the most famous (and
dangerous) experiments in history – that of
Benjamin Franklin who, in 1752, flew a kite with
a dangling key in a thunderstorm to prove that
lightning was electricity. The kite and key were
struck by lightning and electricity flowing through
them was captured in a Leyden jar.

Much later, in 1831, it was Michael Faraday who
showed that mechanical energy could be converted
into electrical energy, which provided the very
foundation for electric power generation and led
directly to the invention of the electric motor. Today
we reap the benefits of all the breakthrough
discoveries behind the scientific principles explored
above. Just imagine what our lives would have
been like today if they had never occurred.

Timekeeping

Instruments for measuring time come from one of the most ancient fields of technology still in existence

▲ Silver pocket sundial
By Butterfield of Paris, late 17th/early 18th century. This piece has a folding bird-form gnomon and an inset compass.
£1,000–1,500/$1,500–2,000 (for a brass version, about half as much).

Throughout history, people have been measuring time by the movement of the earth in relation to the sun and stars. The shadow clock or gnomon – a simple upright stick or obelisk that casts a shadow – dates from around 3500BC. It was the forerunner of the sundial, the instrument that was to dominate timekeeping until the end of the 19th century.

At first it is surprising to find that sundials were the chief device for measuring time until so recently. After all, John Harrison, the clockmaker who famously solved the longitude problem, developed his chronometer in the mid-18th century. But it's important to remember that although Harrison's chronometer was extremely accurate, it was not made in great numbers because it was such an expensive instrument.

At this point it's worth noting that the vocabulary of timekeeping can sometimes be complicated. A clock, strictly speaking, is an instrument that signals the time by striking a bell. A timepiece, on the other hand, is an instrument that does not audibly signal the time. (So most watches are in fact small timepieces, though a watch that chimes is correctly referred to as a clock.) A chronometer is a very precisely built mechanical timepiece used by navigators to determine their longitude at sea, and also to regulate other instruments. For instance, astronomers use it to calibrate their measuring devices.

The chronometer represented a huge step forward in the science of timekeeping. Sundials obviously only worked in the presence of sunlight; other ancient methods existed for telling the time at night or in cloudy weather. The hourglass is almost as old as the sundial, and the notched candle was another widespread way to measure time intervals. The water clock, or clepsydra, was also an early timekeeping device. The hours were marked on either the container the water came out of

▶ **Chronometer in deck case**
By Matthew Norman, 20th century. This
is an unusual example owing to its late
date and its battery-driven quartz
movement. It therefore represents the
last of the purpose-built chronometers.
£300–400/$500–600

▼ **Marble noonday cannon sundial**
Probably German, early 19th century.
Gunpowder was placed in the cannon,
and the magnifying glass was set in such
a way that it would be ignited when the
sun was overhead at midday. This was a
very useful item at a time when watches
were still of dubious accuracy.
£1,000–1,500/$1,500–2,000

▲ **Ivory magnetic azimuth diptych
pocket sundial**
By Charles Bloud of Dieppe, late 18th century. These
were very popular at the time, and, because they
were made in a port city, Bloud's sundials were sold
all over the Western world. They are very occasionally
made of wood. £1,000–1,500/$1,500–2,000

or the bowl it flowed into. Gradually clepsydras became more complex; in about 270BC the Greek inventor Ctesibius of Alexandria built one with gears. Eventually the water was replaced by a weight falling under gravity, an interesting anticipation of the mechanical clock.

Mechanical clocks started to become widespread in Europe in the 14th century, when people began installing clocks with bells, and then with faces, in churches and other public buildings. These early clocks were not especially reliable, and their rates and accuracy would be checked and regulated against sundials. Wound springs were used for power from the mid-1500s, but their force tailed off as the spring unwound, so the clock would run more slowly. High-friction movements also caused erratic operation, and clockmakers had not yet discovered a way to compensate for changes in heat, pressure and humidity.

You should find plenty to collect in this field. Sundials were made in huge numbers from the 16th and 17th centuries onwards, and they demonstrate an enormous range of quality and style. And it's not necessary to spend a fortune. Sundials were made in such vast numbers that even a 400-year-old one can be surprisingly affordable.

Chronometers tend to be very similar in appearance, though their internal construction will vary according to their period, the price level at which they were sold and the skill of the maker. Most of the chronometers found today are from the 19th and 20th centuries, since these expensive devices were not made in great numbers until well into the 19th century.

Quality is the key to value with timepieces. Before you spend serious money, take time to look around. Examine museum pieces to get a feel for top-quality craftsmanship, and handle as many examples as you can. It's worth reading up about makers too, and learning to identify their marks or personal styles.

▼ **Italian fruitwood sundial**
(See p18 for reverse.) 17th century. It can be adjusted for any latitude by hanging it from a cord passed through the holes in the panels. £650–1,000/$1,000–1,500

◄ **Garden dial**
Signed J. H. Bostwick, Auburn, Mass, c.1900. The gnomon is fixed at 41°, the correct degree of latitude for the town of Auburn.
£250–400/$400–600

► **Compass dial**
French, mid-19th century. It is just 5cm (2in) in diameter, and is in a turned wooden case with the initials RH carved on the lid. These initials probably refer to the first owner.
£150–190/$220–280

Sundials

By the first century AD, it was recognized that if the gnomon was angled to lie parallel with the earth's axis, it would mark 24 hours of equal length. A calibrated face was added around the gnomon to show the hours, and the sundial was born. The earliest examples still extant are Egyptian and date from around 1500BC. Small, portable versions designed for personal use first appeared in Roman times and remained popular into the 19th century. Garden sundials are still in common use, and there are many beautiful faces, particularly from the 19th century, to be found. However, most collectors have to consider space restrictions, and so it is the smaller sundials that offer a richer field. Fortunately for most sundial collectors, old does not necessarily mean expensive. Value depends on the quality of the workmanship and on the types of material used.

Portable sundials were the Swatch watches of their era. European workshops made thousands of them from the 16th century onwards, and ordinary people used them every day. Travellers on the roads and farmers out in their fields kept track of time with a handy, reliable sundial. Clocks and watches broke down frequently in spite of their expense, and most people had a sundial by which to set and check their costly new timepieces.

In an early example of international marketing, sundials from Europe were sold across the civilized world throughout the 17th and 18th centuries. The design and construction of a sundial are good pointers to its origin. Regional variations are distinctive – for example, Nuremberg and Dieppe were known for their ivory diptych dials; Augsburg produced brass and gilt-brass dials and Bavarian sundials were typically simple models made of wood and paper.

A lot has been written about sundials, and you may be able to track down information about the maker of a signed piece. Butterfield of Paris is a very desirable name, even though his dials are fairly common, and every sundial collection should include

▲ English pocket sundial
By W. Watkins of Bristol, c.1830. It has a brass folding gnomon and a perpetual calendar printed inside the lid. **£100–200/$200–300**

▶ German cube dial
Signed D. Beringer, early 19th century. It is 19cm (7½in) high. When the sundial is correctly orientated, using the compass in the base, all five faces will show the same time. **£2,000–2,600/$3,000–4,000**

one. However, some are described as "Butterfield dials" but are actually unsigned. They may look exactly the same but are not worth as much as the signed article, as they may not have been made by him. Many sundials are not signed, but, as you become more familiar with the field, you will find that you begin to recognize styles from a particular maker or workshop. Sundials may also have makers' marks instead of signatures and you can identify these with the help of a good reference book.

A sundial that appears to have been made by a skilled craftsman – with high quality engraving or using expensive materials – is very likely to be of superior technical quality too. Its accuracy would naturally have been a key factor in its selling price at the time it was made and is no less essential to its value in today's market.

Every portable sundial contains a compass so that the sundial may be correctly aligned, but the angle of the gnomon is also vital to the sundial's accuracy. All garden sundials, and many portable models, have gnomons fixed at the angles for the particular latitudes where they were sold. However, the better pocket sundials actually have adjustable gnomons. Sometimes these are metal or wooden, while others were made of cord that could be hung according to the latitude scales supplied on the inside of the lids.

Earlier models usually had carved or engraved scales; examples from later dates have scales of printed and coloured paper. Some travellers' sundials include a convenient list of different cities and their latitudes. And of course all sundials should have a table for calculating standard time from solar time, because solar time changes daily with the position of the sun. This aspect of solar time brings us to an interesting feature to look out for in an older, good quality dial – the inclusion of dials that show different systems of hours. Although from the first century the gnomon's shadow was used to mark 24 hours of equal length, both before and after this time other systems of dividing up the day were also in use.

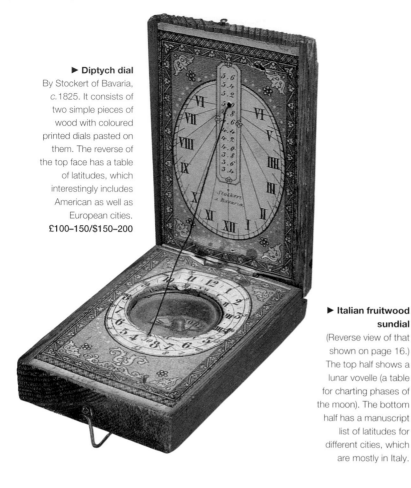

▶ Diptych dial
By Stockert of Bavaria, c.1825. It consists of two simple pieces of wood with coloured printed dials pasted on them. The reverse of the top face has a table of latitudes, which interestingly includes American as well as European cities.
£100–150/$150–200

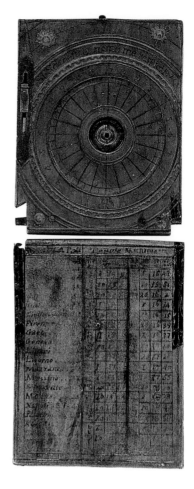

▶ Italian fruitwood sundial
(Reverse view of that shown on page 16.) The top half shows a lunar vovelle (a table for charting phases of the moon). The bottom half has a manuscript list of latitudes for different cities, which are mostly in Italy.

"Planetary Hours", so named by astrologers who believed each hour to be ruled by a different planet, divided day and night into separate periods of 12 hours each. Sunrise and sunset marked the starting-point of each period, which means of course that day hours and night hours were of different lengths, except at the Spring and Autumn Equinoxes. "Babylonian Hours" counted sunrise as the first hour and continued through to the next sunrise as the end of the 24th hour. This meant that midday was marked by a differently numbered hour as the year moved on. "Italian Hours" used the same system but went from sunset to sunset.

The point about all these systems is that they closely relate time to the movement of the earth, sun and stars. The link between time and astronomy remained very close until mechanical clocks began to develop. Because a mechanical clock has a regular movement, the hours had to be uniform in length. The difference between solar time and standard time was already understood, and clock faces were designed to show standard time. There was no reason for them to follow solar time, after

all. However, early clocks were not particularly reliable. The machinery was crude, and the time-keeping was irregular. Church clocks from the 14th and 15th centuries only had single hands, which indicated time to the nearest quarter hour, and they were checked and regulated by sundials, just as their successors were. The first reliable mechanical clock may have been invented in the middle of the 18th century, but the technology of accurate time-keeping relied on craftsmanship of the highest order. It did not become cheap enough to be widely available until the middle of the 19th century. The United States led the way in mass production, and, around the 1830s, Chauncey Jerome of Bristol, Connecticut, invented a low-cost rolled-brass clock movement. This meant that, for the first time ever, most families could afford a clock.

When you come to start your sundial collection, look out for the following leading names: Andreas Vogl of Augsburg, Dollond and George Adams from London, and Bloud of Dieppe. You will find that the majority of examples available now date from after about 1800. There are still some 18th-century

▼ **American "Solarwatch"**
By the Ansonia Clock Co., one of the USA's
larger clock companies, c.1920s. It has a metal
table of American city latitudes, an instruction
booklet, three dials and a folding gnomon.
£50–85/$75–125

▲ **(Top) Nickelled French novelty sundial,**
with crude English instructions in lid.
◀ **(Left) Simple brass novelty sundial,** possibly
English or German, with a fixed gnomon. Both date
from the early 20th century. £50–85/$75–125 each

pieces around, though, so keep an eye out. They tend
to be in brass, silver or ivory with engraved markings
and, surprisingly, needn't break the bank. The
majority, however, will be from the 19th century,
when watches were still beyond the pockets of most
people. Demand for an affordable alternative was
such that cheaper brass or wooden portable sundials,
which had printed paper calibrations, became the
first mass-produced scientific instruments.

You shouldn't turn your nose up at relatively
modern pocket sundials, either. Even well into the
20th century anyone away from a repair shop –
explorers, naturalists and railway construction
workers, to name a few – carried a sundial as a
back-up in case his watch broke. And in the 1920s
some watch companies made novelty "sun watches"
and gave them away as a promotional item.

Twentieth-century dials are still reasonably
priced, and there are some good quality instruments
available as well as fun items. Novelty dials are
fairly crudely made, with directions that are often
of little use. ("Raise the angle to its full length" is
all that one French-made example with English

instructions helpfully tells the user to do, without
giving any information as to how to align the dial to
get a correct reading.) However, there are some very
serviceable simple models around, and some that
were really rather good, such as the American
"Solarwatch" that was still being made into the
1920s. The increased quality of models such as the
Solarwatch suggests that they were intended for
actual use, as does the fact that the makers produced
models calibrated for the southern hemisphere.

A note of warning: look carefully at any garden
sundial faces that are labelled as 18th century. They
are more likely to be Victorian or early 20th-century
reproductions that have been made by taking a cast
from an original. A good indicator is the precision
of the markings on the face. Original engraved
markings are clear and sharp, while cast markings
have blunted edges. Another check you can do is
to study the patina. If you compare the surface
appearance of an 18th-century sundial face to that
of a 19th-century reproduction with an aged finish,
you will see the difference. As a rule of thumb, if
something looks too good to be true it usually is.

▶ **Brass-bound chronometer**

By Molleneux of London, mid-19th century. This fine-looking piece has a strong nautical appearance. Sadly, the top of the case has been lowered, which reduces the value.

£650–1,000/$1,000–1,500 (perhaps £1,000–1,335/$1,500–2,000 if unaltered).

▶ **Novelty lighthouse clock**

German tinplate, probably early 20th century. The main timepiece is in the base and can be set to tell the time for the "home port". The other dials may be set to tell times in ports (or cities) around the world.

£450–700/$700–1,000

Chronometers

The need for an accurate method of measuring time was particularly acute in an island nation that depended on the sea for its defence and strength. By the beginning of the 18th century, Britain's safety and prosperity were increasingly underpinned by its sizeable navy. But sailors, once out of sight of land, relied on frighteningly little information to work out their positions (*see* pp. 36–7). Of the two essential co-ordinates of latitude and longitude, only latitude could be calculated with any certainty.

To work out longitude, sailors needed to know both the local time and the time at the home port, as precisely as possible. Local time was not a problem – sundials were reliable instruments, as has been shown. However, they were obviously of no help in telling the time of the home port. The most reliable mechanical timepieces around were clocks that depended on pendulums to regulate the movement, but temperature changes and humidity rendered them almost useless, even when gimballed.

Navigators therefore relied on astronomy when the skies were clear and guesswork when they weren't. The slightest degree of inexactitude could be fatal, as was horribly demonstrated on the foggy night of 22 October 1707, when 2,000 British troops perished on the rocks of the Scilly Isles. The problem became a matter of public awareness in 1714, when the British Parliament offered an astounding reward of £20,000 to anyone who could find a way of calculating longitude to within half a degree.

The difference between the astronomical and the mechanical approach to time measurement became immediately apparent. Leading scientists of the time favoured an astronomical solution to the longitude problem, and their opinion carried a great deal of weight even though their ideas relied on clear skies. To be fair, the clocks and watches of the time were still few and unreliable, and had to be checked and regulated against sundials.

Fortunately John Harrison, an English clock-maker, pursued the mechanical solution. He had

◄ **World War II chronometer**
By Elgin National Watch Co., USA, c.1940. This utilitarian example is not of top quality – its construction is simple, and it only runs for 48 hours – but it has a stem-wind, much easier than key winding. **£400–550/$600–800**

◄ **Regulator timepiece**
By Blunt & Co., New York (specialists in nautical instruments), c.1840. The main dial is for minutes; the subsidiary dials tell hours and seconds. The signature and Gothic Revival style case add to its value. **£6,500–10,000/$10,000–15,000**

► **World War I chronometer**
By the Hamilton Watch Co., Lancaster, Philadelphia, c.1915. This has a better appearance than the 1940s example above and is of better quality. It has a 56-hour movement. **£650–1,000/$1,000–1,500**

already built clocks with friction-free escapements, self-lubricating clocks with wooden works that did not require oil and pendulums that swung evenly in all temperatures. Against extraordinary opposition it was he who solved the longitude problem and severed timekeeping from the stars.

Today, chronometers are still made and used, although atomic clocks and satellite technology have overtaken them. The collectable examples you will find will be mostly from the 19th and 20th centuries because so few were made earlier than that. They were very expensive instruments to build, requiring craftsmanship of the very highest order, and the market for them was small.

It was the combination of the threat of war and cheaper manufacturing that increased production in the early 1900s. These wartime chronometers are the most commonly found nowadays – but be warned, they are still not cheap.

One problem for collectors is that chronometers can look very similar, at least as far as their external appearance goes. Inside, it is a different story. Look for quality above all. The better the movement, the more valuable it will be. Long running times also increase value. The cases will nearly always be of mahogany or teak and sometimes have brass bindings. Chronometers commonly survive well and the glass inner lids are usually intact, so that will not raise the value. They are also usually lockable. This all means that any obvious damage will lower the value considerably.

To vary your collection, you can include other scientific timepieces, such as a regulator. This is a timepiece of unusual precision, used to regulate other instruments. When looking for scientific timepieces, look for extra dials. An apparently ordinary looking clock with separate dials for hours, minutes and seconds has obviously been built for accuracy. This is particularly the case if the minute dial is the largest. Some clocks have a number of dials for telling the time in different cities, and these novelty pieces are fun additions to a collection.

Surveying

The beauty and varying complexity of surveying instruments tell the story of the expansion of mankind and the transformation of the world

▲ **Cam pedometer**
French, *c.*1875. A pendulum moves as the wearer walks, and the instrument then converts the wearer's paces into distance. Pedometers were never very accurate. £100–200/$200–300

Wh* hen people settled down and began farming, land measurement became very important. As mankind spread across the globe, different peoples began elbowing each other for the available land, and markers such as rivers and trees were no longer precise enough. Basic measuring instruments such as cords, rods and simple sighting devices were used around the Tigris and Euphrates rivers as long ago as 1000BC. By about AD100, the Greek engineer Hero of Alexandria had written a book on surveying.

In England, Henry VIII's dissolution of the monasteries in 1536–9 and the acts of enclosure in the late 18th century brought sweeping changes in land title. Arguments over boundaries were rife and the need for accurate land measurement and valuation became vital. The science of measurement flourished, and soon individuals could say with certainty, "Your land stops there. My land begins here".

The mathematics of measurement developed from simple arithmetic to sophisticated geometry and trigonometry. The units of measurement changed from paces to relatively standardized rods, poles and chains. The instruments for taking the measurement developed too, from the simple plumb line to the complex theodolite.

Many of these technical advances took place in the 18th and 19th centuries, when Western Europe was colonizing the world and the Industrial Revolution was changing lives forever. Miners had to burrow more deeply to feed the demand for iron. Canal diggers and the builders of roads and railways needed to find true levels. Settlers in America and Africa needed decent maps and a reliable way to make their land claims. Structures were becoming more complex, and their measurements needed to be precise if they were not to fall down. And, as always, war played its part in hastening technological development. The military needed more

◀ **English brass box sextant**
By A. W. & S. Jones, mid-19th century. This compact instrument is the descendant of the semicircumferentors shown below.
£150–200/$225–300

▶ **Two American semicircumferentors**
18th century. Both instruments have inset compasses and 180° scales, and both lack their sight vanes.
£250–300/$375–465

accurate ways to lay its artillery and more reliable ways to get across rivers or mountain ranges. Surveying was becoming a specialist, high-prestige science.

The instruments used by those 18th- and 19th-century pioneers are often spectacular objects in their own right, and this has become one of the most popular areas of collecting, both with today's surveyors and with people who love the instruments for their own inherent beauty. England was the centre for precision-instrument making, and most of the collectable names are therefore English. Look for Jonathan Sisson, George Adams, Thomas Jones, William Cary, Dollond, Troughton, Negretti & Zambra, Elliott Brothers, J. H. Steward, W. F. Stanley and T. Cooke & Sons. Jesse Ramsden (1735–1800) is the outstanding English name: he developed the dividing engine, which standardized the scales and guaranteed true replicas. He developed it with a grant from the Board of Longitude but was not allowed to patent it, so his ideas were quickly copied in Europe and

the USA. But instruments with scales made using his dividing engine will have extra value.

Names to look for on European instruments are F. W. Breithaupt & Sohn and Kassel from Germany, Claude Langlois and Etienne Lenoir from Paris, Beaulieu in Belgium, and W. Schenk & Co, a Swiss company. The outstanding American name is that of the Rittenhouse Brothers who made surveying instruments in the 1780s.

There are plenty of fascinating instruments to choose from. The more complex ones, such as theodolites, are likely to be more expensive, but many compasses, graphometers and levels are surprisingly affordable. The simpler instruments are of great interest because they tend to be the early pieces. Condition and decoration are important factors in value, and also in interest, as instruments that were made for use in the field are very likely to show signs of wear and tear. Anything with a history attached to it will be of greater value.

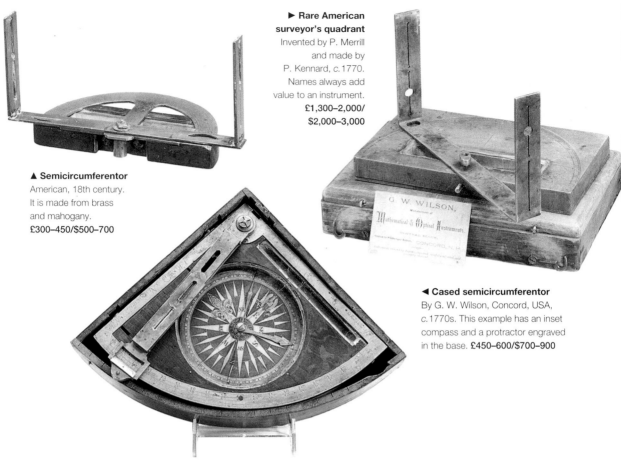

► **Rare American surveyor's quadrant** Invented by P. Merrill and made by P. Kennard, *c.*1770. Names always add value to an instrument. £1,300–2,000/ $2,000–3,000

▲ **Semicircumferentor** American, 18th century. It is made from brass and mahogany. £300–450/$500–700

◄ **Cased semicircumferentor** By G. W. Wilson, Concord, USA, *c.*1770s. This example has an inset compass and a protractor engraved in the base. £450–600/$700–900

Compasses

A compass was the basic instrument for anyone who needed to calculate angles and distances in order to make a map, plan a railway line or simply dig a drainage ditch. Theodolites were more precise than surveying compasses but they were also more expensive and less portable. A wooden compass, set into a 180-degree scale fitted with sights, formed an instrument that was easy to make, carry and use, and was precise enough for on-the-spot surveying by laymen. This early surveyor's compass was known as a semicircumferentor. and that is the term that is still used, even for those that have a smaller scale.

Semicircumferentors were especially useful in the United States during the 18th and 19th centuries. The western states were plotted in a grid pattern of townships centred on schools. Settlers chose their township and marked out and registered for themselves the 160 acres (or quarter-section) to which the Homestead Act of 1862 entitled them. There was less of a need for semicircumferentors in Britain, but they were occasionally found on country estates in the land agent's office. A land agent would have used a semicircumferentor for checking the line of irrigation and drainage ditches, and when building roads on the estate.

American semicircumferentors are nearly all made of wood. Many of them were homemade, and few of them are signed. They were frontiersmen's instruments and therefore were made from the materials that were ready to hand. Brass was an expensive import, and difficult to find, so it was usually just used for the alidades, or sighting rules. However, these instruments are not the rough carvings of backwoodsmen but the fine work of skilled craftsmen. Many makers of brass compasses also made wooden ones, which sold for about half the price or less and, again, are rarely signed.

Some simple surveying instruments were made to suit the needs of the moment, such as the quadrant pictured above. These are very interesting and may have been based on engravings of European instruments or the information in the books on

◄ **Brass surveyor's compass**
By Loring & Churchill, Boston, early to mid-19th century. It comes in a fitted case with the label of Thaxter & Son, Boston. It also has twin sights and bubble levels.
£500–800/$800–1,200

► **Graphometer**
French, c. 1825. It has fixed and movable sights and a brass finish.
£250–400/$400–600

basic surveying that were published in the USA in the second half of the 18th century.

The compass that was used in combination with the semicircumferentor or the quadrant was sometimes inset and sometimes a separate instrument. A simple wooden compass, with a paper (or brass) rose, in its own mahogany case was part of a surveyor's standard equipment. The compass above is a typical example. The outer scale of a surveyor's compass is usually divided into 360 degrees and the inner scale into four quadrants of 0–90 degrees. Twin bubble levels and twin sight vanes help the user to hold the compass flat and take an accurate reading.

Sturdy and reliable, these compasses were taken into the fields and down mines. Miners' compasses were, for example, used to take bearings above and below ground so that the mineral deposits and the mine shafts could be charted. Surveyors' compasses are characterized by a ridge on the scale opposite north and south, so that they could be read in the dark. In simpler, less expensive models, the glass

was held on with wax, so that the user could mark the bearing needed with a thumbnail. Complex compasses from the late 19th century are often mounted on tripods with universal joints so that they can be lined up with the horizontal plane.

The French version of the semicircumferentor is known as a graphometer and is virtually the same instrument. It was invented in about 1597 by Philippe Danfrie of Paris, and also works in both the horizontal and the vertical plane. It is made up of two alidades, one fixed to a semicircular 180-degree scale while the other can be moved over the degree scale. The graphometer was popular in Europe in the 19th century, when enclosure acts began to affect land titles across the continent. Like the semicircumferentor in America, it met the need for a simple, accurate instrument that was compact and sturdy enough to be carried in the field and used in all weather conditions. However, the French graphometers are mostly of a later date and tend to be made of brass rather than wood.

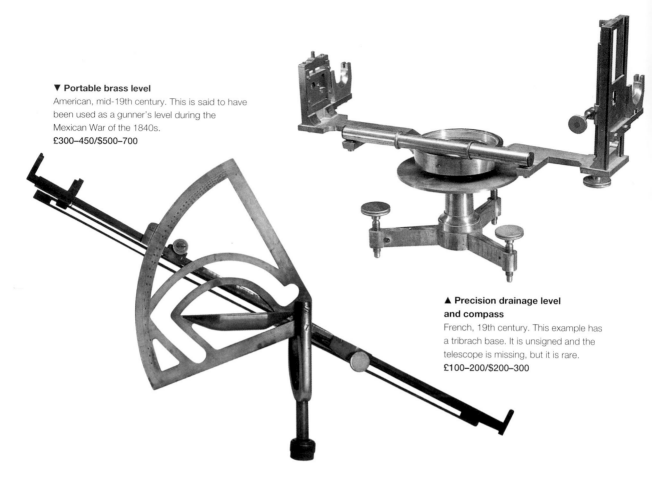

▼ Portable brass level
American, mid-19th century. This is said to have been used as a gunner's level during the Mexican War of the 1840s.
£300–450/$500–700

▲ Precision drainage level and compass
French, 19th century. This example has a tribrach base. It is unsigned and the telescope is missing, but it is rare.
£100–200/$200–300

Levels

As roads and railways branched out across Europe and the United States, the level came into its own. Levelling is the science of finding a horizontal line among one or more points in order to find out how much higher one point is than another. When road builders needed to calculate an acceptable gradient for a loaded wagon, they reached for their levels. Railway construction teams faced with a mountain range used a level to work out the grading for the track bed. And it wasn't only professional surveyors who used levels; farmers used them for their irrigation ditches, and artillery officers found that they came in very handy for calculating the trajectory of their shots. Not all levels are easy to identify, though. One of the attractions for collectors is that in many cases you are buying an enigma – it's up to you to discover exactly what a particular level was used for.

The first levels relied on still water being the guide to indicate the horizontal. The familiar spirit level is a variation on this – a tube filled with alcohol

or ether with a space for air to make a bubble. The next refinement to the level was the addition of sight vanes. The user could line up the vanes with the horizon to take a more accurate sighting, and then read off the angles from a scale attached to the level. One example of this is the American brass level pictured above, which is said to have been used as a gunner's level during the Mexican War. Instruments made in the field are characteristically crude and inaccurate in comparison with the precision instruments that were produced in the London workshops. However, a gunner did not need to be a marksman – as long as his shot passed over his own side and landed among the opposing troops, it would count as good shooting.

Less exciting, but more widespread, are drainage levels. These were used for construction, mainly of roads and railways. The nature of the job meant that the user's unaided eye was not sufficient for taking accurate sightings over the distances that the road or railway would cover. The next technological

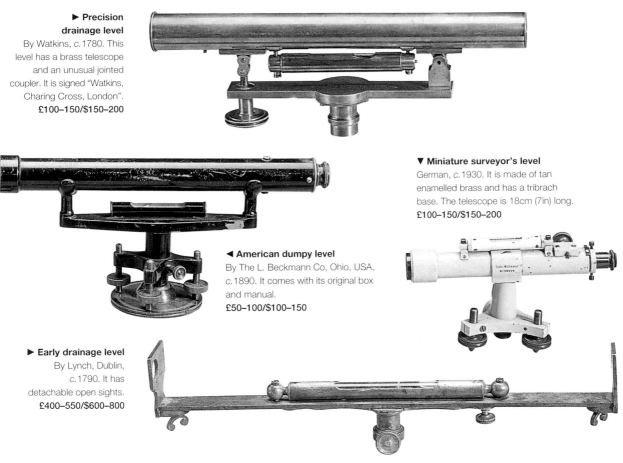

▶ Precision drainage level
By Watkins, c.1780. This level has a brass telescope and an unusual jointed coupler. It is signed "Watkins, Charing Cross, London".
£100–150/$150–200

▼ Miniature surveyor's level
German, c.1930. It is made of tan enamelled brass and has a tribrach base. The telescope is 18cm (7in) long.
£100–150/$150–200

◀ American dumpy level
By The L. Beckmann Co, Ohio, USA, c.1890. It comes with its original box and manual.
£50–100/$100–150

▶ Early drainage level
By Lynch, Dublin, c.1790. It has detachable open sights.
£400–550/$600–800

advance was the addition of a telescope. Levels that incorporate telescopes can be big, elaborate instruments, and they are very popular with today's collectors. They were less popular with their users at the time, though, because such early telescopes were so unwieldy. Portable levels continued without telescopic sights for some time, so don't be tempted to use the presence of a telescope as a guide to dating a level.

The first version of the modern surveyor's level was the Y-level, which was invented by Jonathan Sisson in the second quarter of the 18th century. He was an instrument maker in London, and his Y-level incorporated a large telescope held in Y-shaped bearings by brass straps. It originally stood on a tripod but later levels used a tribrach (three-armed) base with screws that could be adjusted to give the instrument a level base on uneven ground.

By the end of the 18th century, improved lenses meant that telescopes could be made much smaller. In the 1840s a civil engineer named William Gravatt

designed the dumpy level, which made the Y-level obsolete. Gravatt designed the dumpy to be used in the railway boom of 1848, and it is the first portable level with telescopic sights. Its telescope is about 30cm (12in) long, whereas the Y-level's measured 50cm (20in) or more. Sturdy, compact and reliable, it was immensely popular, and several fine examples have survived.

Condition affects the value of levels, especially if parts have been lost. Telescopes are often missing, and the adjustable screws in the tribrach feet may have been replaced. Any level will be of more interest to collectors if it has documentary proof of its history – for example, if it was used to build the Panama Canal. And a level that was used, say, to build the Union Pacific railway will provoke more interest in the western United States than in Europe. Finally, an instrument with a connection to the English inventor Jesse Ramsden (*see* p.23) will have increased value, even if it is only that its degree scale was made on his dividing engine.

▼ **Early Swiss theodolite/compass**
By Schenk, mid-19th century. It has a
lacquered brass finish and dovetailed
mahogany box. £450–600/$700–900

▶ **Brass theodolite**
By W. & S. Jones,
c.1825. Note the
downward curve of
the vertical arc,
typical by this date.
£500–650/$750–1,000

Theodolites

So far the simple, single-purpose instruments
used by laymen and semi-professionals to
chart and measure tracts of land have been
discussed. However, there are also instruments that
were capable of doing more than one thing; for
example, the theodolite does everything the
compass and the level can do and does them more
accurately. It's also compact and easily portable –
most theodolites are less than 30cm (1ft) high. But
its elegance lies in more than just its technical
sophistication. Collectors love theodolites for their
beauty and for the harmony between design and
science which they illustrate.

The early 19th-century theodolites are therefore
the most desirable as a result of their design quality
and finish. The characteristic arcs and parallel lines
are put together in combinations that delight the
eye with their flowing lines. These, and the deep,
soft glow of lacquered brass, evoke a time when
scientific instruments were made to be things of
beauty as well as function.

The theodolite is the most useful of surveying
instruments because it can measure the horizontal
angle between two points and their angle of
elevation at the same time. The basic theodolite was
made up of the following elements: a horizontal
circle divided into degrees; a compass; a vertical
semicircular arc divided into degrees; and a
telescope with a bubble level. This instrument was
first invented in the mid-16th century, but little
improvement was made on it until the 18th century
when Jonathan Sisson (c.1694–1749) replaced the
sight vanes with a telescopic sight, and Jesse
Ramsden made the division of the degree scales
much more accurate.

The size of a theodolite is measured by the size
of its horizontal circle. If it is 15cm (6in) across, then
it is a 15-cm (6-in) theodolite. Ramsden's great
theodolite of 1791 had a 91cm (3ft) horizontal circle
and weighed 90kg (200lb). It had to be so big
because, at the time, greater size in the scales
meant greater accuracy, and also because early

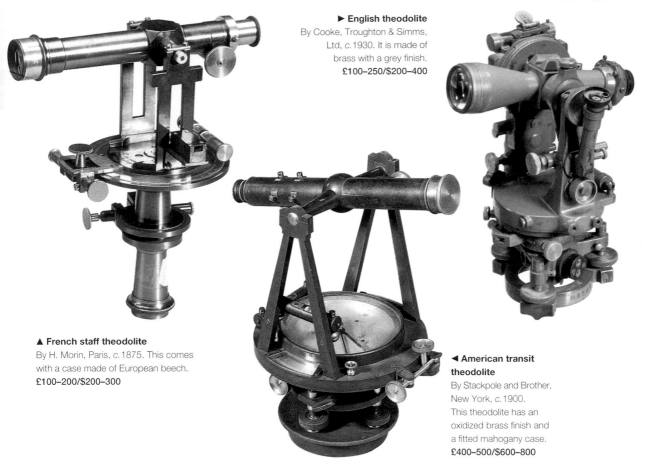

▶ **English theodolite**
By Cooke, Troughton & Simms, Ltd, *c*.1930. It is made of brass with a grey finish.
£100–250/$200–400

▲ **French staff theodolite**
By H. Morin, Paris, *c*.1875. This comes with a case made of European beech.
£100–200/$200–300

◀ **American transit theodolite**
By Stackpole and Brother, New York, *c*.1900. This theodolite has an oxidized brass finish and a fitted mahogany case.
£400–500/$600–800

telescopes were very large. But engineering was taking great strides forwards, and inventors in related fields kept pace. It wasn't long before lens technology improved and telescopes were made smaller (*see* pp.54–9).

At the same time, precision mechanics made advances. Pierre Vernier invented the vernier, a scale with fine divisions that could be moved over a fixed scale of larger divisions to give more accurate readings. A horizontal circle could be made much smaller by incorporating a vernier, which meant that, at last, the theodolite could become a portable instrument.

Very few of the theodolites you will find in the collectors' market today date from before 1850. Not many were made early on as they were expensive, specialist instruments, and they were not cherished in the way that, for instance, microscopes were. It is thought that many were destroyed for scrap metal. Most of the theodolites around now date from the late 19th and early 20th centuries.

The theodolite changed very little over the second half of the 19th century, at least technically. Its style, however, began to evolve, and the way in which the components are fitted together on a particular model can help to date it. Another useful way to date a theodolite is by its finish. Early 19th-century examples are usually finished in lacquered brass. Those made in the third quarter of the 19th century are generally finished in oxidized brass, which has a bronze colour. If a theodolite has a finish of grey or green lacquer, either it is a military instrument or it dates from after World War I. Black lacquer was also often used. Early 20th-century theodolites can be recognized by their matt finishes, but most of all by their compact sizes – they are likely to weigh less than 4.5kg (10lb). They may be less easy on the eye, but these theodolites retain their place in the story of man's exploration of the world, as such portable ones were used by Scott on his expedition to the Antarctic.

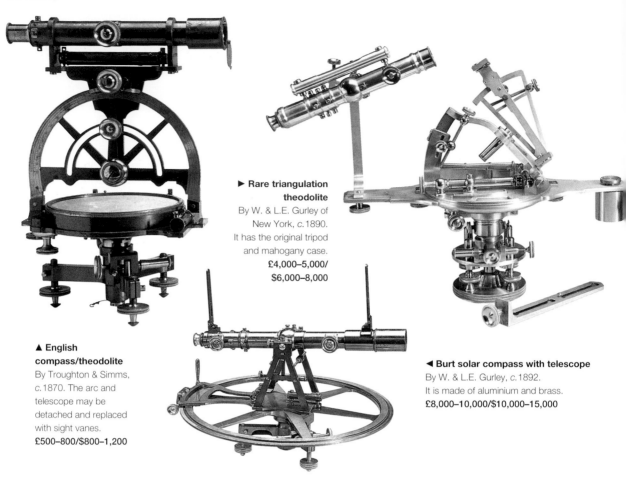

▶ **Rare triangulation theodolite**
By W. & L.E. Gurley of New York, c.1890. It has the original tripod and mahogany case.
£4,000–5,000/$6,000–8,000

▲ **English compass/theodolite**
By Troughton & Simms, c.1870. The arc and telescope may be detached and replaced with sight vanes.
£500–800/$800–1,200

◀ **Burt solar compass with telescope**
By W. & L.E. Gurley, c.1892. It is made of aluminium and brass.
£8,000–10,000/$10,000–15,000

Theodolites were the tools of progress. The simple levels and compasses used by farmers and settlers were not up to the job of surveying areas larger than about 10 sq km (3.86 sq miles), as the curvature of the earth then had to be taken into account. The theodolite provided the data for these complex calculations with speed and precision, and was used in every field of civil engineering.

There is a surprisingly wide range of theodolites available to the collector, and many were made with extra components such as a further fixed telescope below the compass. Some have detachable sight vanes, which can be mounted in place of the telescope. Compasses were actually of less importance on the theodolite than the bubble level, which came into its own on this instrument. The user needed at least one bubble level to ensure that the horizontal base had been set up properly. The bubble level is contained in a vial on the theodolite and many of them have twin vials.

The transit is another version of the theodolite. The main difference is that it has a 360-degree vertical circle, where the traditional theodolite has a semicircle. As a result of this it has a different mounting for the telescope, which is fixed to a horizontal axle on a frame. The telescope can be rotated on its axis in a vertical circle, and the frame can be turned in a horizontal circle. In this way the line of sight can be directed to any point. Where the theodolite's scales and controls are hidden in the telescope casing, the transit's are exposed. Vertical angles are read from a calibrated circle that rotates with the telescope and from a vernier mounted on the frame. Horizontal angles are read with an index and a vernier that rotate with the frame past a calibrated circle.

By the late 19th century, American instrument makers had caught up with their counterparts in Britain and Europe and were also producing high-quality precision instruments. A particular name to look for is that of W. & L.E. Gurley of New York. This company was the major maker of surveying instruments in the USA and some fine examples of its work exist today.

William Austin Burt of Michigan invented the solar compass in 1835. He had discovered the rich

▼ Light mountain transit
By W. & L.E. Gurley, NY, c.1895. It has a Burt solar attachment and an auxiliary telescope. Price includes a leather-covered case with accessories (not shown).
£2,500–4,000/ $4,000–6,000

Collecting Wooden Theodolites

▲ An early American wooden theodolite
Homemade by Solomon Drown Junior of Providence, New England, 1791. Its telescope is missing.
£1,400–1,600/$2,100–2,400

deposits of iron ore in his home state and realized that their effect on an ordinary compass would make it useless. The solar compass takes observations from the sun and other stars to determine true north. It can also measure horizontal angles, rather in the way that a transit can. It was such a useful invention that within a few years American law required a solar compass to be used in surveys of public lands. Solar compasses were made as separate instruments, which are very collectable in their own right, and were also incorporated into theodolites.

Do not be put off if you cannot afford the old and beautiful theodolites. This is a dynamic collecting area, and interesting pieces are constantly appearing on the market. Later instruments are just as collectable and may have fascinating histories attached to them. Documentary proof that a specific theodolite went on a particular expedition, or was used for a particular undertaking, will always increase its value and interest. Many early 20th-century theodolites have all kinds of interesting accessories. A complete theodolite with its original box will have the most value.

This is an extremely rare theodolite that has been entirely hand-carved out of wood. Its maker, Solomon Drown, must have copied the design from an English brass theodolite, which would have been expensive to import. This theodolite is a working instrument of surprising accuracy so it is of great scientific interest. It would have had a telescope, probably a fairly simple brass one, bought separately. The lack of this telescope has lowered the value today, but this wooden theodolite is still an exciting piece as it is an important scientific instrument as well as a rare example of American folk art.

This theodolite sold in the USA in April 2000 for $2,300/£1,535. It's a very desirable item, and if you ever see anything similar you should get your cheque book out at once.

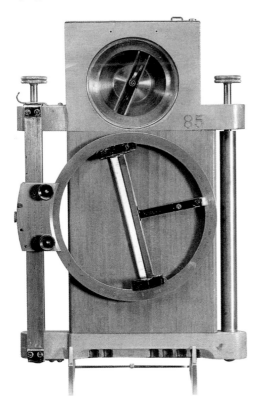

▲ Batson sketching case
By W. & L .E. Gurley, New York, late 19th century.
It is made of varnished hardwood and lacquered brass.
£300–450/$500–700

▼ Student's set of drawing instruments (incomplete)
Made in England, c.1900, in a fitted walnut case. Students' sets
are nearly always incomplete. This does affect the price, but
these sets tend to be very cheap anyway.
£35–50/$50–75

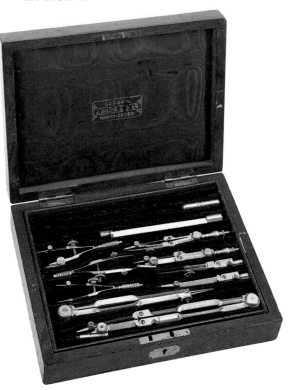

Drawing Instruments

If you think collecting drawing instruments sounds as much fun as watching paint dry, think again. Drawing instruments from the 19th and early 20th centuries are miracles of precision engineering. Great names such as da Vinci (who, in the 15th century, invented beam compasses for drawing large circles) and Brunel (who gave compasses tubular legs) are associated with their design, while their changing materials tell a marvellous tale of human ingenuity.

Rulers, set squares and protractors were originally made of wood. Dense, fine-grained pearwood and mahogany were especially valued for such instruments owing to their resistance to temperature and humidity, but they still shrank and expanded enough to spoil the accuracy. Some makers tried to solve this by edging instruments with ebony or binding them with brass. Others made their instruments entirely of brass, but it was more expensive and was quickly dropped when nickel silver (brass made whiter by adding nickel) was invented in the 1820s.

Other instrument makers tried making their rulers and protractors from horn. However, draughtsmen realized that they could mark lines and angles more accurately if they could see through their measuring instruments, and horn wasn't sufficiently transparent. A patent was taken out in 1854 for glass set squares, but they broke too easily to become truly popular. In the 1860s instrument makers tried the latest new invention: Goodyear's vulcanized rubber. Unfortunately it didn't work, as static electricity built up, attracting dirt and making grubby marks on the paper. In 1869 celluloid knocked spots off all its predecessors, but, even by 1900 it was still three times as expensive as pearwood.

By the late 19th century, draughtsmanship was a basic skill, and anyone with a decent education knew how to use drawing instruments. The Industrial Revolution had transformed technology, engineering was the subject to study, and technical colleges flourished. Every student who went off to

▲ **Proportional dividers**
English, early 19th century.
It comes in a fish-skin case.
£100–125/$150–200

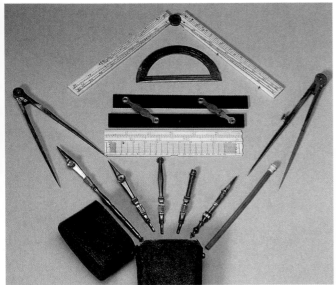

▲ **A complete set of brass and ivory drawing instruments**
From 1860. This high-quality set comes in a fitted fish-skin case. If any pieces were missing, the value would be lower.
£250–400/$400–600

▶ **An Allbrit planimeter**
English, 1950s. This typical 20th-century planimeter is in a fitted case with accessories. It is important to check that all the pieces are present before buying a planimeter like this.
£30–45/$45–70

enrol took a case of drawing instruments. The big names of instrument making who have appeared in the earlier chapters – Troughton & Simms, W. & L. E. Gurley and so on – relied on such drawing instruments as their bread-and-butter work. As a result, this is a wonderfully rich field for collectors. If you are interested in craftsmanship, there are drawing sets with beautifully turned handles in fitted cases of finely worked hardwood. If you are interested in technical design, concentrate on 19th-century instruments as they are astonishing examples of engineering in miniature. There are also some specialist pieces around that fulfil both criteria, such as the Batson sketching case that was patented in 1897. It's a portable forerunner of today's draughtsman's desk.

Cased sets remain the backbone of this field. They come in two kinds: those for students and those for professionals. If you studied geometry at school you will be familiar with the ruler (for straight lines), protractor (either circular or semicircular, for

measuring angles), set square (for right angles), compasses (for drawing circles) and dividers (for measuring lengths). A typical student's set of drawing instruments will include these as well as parallel rulers, a rectangular protractor, spring bows for drawing small circles, and pens and pencils for attaching to the legs of the compasses. The rulers and scales will probably be of boxwood, while the compasses and dividers are likely to be made of brass with steel points. Parallel rulers are usually made of ivory, ebony or brass.

Many additional instruments were also sold separately from the cased sets. The planimeter was used for measuring areas on maps and plans. One arm has a pin to fix it to the board and the other has a tracing point. As the tracing point moves around the area to be measured, a wheel at the joint rotates. The measurement of the traced area is then read from a dial.

The proportional compass (also known as proportional dividers) has two pairs of points. A

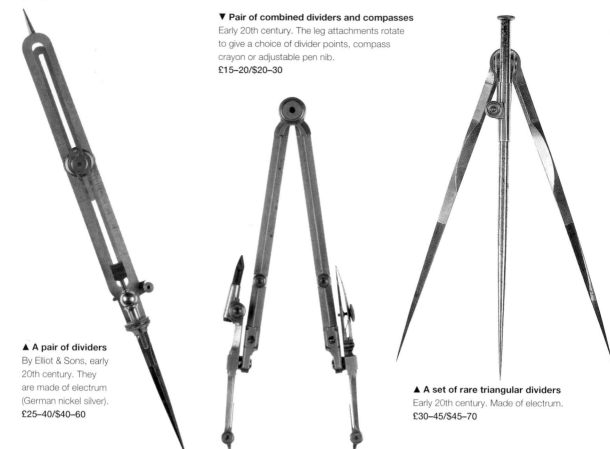

▼ Pair of combined dividers and compasses
Early 20th century. The leg attachments rotate to give a choice of divider points, compass crayon or adjustable pen nib.
£15–20/$20–30

▲ A pair of dividers
By Elliot & Sons, early 20th century. They are made of electrum (German nickel silver).
£25–40/$40–60

▲ A set of rare triangular dividers
Early 20th century. Made of electrum.
£30–45/$45–70

pivot partway along the arms allows the user to open them out to different lengths, usually in a ratio of 2:1. It is used for reducing or enlarging drawings. (Note: in Europe the name "proportional compass" is used for an instrument that in England is called a sector. This looks like a jointed ruler marked with scales and is used for making calculations.)

The only difference between compasses and dividers is that compasses have an attachment for a pen or pencil on one leg. Dividers have a point on each leg. The points are usually detachable so that they can be replaced if blunted or damaged. Sometimes they are interchangeable with pencil attachments, such as the combined dividers and compasses shown above.

The pantograph was an evolution of the proportional compass. Drawings often had to be enlarged or reduced and, even with a proportional compass, it took a long time. The pantograph has two jointed arms, one twice the length of the other. One arm has a tracing point and the other has a pen. The German astronomer Christoph Scheiner invented it between 1603 and 1605, and Claude

Langlois, the Parisian instrument maker, improved Scheiner's design in 1743. The pantograph became very useful in the 19th century when the building of railways boomed. Hundreds were made, and there are some nice examples still available today.

Triangular dividers or compasses were also sold separately. They are used to fix three points at once on a plan and can transfer them accurately to another drawing without having to measure their distances and angles separately. These instruments were obviously very useful, especially for copying mechanical drawings, but weren't made in great quantities so are quite rare and hard to find today.

Opisometers were very useful for measuring irregular lines on charts and maps. An opisometer looks like a pen with a wheel on the end instead of a nib. A screw-threaded rod runs through the centre of the wheel. As the wheel traces the route, it "winds" around the rod. It is then wound back along the scale at the edge of the map. Opisometers are rare; you are more likely to find a chartometer, which does the same thing but has a dial that gives the measurement immediately.

▼ **English architect's set of drawing instruments**
By Thomas Armstrong & Brothers, *c.*1880. The case is of walnut.
£800–1,200/$1,200–1,800

THOMAS ARMSTRONG & BROTHER
MANCHESTER & LIVERPOOL.

▲ **A pair of Swiss-pattern folding compasses**
Mid-20th century, the leg attachments feature divider points and pen nibs.
£15–20/$20–30

The cases for separate instruments were often made of expensive lizard or fish skin. Professional sets of drawing instruments include some of the instruments described previously and additional ones that were particular to the owner's trade.

The sector mentioned earlier was much used by navigators, surveyors, gunners and draughtsmen. It was the most versatile of the 19th-century rules, dating originally from about 1600. At first sight a sector looks like a jointed ruler, but it is in fact a geometrical calculating device used in conjunction with a compass. It has lines of sines, tangents, logarithms and chords ruled on it. The sector went out of fashion in the mid-19th century when comprehensive tables began to appear. By 1900 it was of little more than ornamental use, but today it is a very desirable collectable.

The most basic instruments of all, the pens themselves, are also highly collectable. A draughtsman has to be able to draw a clear, even line, so the quality of the pen is of vital importance. Early draughtsmen struggled with smudgy charcoal (they welcomed graphite with open arms in the 1560s) and crude nibs of quill, bronze, silver or gold. By the 19th century they had access to a bewildering array of steel nibs for drawing fine lines, parallel lines and even dotted ones. The nibs were made in all kinds of different ways, incorporating tiny screws and springs to help in the search for the perfect line. Pens were often sold in sets of six nibs fitting a single, beautifully turned ivory handle, which was presented in a velvet-lined case.

Be wary when buying sets of instruments as most students' sets are incomplete. Many makers inscribed each instrument in a set with their name – check for these inscriptions and also make sure that all the instruments match. It is a good idea to do this even with an apparently complete set, just to make sure that it hasn't been padded out with odd pieces. However, you shouldn't worry if the set isn't complete. It will be more affordable, and part of the fun of collecting lies in searching for instruments to fill in the gaps. They can turn up in odd places; 19th-century rulers and compasses are often discovered in the backs of old desk drawers. These won't cost a fortune and will increase the value of your set.

Navigation

The instruments that were used to chart the oceans speak of courage, ingenuity and the golden age of exploration

▲ Early cross staff
Late 17th/early 18th century. Early cross staffs are very rare, especially those that are completely intact. This example still has all four transoms in place.
£16,000–21,000/$24,000–32,000

In 1492 Columbus discovered America, and suddenly the European powers were competing for the New World's wealth. Sailors who knew their way around the seas held the keys to discovering and controlling trade routes, and they guarded their knowledge jealously. Sir Francis Drake has gone down in history for his epic circumnavigation of the world in 1577–80. His voyage depended partly on information that he had gathered by kidnapping foreign pilots and stealing their charts and instruments.

Britain, in particular, depended on the sea for trade, and the government quickly realized that it made sense to promote the dissemination of knowledge and encourage research. The problem of direction had been more or less cracked by the compass, which was used by Europeans from about 1400, and latitude is known to have been accurately charted some three centuries before Christ. However, the calculation of position remained an inexact science until the Yorkshire clockmaker John Harrison, solved the problem of measuring longitude in the 18th century.

Before that longitude had been measured with crude adaptations of astronomical instruments and even latitude at sea could only be roughly measured. The cross staff was invented by the astronomer Levi Ben Gershon in about 1342, and it remained the most popular navigator's tool until the end of the 16th century. The staff was held against the cheekbone and the crosspiece, or transom, was moved until one end appeared to touch the horizon when the other end touched the sun or Pole Star. The altitude could then be read off a scale on the side of the staff.

A major problem with the cross staff was that the user had to look directly at the sun. Then, in about 1594, an English sea captain named John Davis invented a purpose-built back staff. It followed the same principles as the original cross staff, but the user turned his

▼ **Davis-pattern back staff**
By Benjamin King, 18th century. Early American instruments are rare and much sought after in the USA, and are therefore automatically valuable. Most back staffs are unsigned – those that are signed are usually British or Dutch.
£3,000–5,000/$5,000–7,000

◄ *Detail of back staff*
The signature on the cross member reads: "Made by Benjamin King in Newport, Rh⁰ Island 1768" (Rh⁰ meaning Rhode).

back to the sun. This back staff was also known as the Davis quadrant or the English quadrant because it could measure 90 degrees.

Eighteenth-century back staffs crop up now and then at sales but are not cheap. You rarely see original sighting vanes, though, so always check to see whether the vanes have been replaced. Other instruments are more common; the octant and the sextant were made in great quantities. The difficulty of looking into the sun to take readings has already been mentioned, but there was a second, more obvious, problem common to all sighting instruments. It was very hard to keep such instruments steady on the horizon while standing on the deck of a ship at sea. To counter this, every officer would take several readings, each with his own instrument, and the readings would be averaged out. Every young midshipman joining the navy would arrive on board with his own sighting instrument. The USA and Britain had huge

navies and merchant marines in the 19th century, and the making of navigational instruments formed quite an industry.

Navigational instruments were tools for working men and so were often strictly functional. They were designed for use in extreme conditions so the materials used were chosen for their sturdiness. Ebony was often used for its hardness and resistance to splitting. Other woods such as mahogany had to be bound with brass, and such reinforcements are sometimes found on teak instruments as a failsafe. The cases were often made of cheaper woods, which usually split.

If you find an octant or a sextant with its case, it is worth taking the time to examine the case closely. This is because repairmen would frequently stick their own label over the original retailer's label, and they often wrote the date of repair on it too, so the instrument you have found may in fact be older than it looks at first glance.

▼ ▶ Large ebony octant
By Robert Merrill, c.1825. This has a 36-cm
(14-in) radius and brass arm and glass
shades (below left). It lacks a maker's
plate, but the case has the label of
Robert Merrill, New York (right).
£200–250/$300–400

◀ Ebony octant
by H. Duren, New York,
c.1850. It has a 25-cm
(10-in) radius and ivory
scale, vernier, brass
arm and shades in a
shaped oak case.
£250–400/$400–600

Octants

By the early 18th century the European powers were working feverishly to improve their navigational methods. The British government famously offered the breathtaking sum of £20,000 to whoever could devise an accurate method of determining longitude at sea. The Royal Society, Britain's highly distinguished scientific association, similarly offered cash prizes for any worthwhile inventions. Other countries put up prizes too, and scientists on both sides of the Atlantic competed to improve on the back staff.

In 1731 the Royal Society published details of a brilliantly simple navigational instrument devised by the British scientist John Hadley. Hadley's octant featured a mirror that moved over an arc and reflected the sun into a second, fixed mirror. Cleverly, the second mirror was only half-silvered. The user looked through a pinhole sight to catch the reflection of the sun on the silvered half while also being able to sight the horizon through the clear half – in other words, he "brought the sun down" to the horizon instead of "shooting it" above the horizon.

At the same time, and working independently, Thomas Godfrey, a Philadelphia glazier, built an improved altitude-measuring device that worked on the same principles. The Royal Society recognized the worth of Godfrey's work and awarded a prize of £200 each to Hadley and Godfrey.

At first Hadley's invention was known as the Hadley quadrant. This was because it could measure up to 90 degrees, or a quarter circle. However, the actual arc only needs to occupy an eighth, or octant, of a circle because, by using a mirror, the instrument halves the angle through which the radial arm needs to move. This meant that the octant was smaller and handier than the back staff.

Other improvements to instruments during this time included a vernier for finer readings and a telescope instead of the ordinary sight vane. Sets of coloured glass shades were fitted for use with the sun. The wooden limbs were usually made of ebony as this withstood temperature and humidity changes well. Less expensive octants were made of wood that was "ebonized" or blackened to reduce glare while the scale was created from ivory or boxwood.

▲ **From left to right: Ebony, ivory and brass octant with two telescopic sights** by H. Duren, New York, c. 1865. The case is decorated with the name of a New Brunswick captain. **£450–650/$700–1,000; Deck watch chronometer** Waltham Watch Co, c. 1913. Has a mahogany deck case and a weighted brass case in brass gimbals. The cover is cracked but the chronometer is still in good working order. **£300–450/ $500–700; Ship's chronometer** Hamilton Watch Co., Pennsylvania, c. 1944. This chronometer still works well. **£700–1,000/$1,000–1,500**

As a rough guide to dating, octants were made entirely of wood and ivory up to the mid-18th century. After about 1750, when the octant came into general use, the index arm was often made of brass. However, navigational instruments are not easy to date. Heavy wear from use at sea can make instruments appear older than they really are. Different instruments also existed at the same time, so it is a mistake to assume that an octant must be more recent than a back staff. The back staff had been phenomenally successful, dominating navigation worldwide for almost 200 years, and it took a long time to die out. (However, the Dutch navy actually stuck firmly to the cross staff and continued to use it well into the 19th century). While the octant was made in a range of qualities, it still represented a considerable expense for seamen, who usually had to provide their own instruments. These sailors were also on the whole poorly educated, or not educated at all. They mostly learned parrot fashion on the instrument they brought with them and preferred to stick with it rather than learn to use a new and strange-looking device.

The most reliable way to date an octant is from the maker's signature on the instrument. The presence of a label also makes a big difference to an octant's value. If you don't find one on the instrument itself, look inside the case as there may be one there. There are often several labels, from the retailer who sold the instrument, the chandler who repaired it or maybe from an instrument maker's where it was taken to be adjusted. They make fascinating reading and tell the tale of the owner's travels as well as adding extra value.

Octant owners took very good care of their instruments, and many of those available today are still in working order. It is also possible to find chronometers to use or display with them. An accurate chronometer is of course vital to the precise calculation of longitude, and a nice example such as one of those on pp20–21 will round off your collection of navigational instruments. Choose one that appeals to your taste and pocket and place it with your octant. After all, the octant was a giant step forwards in precision measuring and, together with the chronometer, took British navigation into a new era.

▶ **English sextant**
By Spencer, Browning
& Rust, *c.*1840. It has
a brass truss frame,
glass shades, four
eyepieces and
a shaped case
(not shown).
£300–450/$500–700

▲ **An artificial horizon**
Unsigned but possibly by Keuffel & Esser,
*c.*1900. The container is filled with mercury.
£250–400/$400–600

◀ **English sextant**
By Norris & Campbell,
*c.*1875. It is displayed
in a shaped mahogany
case with a label from
Thaxter of Boston.
This example still has
its magnifier, shades
and telescopes.
£200–300/$300–500

Sextants

The birth of the sextant is an entertaining tale of flawed research and much underhanded scientific elbowing for position. By the mid-18th century the search for the answer to the longitude question had developed into a competition that was as intense as it was blatantly (and now famously) unsporting. The scientific élite who controlled the Board of Longitude turned up their well-bred noses at John Harrison's "tradesman's" work on accurate timepieces (*see* pp.20–1). They loftily resolved to tell the time by "heaven's clock" – the stars – while at the same time changing the rules for the longitude prize to exclude Harrison's chronometers. In about 1767 they came up with the "lunar method" for finding longitude at sea by measuring the distances of certain stars from the moon.

The octant's 45-degree arc was not great enough for observations of the moon. The lunar method also required greater accuracy than the octant could provide, and work began on the octant's successor, the sextant. The sextant is named for its arc, which

occupies 60 degrees, or a sixth of a circle, and it can measure up to 120 degrees. The great names of instrument making from the period each made their own versions, improving them all the time: those associated with Jesse Ramsden (1735–1800), John Bird (1709–76) or Edward Troughton (1753–1835) will have great value. Thanks to these men, the sextant was vastly more accurate than the octant. A few early models were made of ebony but most were of metal, which didn't distort, and had telescopic sights and precision scales. Sextants were made in quantity from about 1800, and the design evolved from simple brass bars to light, strong constructions with grids, ovals and circles between the outer limbs and the arc. Sextants were more expensive than octants and were bought by wealthy mariners, such as the officers of the East India Company.

The artificial horizon, which was another technical breakthrough of the time, is associated with the sextant. All angle-measuring instruments up until this time had been hampered by their

▲ **Training sextant**
By Einson-Freeman, New York, c.1940s. It
has a cardboard body and a simple telescope.
£25–40/$40–60

reliance on a clear view of the horizon – in other words, they didn't work in the dark or in most of the weather conditions encountered at sea! So the artificial horizon was the answer to a navigator's prayer. Spirit levels and pendulums had been tried and found inadequate. Then, in about 1812, the mercury-level artificial horizon appeared. The earliest version was a trough of wood or iron into which the user poured mercury from a stone bottle, to get an absolutely flat surface. A triangular roof with glass sides fitted over the trough and prevented wind from ruffling the surface of the mercury. After use it was taken to pieces and stored in a box, and today old artificial horizons are actually often not recognized for what they are.

By the end of the 19th century the bubble sextant had been invented to help followers of the new ballooning craze find their positions. The bubble sextant has a bubble level fixed to one limb, and the user looks at the image of the bubble in a mirror set at 45 degrees above it.

The lunar method wasn't particularly helpful for finding longitude (it could only be used at night, and also required clear skies) but the sextant went on to become the sailor's most popular instrument. As well as being more accurate than its predecessors it could measure horizontal and vertical angles, and was also easily portable, so sailors could carry it up masts to extend their field of observation. Cook used it for his work in the Pacific and charted 4,445km (2,760 miles) of coastline in just six months when he sailed round New Zealand in 1769–70. In fact sextants have remained in use right up to the present day. During World War II they were made with battery-powered lights so that the user could see the vernier in the dark. Just as wooden guns were issued for drilling new recruits, so cheap cardboard sextants were provided for training the men in the basics of calculating their position. These later examples are an affordable and fascinating piece of history so it is well worth keeping your eye out for them to add to your own collection.

▼ **Boxed and gimballed ship's liquid compass**
By E. S. Ritchie, Boston, mid-19th century. It is made
of brass and mahogany and has a floating dial.
£200–300/$300–500

▲ **Simple dry compass**
By James Gale of Salem, c.1800. This
compass is made of wood covered in
gesso and is 19cm (7½in) in diameter.
£200–300/$300–500

Marine Compasses

The compass was first used at sea by Europeans
in about 1400. It transformed sailors' lives and
changed the course of history: in 1447 the Cape
Verde islands were rediscovered (they had been
found before, but without reliable navigational
instruments people couldn't get back there), Sierra
Leone was discovered in 1460 and America in 1492.
Columbus's compass bearing took him across the
Atlantic along a parallel. His intended destination
was the Indies (today's Indonesia), and he probably
would have made it had the New World not got
in the way.

The magnetic compass was known to European
sailors long before it became an instrument suitable
for taking to sea. Alexander Neckham, an English
monk who studied in Paris, described a magnetized
needle floating in a bowl of water in 1187. However,
the card with the directions on it is actually much
older than that. The term "mariner's compass"
originally meant the division of the circle of the
horizon into 32 points (north, north by east, north by

north-east etc) in order to determine wind direction,
or rhumb. With a compass, sailors could find the
rhumb and continue to sail along it in a line that
could be plotted on a chart, known as the rhumb line.
Wind dominated the sailor's life, and early compasses
were marked with the eight principal winds.

It is worth noting that the term "compass rose"
doesn't only mean the printed card; it often includes
the needles that point the direction and the cap,
which is the piece that holds the needles so that they
swing smoothly round the pivot. The cap is usually
jewelled, in the same way that clockwork watches
used to be, to ensure a smooth bearing that doesn't
rust, distort or require lubrication. The sensitivity of
the compass depends on how light the whole rose is.

Like all a ship's instruments, the compass needed
to stand up to hard wear in extreme conditions and
to have some way of dealing with the ship's motion.
Early marine compasses consist of a compass rose
enclosed in a circular wooden box, and there are
not many that survive today because they were so

▼ **Ship's sighting compass**
By the famous firm of Keuffel & Esser, New York, late 19th/early 20th century. The cast-brass compass rose is in an iron gimbal with a weighted base. £200–250/$300–400

◄ **Pleasure yacht's deck compass**
By E. S. Ritchie, Boston, early/mid-20th century. Boston, as a harbour city, was one of the big centres of navigational instruments, and Ritchie was a leading maker.
£250–400/$400–600

delicate. Brass quickly became the preferred material for the compass, although the box continued to be made from wood. However, the problem of the ship's motion was not so easily solved. A dry compass described in 1269 relied on a non-magnetic pin fitted at right angles to the needle. This pin cleverly compensated for moments of inertia when the ship rolled. Later compasses had at least two needles to compensate for moments of inertia, as a single needle might have given a false reading. If the two needles diverged, the user knew that one had got stuck and could give the compass a light tap to free it and confirm the true reading. When the friction-free bearing had been perfected, compasses went back to having one needle.

The liquid compass, first suggested around 1779, countered rough weather by floating the card in a reservoir of alcohol and water. Gimbals, a technique known since at least the 16th century, held the liquid compass level. True north is marked by the North Pole, which is an imaginary point indicating the

most northerly point of the globe. However, the magnetized compass needle is attracted to a particular point in the earth's magnetic field some 1,300km (800 miles) from the North Pole. The variation of magnetic north from true north became a big problem with the advent of iron ships, and was countered by the British Commander Matthew Flinders between 1800 and 1803. After several experiments, he found a way of correcting for deviation with Flinders bars – a combination of magnets and iron placed near the compass, which was then often included as part of the binnacle.

The binnacle took its name from a place near the helm where the compass was kept. The term came to mean the box or cupboard the compass was housed in, which had a glass lid. Binnacles are handsome objects and surprisingly affordable, as are all marine compasses. Most of the compasses you will find today are well within the average collector's budget and they are an essential part of any good collection of navigation instruments.

Geography and Meteorology

Developments in 19th-century instruments confirmed our understanding of the world and its place in the solar system

◀ **Mahogany stick barometer**
By Harris & Company, London, early to mid-19th century. This is a typical, good quality stick barometer of classic form, which is more collectable than a banjo barometer.
£500–800/$800–1,200

The 18th century saw a flowering of interest in the sciences, as Western thought gradually moved away from theological explanations of the world towards scientific explanations of our planet and its place in the universe. This movement had begun among a small group of learned people in the Renaissance period, but new scientific knowledge and discoveries could not be widely disseminated until communications improved (*see* p.78).

The increased prosperity in the 19th century brought by the Industrial Revolution meant that more people received an education. Education was a mark of wealth and status for the new urban middle classes, and scientific hobbies became very fashionable. No gentleman's house was complete without a barometer for monitoring and predicting the weather. A pair of globes (one terrestrial, the other celestial) displayed in the library similarly signalled the owner's learning.

Globes are far older than you might think. It is a popular myth that most people believed the earth was flat until Columbus discovered America in 1492. Anyone living on the coast can observe the curvature of the earth with the naked eye. A ship coming into port first shows the tip of its mast over the horizon. Gradually the rest of it comes into view, just as if the ship were coming over a hill. This phenomenon was observed by the ancient Greeks, and the first globe is said to have been built by the scholar Crates in 150BC.

Globes made before about the mid-19th century are hard to find and very expensive. Fortunately for most collectors, advances in printing techniques meant that globes could be mass produced and examples from the second half of the 19th century and the early 20th century are plentiful and affordable.

Because so many schools and universities began to have globes in the late 19th century, the prestige of owning one became rather

► A pair of maximum/minimum thermometers
By Negretti & Zambra of London, late 19th century. The thermometers are mounted on nickelled plates in a mahogany case. The logo on the silk lining, "makers to Her Majesty", refers to Queen Victoria and dates the thermometers before 1901. £100–150/$200–250

◄ Loring 10-inch terrestrial globe
By Josiah Loring, a Boston bookseller and noted globemaker. This one was actually sold after his death in 1840 by his successor, Gilman Josling. It has a brass meridian ring and a walnut stand with a coloured horizon ring showing the months and houses of the zodiac.
£2,000–3,000/$3,000–5,000

diminished. However, celestial globes remained status symbols for the wealthy because astronomy was such a popular 19th-century hobby. Mechanical models that demonstrate how different bodies move around each other are very collectable today, although they are likely to be at the higher end of the price range.

Instruments for recording and predicting the weather offer a great deal of variety, and can be more affordable. Barometers and thermometers were used by people from all walks of life. Everyday life was heavily influenced by the weather, and until the 20th centuries individuals had to do their own weather forecasting. As a result, barometers and thermometers were made in several different qualities to suit the varying markets.

Barometers also demonstrate a huge diversity of designs. Many, such as the popular banjo barometer, were designed as home furnishings and are highly decorative. Marine stick barometers are

also beautiful instruments and, because they were built to last, have often survived well.

Thermometers are especially varied. They range from elaborate 19th-century desk ones to 20th-century promotional giveaways, so there is plenty to choose from.

The key to building a good collection of geographical and meteorological instruments is to focus on what interests you. Don't let the high prices of antique globes, for instance, frighten you away. Early 20th-century globes are much more affordable and are fascinating examples of early production techniques. Some were also made with attachments to show the sun or moon.

You are unlikely to have space for many globes, especially of the larger and more expensive sort. Therefore, use a selection of meteorological instruments to round out your collection – again, early 20th-century examples are mostly very affordable, and even 19th-century pieces are often within reach.

▶ **Andrews 18-inch terrestrial globe**
By A. H. Andrews & Co. of Chicago, c.1890. A typical mass-produced globe, this has a plaster sphere with coloured gores on a bronzed stand with paw feet.
£300–450/$500–700

▲ **Loring 10-inch celestial globe**
From 1854. Companion to the terrestrial globe on page 45. Celestial and terrestrial globes are usually sold in a pair so it is unusual to find one by itself. Less decorative, interesting and expensive than terrestrial globes. **£1,000–2,000/$2,000–3,000**

Globes and Orreries

Around 150 AD, the great astronomer and mathematician Ptolemy of Alexandria wrote two books that were to be of great importance to the development of the globe. The first was called the *Almagest* (from the Arabic "al-Majisti", which means "Great Work"). The *Almagest* contained Ptolemy's geometric theory to account for the apparent motion of the sun, moon and planets around the earth and against a background of non-moving stars. The second was called *Geography* and charted the world as it was known in his time, using a system of longitude and latitude. With Ptolemy's work behind it, the globe became a true scientific instrument.

Ptolemy's earth-centred model of the universe was to dominate scientific thought for over a thousand years, until it was superseded by the work of Nicolaus Copernicus in the 16th century (*see* pp.54–5). During this period very few globes were made, and those that were are known as manuscript globes. They were all handmade from metal with the features engraved directly on the surface of the sphere. Printed globes didn't appear until the early 16th century, when the printing was done on elongated ovals of paper called gores. The printed gores were then applied to the surface of a hollow plaster sphere, with the narrow ends lying at the poles and the wide mid-section at the equator. This was clearly a time-consuming, highly skilled process. Early globes were immensely expensive instruments, and only royalty, the nobility and a few of the very wealthiest scholars could afford them.

In the mid-18th century, as trade expanded and prosperity began to increase, globes became slightly more accessible. Most of the major European countries produced them, but they were the work of cartographers. In England, however, globes were made by instrument makers. Great names of the day, such as George Adams, Dudley Adams, John Moxton, Nathaniel Hill, John Newton and William Cary, all included globes in their catalogues. England, and in particularl London, became a centre for globemaking.

▼ **Fitz six-inch globe**
By Ginn & Heath of Boston, *c.* 1880. This unusual globe was designed and patented by an American governess named Ellen Eliza Fitz in 1875. It has a small sphere on the left representing the position of the sun and therefore can show the sun's course and the lengths of day and night. **£2,000–3,000/ $3,000–5,000**

▲ **A pair of 21-inch library globes**
By Bardin of London, early 19th century. Bardin globes were considered to be the best available, and many makers sold them under their own names. Signed Bardin globes are therefore especially rare. **£20,000–35,000/$30,000–50,000**

The second half of the 18th century was also an age of exploration and of changing boundaries. British and other European colonization was spreading across the world, and borders within Europe were hotly disputed too. This meant that a globe was technically out of date almost as soon as it was published. However, people didn't really need the very latest edition, and these were still extremely costly instruments to buy or produce. Not only were the expensive plates for printing the gores used for several years before being updated, but also the successor to a famous maker would often use the eminent name as a selling point. This is why some globes have a date of manufacture that occurs long after their maker's death. Gilman Josling, for example, the successor to the Boston globemaker Josiah Loring, used Loring's name for years.

There are two kinds of globe: terrestrial and celestial. A pair of globes was a very popular item of library furniture in the late 18th and early 19th centuries and is very valuable today. The map of the

heavens on a celestial globe of this type is inside out, because the gores are necessarily on the outside of the sphere. Celestial globes were not updated as often, partly because celestial discoveries did not keep pace with terrestrial discoveries or additions, but also because they were considered less important. The terrestrial globe of a pair is therefore likely to be of a more recent edition.

English instrument makers led the way in new globe designs and were the first to make the pocket globe. As its name suggests, this globe was small enough to be carried in the pocket. Examples are usually about 8cm (3in) in diameter and have celestial gores on the inside. They couldn't carry as much information as the larger globes, but did include all the major features, including the tracks of the latest voyages of discovery. Another interesting English design, dating from the late 19th century, is the folding globe, which was often bought as a teaching aid. This works like an umbrella and is easily portable.

Globe production began in the USA around the beginning of the 19th century. Boston and New York, the intellectual and commercial centres of the country, were the chief sources. Globes became cheaper from the middle of the century as printing techniques advanced, and the United States became the leader in producing affordable, accurate globes. The large publishing companies, especially Rand McNally of Chicago, used the technique of wax engraving to mass-produce globes for the first time.

The companion instrument to a globe is a model showing the relative positions and movements of heavenly bodies. Some globes have attachments showing the sun and moon, but mechanical models dedicated to demonstrating the solar system, in part or in full, have existed for thousands of years. An armillary sphere consists of a sphere representing the earth encircled by bands or rings. Some rings move, showing, for example, the sun and moon and their paths of movement, but most of the rings on an armillary sphere are fixed. Some of them represent the paths of other planets while others are purely ornamental, perhaps engraved with the signs of the

zodiac. The first armillary spheres were made by the ancient Greeks. These instruments were very fashionable in the 16th and 17th centuries. Their popularity waned around the beginning of the 18th century, although they were still made as teaching aids in the late 19th century. There are 20th-century armillary spheres around too, but many aren't scientific instruments at all; they are decorative and have often been used as garden ornaments. In private homes, armillary spheres had been replaced by orreries.

The first orrery was made by a clockmaker called George Graham and his famous uncle, the master clockmaker Thomas Tompion, in about 1709. It was copied a few years later, around 1712, by John Rowley. He made it for his patron Charles Boyle, fourth Earl of Orrery, and that is where it gets its strange name. Rowley's orrery was more for decoration than for scientific use. It was lacquered and engraved and showed the relative motions of sun, moon and earth. When the user turned a handle, flat metal plates carried the spheres around their designated paths.

◄ Brass armillary 12-inch sphere
French, late 19th century. The plain design of this example reveals that it was made for use as a teaching aid. The planets are represented by cardboard discs whereas earlier, better quality pieces would have had spheres. It is operated by a simple gear mechanism with a flat handle awkwardly located in the centre.
£1,000–1,500/$1,500–2,500

▼ Demonstration tellurium
By Berg of Stockholm, late 19th/early 20th century. This would have been used mostly in schools. When the user turns the handle, intricate gearing allows the moon ball to rotate around the earth and the earth to rotate around the sun (represented by a candle placed in front of the reflector).
£700–1,000/$1,000–2,000

The orrery caught on immediately, and demand was huge. Other instrument makers hurried to copy and improve on Graham and Tompion's idea. In the 1760s, Benjamin Martin invented an orrery in which the spheres were on thin brass arms connected to an upright central rod, so they looked more as though they were moving freely in space.

The naming of this type of device can be confusing. Sometimes it is known as a planetarium but at other times as a tellurium. However, the term planetarium today usually means a building inside which you can see representations of the heavens projected above and around you, while a tellurium is a model that shows only the movement of the earth and moon around the sun and therefore doesn't include the planets. Today the generic term for a mechanical model of the solar system, however few or many bodies it includes, is orrery.

Such models are very popular with collectors, and there is no such thing as a cheap orrery or armillary sphere. Even a comparatively recent example, of plain design and in less than perfect condition, will be worth a very substantial amount.

Globes from the 19th and 20th centuries are much more affordable. Early globes are rare and difficult to find, so unless you have a hefty budget you should stay away from anything earlier than about 1870. Whichever period you choose, look for unusual features. The changing map is of special interest: an 18th-century globe that shows the new United States will be worth more than twice as much as a globe without that feature. More recent globes might show shipping lanes or even undersea telegraph lines. Pairs of globes are also valuable: matching terrestrial and celestial globes will often be worth more than the sum of the individual pieces. The style of the stand will also affect the price. The best early examples were made to blend in with the furniture and may feature reeded or cabriole legs.

Always check the condition carefully before buying. Globes are fragile items and plaster spheres are subject to cracking and chipping. Small cracks are to be expected, especially around the axis, but holes or crushed areas are expensive to restore. Paper gores are likely to be rubbed and worn, but the less damage the better.

◄ American Fortin-pattern stick barometer
By J. H. Temple, *c.*1840. This barometer is made of rosewood rather than mahogany, which indicates that, although it is of a marine style, it was not intended for marine use.
£700–1,000/$1,000–1,500

▲ Detail of the maker's signature
This adds to the barometer's value, as very few known examples of John Temple's work exist.

◄ Marine Fortin-pattern stick barometer
By Spencer, Browning and Co., London, mid-19th century. This example is made of mahogany, and is mounted on a gimbal.
£1,000–1,500/ $1,500–2,000

► US Signal Corps Fortin-pattern laboratory barometer
Henry J. Green, Brooklyn, *c.*1900. The plain mahogany case indicates that this particular barometer was intended for scientific use. It includes a °C and °F thermometer.
£300–450/$500–700

Barometers, Thermometers and Ancillary Instruments

Even today our lives are dominated by the weather, and in the days before newspapers and radio, thermometers and barometers were an essential part of home technology. Farmers, market traders, builders and anyone dependent on the shipping business would each have pressure and temperature instruments ready to hand. Skilled craftsmen made elegant casings for the instruments, and by the mid-19th century, every middle-class home had a barometer. Once it was realized that air pressure changed with altitude, experimenters began taking barometers up mountains. Workshops made barometers in their thousands, in an array of designs that offer an exciting field to today's collectors.

The barometer is the single most important meteorological instrument there is. It measures atmospheric pressure and was invented in 1643 by an Italian mathematician and physicist named Evangelista Torricelli. It was he who realized that

air has weight – the principle that makes weather forecasting possible. Within a few years, any man who considered himself to be educated had a barometer. These were made in beautiful and exotic woods with silver and ivory inlays by skilled craftsmen, usually clockmakers. This is why early barometers so often resemble longcase clocks in their finishing and ornamentation.

Very few 17th-century barometers have survived, so those available are mostly from the 18th and 19th centuries. Some names to look out for on the maker's plate are John Joseph Hicks, a leading London craftsman, Negretti & Zambra, an Italian firm, also in London, and J. H. Temple of Boston, whose instruments are particularly rare and fine.

Barometers fall into three main groups: the stick, the wheel, or banjo, and the aneroid. The stick barometer replaced the early clock-shaped one as demand grew for more portable barometers to be

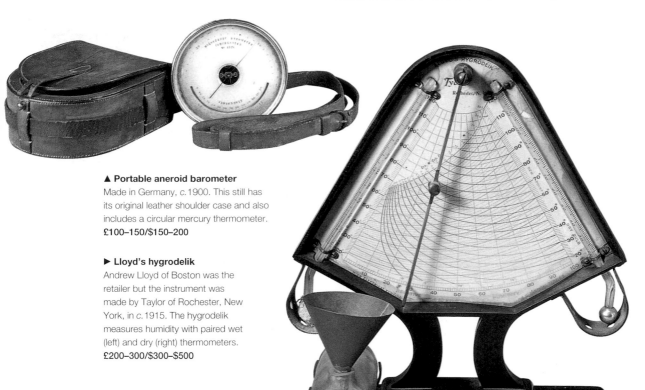

used on ships, down mines and for research trips
and expeditions. Original stick barometers are
especially valuable for their greater age and their
Georgian appearance.

The banjo barometer dominated the 19th
century and it still remains the most familiar form.
It was invented by Robert Hooke (1635–1703) and
has a float in the cistern attached to threads that run
over a pulley and move an indicator on a dial. The
banjo is the most sought-after barometer purely
because of its beauty. It wasn't popular as a scientific
instrument because its construction gave unreliable
results. However, the banjo was accurate enough
for domestic use and replaced the stick barometer in
many households. Many banjo barometers were
made to order from exotic woods, silver, ivory
and mother-of-pearl, but stick ones were usually
made of mahogany.

The technology of the barometer continued
to improve during the 19th century. A Frenchman
named Fortin developed a system using a cylindrical glass cistern with a leather base. An adjusting
screw regulates the mercury level in conjunction
with a pointer so that point zero is standardized
before a reading is taken. The Fortin pattern
proved very popular, especially for marine
barometers. A vernier (sliding indicator marked
with finer calibrations) was also introduced, which
made it possible to take more accurate readings on
a stick barometer.

The next major advance was the aneroid
barometer, invented by the Frenchman Lucien
Vidie (1805–66) around 1840. It contains a metal
box from which all the air has been pumped.
Springs prevent the box from collapsing, and the lid
moves up and down as the external air pressure
changes. Aneroid barometers were cheap to make
and much better at resisting tilting and bumping

▶ English pocket barometer
By Negretti & Zambra, c.1875. This example is in a gilt pocket-watch-style case.
£100–150/$150–200

◀ A pair of maximum and minimum thermometers
By Negretti & Zambra, c.1900. They are still in their original case.
£200–250/$300–400

than mercury was. Another advantage was that aneroid barometers could be made very small. By 1860, pocket barometers had become popular.

Pocket barometers are very collectable and affordable. Some have sturdy, leather-covered wooden cases as they were designed for taking on expeditions. Most barometers are made of brass, though gold or silver was sometimes used. A gilt pocket barometer was a real status symbol.

The science of meteorology led to an explosion of new instruments, some rivalling the barometer and others designed to be used in conjunction with it. The sympiesometer relied on a gas, usually hydrogen, rather than a vacuum. The tube had a cistern at the top containing hydrogen, which was sealed from the air by coloured almond oil in the tube. Changes in air pressure made the oil move up and down. The oil responded more quickly than mercury, but changes in temperature could make the hydrogen expand and move the oil, so a sympiesometer always has a thermometer mounted beside it. It is a technically elegant instrument but was not as popular as the barometer.

Thermometers were commonly used alongside barometers. High temperatures cause the mercury to expand in barometers and give an inaccurate reading, so it is necessary to correct for it. Galileo is credited with the invention of the mercury-in-glass thermometer, although the sealed thermometer didn't come into existence until after his death in 1642. The modern alcohol and mercury ones were invented around 1720 by a German physicist named Gabriel Fahrenheit. He also proposed the Fahrenheit scale. The Centigrade scale, however, is the more widely used today. It is also known as the Celsius scale in honour of its inventor, Anders Celsius, a Swedish astronomer and a contemporary of Fahrenheit. Scientific thermometers use the Kelvin scale. These three are the main survivors of a host of scales that were used in the 18th century.

On the whole, thermometers were instruments of science rather than decoration. They are nearly always found cased with other meteorological instruments. But keep an eye out for thermometers that were given away as promotional items in the early 20th century. There are also advertising

▼ **Biram six-inch anemometer**
It was made in England and retailed in
Philadelphia by Queen & Co, *c*.1900. This
instrument was used for measuring wind speed.
£150–200/$250–300

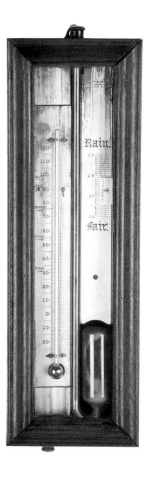

▲ **(Above) 2¾ inch anemometer**
c.1875, with the dial perpendicular
to the blades. **£150–200/$250–300**
▶ **(Right) Currier & Simpson**
station barometer and thermometer
Late 19th-century, enclosed in a glazed
mahogany case. **£400–500/$600–800**

thermometers, ranging from late Victorian ones
mounted on tin for display in village shops through
to 1990s fridge magnets. The older thermometers
will be worth more, especially if they are attached to
an attractive advertisement, but it's worth holding
on to relatively modern ones to bring your collection
up to date. Well-known brand names are always
collectable, as are designs particularly evocative of
their periods.

A lesser known instrument is the hygrometer,
which measures humidity. Early hygrometers relied
on humidity-sensitive materials such as oat-beard or
catgut, glued to a pointer that moved as the material
changed shape. Not surprisingly, they were very inaccurate. However, they often have pointlessly precise
calibrations to make them look scientific. From the
second half of the 18th century, hygrometers began to
be included on barometers to help with forecasts.
They still didn't work very well; in fact, some
barometers have the non-operative hygrometers
with pointer glued on, just to look good. Spirit levels
are another decorative feature, as using your eye to
hang a household barometer straight is good enough.

Hygrodeliks were popular home weather
stations in the early 20th century and consisted of
paired wet and dry thermometers (also known as
psychrometers) and a humidity chart with a moving
indicator. The wet thermometer has its bulb in
water, which evaporates and causes cooling. The
difference in the two thermometers indicates the
relative humidity of the air. Anemometers were
also important instruments as they measured wind
speed. Portable models in wooden carrying cases
were popular for measuring air flow in mines.

All these ancillary instruments are intriguing in
themselves and will add interest to a collection of
barometers. Remember that all meteorological
instruments, particularly mercury barometers, are
fragile. Careless or rough handling can cause the
heavy, and hazardous, mercury to slosh and break
the tube. Any damage reduces the value, so check
carefully for missing knobs, pointers or screws on
any instrument. The older a barometer, the less
likely it is to work, especially in the case of banjo
barometers. Restoration may not harm the value
but must be done by a skilled specialist.

Telescopes

If any single scientific instrument can be said to have changed the world completely, then it is the telescope

Considering how the telescope has shaken the foundations of our thought and attitudes, surprisingly little is known about its precise origins. Lens technology is very old indeed – simple lenses of rock crystal dating from the 7th century BC have been found at Nineveh (in present-day Iraq) – and spectacles seem to have been invented around 1286 in Italy. The basic optical principles of the telescope were first described in the 13th century by Roger Bacon, an English scientist. Obscure references to similar devices in the 14th century exist, but the telescope itself did not appear until the 17th century.

A Dutch spectacle maker named Hans Lippershey is credited with the telescope's invention in 1608. He worked on his device with a colleague, Zacharias Janzoons, and they offered their telescope to the Dutch Estates General as a military instrument.

News of the exciting new invention spread rapidly across Europe. By June of 1609 telescopes were on sale in Paris, and, at the same time, word of the instrument reached the Italian physicist and astronomer Galileo Galilei (1564–1642). This was the moment that marked a revolution in the way mankind perceived the world.

The dominant view of the universe at the time was that proposed by Ptolemy in the 2nd century AD. According to the Ptolemaic system, the earth lay still at the centre of the universe and the sun and the planets revolved around it. By the 16th century astronomers had noticed that a geocentric (earth-centred) model of the universe did not explain certain phenomena. One Polish astronomer, Nicolaus Copernicus, had postulated a theory that the sun lay at the centre and the earth moved around it, spinning on its own axis. This theory made sense, but it was very hard to accept the idea of a moving earth, and besides, Copernicus' calculations were no simpler or more accurate than those of his predecessors. As a result, between 1543 and 1600 only a

▼ Hand telescope

By Broadhurst, Clarkson & Co., London, early 20th century. It is known as a three-draw telescope because it has three sections, or draws. It is covered with leather and has a pull-out shade for the main lens; it is also engraved with the words "Rifle Club". £100–150/$150–250

◄ Astronomical telescope

By Alvan Clark & Sons of Cambridgeport, Massachusetts, 1891. The small telescope on top is a star finder, or position finder, used to aim the large refracting telescope. £7,000–10,000/$10,000–15,000

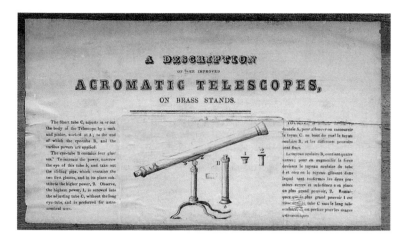

◄ Telescope label

This label was from a telescope made by Dellatour & Co., London, c.1850. The typeface and illustrations can help to date the instrument – such labels increase value because of the added interest. The telescope with its case and label intact is worth £1,000–1,500/ $1,500–2,000

handful of astronomers followed the Copernican theory. Galileo was the man who rescued it, using his own telescope to confirm the earth's true place in the solar system.

Galileo's work landed him in deep trouble with professors of philosophy and the leaders of the Roman Catholic Church, who held that belief in a moving earth was heretical. He was imprisoned, and after his trial, in 1633, Copernican theory was suppressed. Galileo died under house arrest nine years later, but he had planted the seeds of the scientific revolution that flowered under Isaac Newton.

There are two main kinds of optical telescope: reflecting (which use mirrors) and refracting. Early (17th-century) telescopes are all refracting – they use a lens to magnify an object by bending the light to a focal point. Unfortunately, every colour of light has its own degree of refraction, so the lens will bring different colours to a different focus. This is known as chromatic aberration and causes the image of the object to be surrounded by rings

of different colours. In 1757 a British optician, John Dollond, found that using two lenses made of glass with different refractive indexes solved the problem. The resulting achromatic telescopes were very popular.

John Dollond is an important British telescope maker, as is the Scotsman James Short. The firm of Alvan Clark & Sons is a highly regarded American maker, and its instruments always fetch a high price.

Tripod telescopes can be very valuable indeed, depending on their size, age and quality. However, there are plenty of more affordable telescopes around. Hand telescopes are generally within reach of the average pocket as they were made in their thousands in the 19th and early 20th centuries.

Whether your interest lies in full-sized telescopes or in binoculars and hand telescopes, look for good condition. An example that does not work will need to be extremely rare, very old or connected with a famous name if it is to be worth much at all.

▶ Reflecting telescope
By John Cuthbert, 1838. This is an
example of an English 4¼-in (10-cm)
brass reflecting telescope. It has a 15½-in
(40-cm) body tube and a star finder on a
folding tripod stand 16½in (42cm) high.
£1,500–2,000/$2,500–3,000

▲ Detail of signature
John Cuthbert's signature, showing
the date and place of manufacture of
this, the last recorded telescope that
was made by him.

Classic Forms

The refracting telescope was the first to be built.
Early lens makers dealt with the problem of
chromatic aberration by reducing the curvature of
the object glass (the one at the far end of the barrel).
Unfortunately, this meant that the telescope had
to be made much longer to accommodate the
increased focal length of the flatter lenses, and some
telescopes were built that were 45m (150ft) long.
In 1656 a Dutch mathematician, physicist and
astronomer named Christiaan Huygens (1629–95)
laid the groundwork for John Dollond's achromatic
telescope when he used two convex lenses in the eyepiece in an attempt to cut down on chromatic
aberration. He wasn't the first inventor to use more
than one lens, and his system was nowhere near as
sophisticated as Dollond's work with refractive
indexes. However, it should be remembered that
the reason for chromatic aberration was not yet
understood – and wouldn't be until 1666, when
Isaac Newton passed sunlight through a glass prism
and realized that it was made up of different colours.

Meanwhile, inventors and instrument makers
were struggling with the problem of unmanageably
long telescopes. They realized that if they could
reflect the light back and forth within the barrel it
wouldn't need to be so long. However, if it was hard
to make a good lens, it was even harder to make a
good mirror. They began with speculum metal, a
mixture of copper and tin, but it tarnished quickly.

By the middle of the 18th century, reflecting
telescopes had improved considerably in quality.
The best of them were made by James Short.
Short used a mirror made of glass backed with
quicksilver. He signed and numbered all his
telescopes – the highest number known is 1,370, and
they are all very valuable. Short also put the power
of the telescope on each one, but it would be wise
not to believe his rating. Telescopes were sold by
their power then, so the higher the magnification,
the higher the price. Regrettably, Short was not
above overrating his instruments in order to get
them into the next price bracket.

▲ A pair of marine telescopes
(Top) A single-draw marine telescope by the famous Jesse Ramsden, late 18th century. (Bottom) A marine telescope by Pistor & Martins, Berlin, mid-19th century. Both are made of mahogany and brass.
£300–500/$500–800 each

▲ Library telescope
Made by Spencer, Browning & Rust of London, mid-19th century. This is a classic brass refracting telescope of the type bought by gentlemen for use in the library.
£600–1,000/$1,000–1,500

It is always worth checking a telescope for the maker's name. They were expensive, high quality instruments, and a good maker would usually sign his work. John Cuthbert was a noted London maker in the early 19th century. The first telescope shown above is the last recorded telescope by him, so it is especially interesting although it has lost its original lacquered finish. This finish is an important factor in valuing an instrument. Many older examples have deliberately been polished to a high shine, which ruins their appearance and reduces their value a lot.

Refracting telescopes continued to be made alongside reflecting ones, and there are some very nice early examples still around today. Marine telescopes are popular with collectors, being sought after partly for the romance associated with marine instruments and partly for the beauty of the classic marine materials of mahogany and brass. Sturdily built to withstand damp and extreme temperatures, they have usually survived well. Classic marine telescopes usually have a single draw (one tube that slides inside the outer barrel) and are covered in mahogany. Like all hand telescopes they are often signed on the draw, and the signature can be used to date an instrument. Take a look at the direction of the signature. If it begins at the eyepiece and runs down the barrel of the draw, it is likely to be late 18th/early 19th century. If it starts on the draw and runs towards the eyepiece, it is probably from the 19th century or later.

In homes, the library telescope was very popular throughout the 19th century. It is so called because educated gentlemen would often keep one in the library, together with a pair of globes. It was used for looking over land or sea; landowners might use one to keep an eye on what was happening on their property, and if you lived near a port it was fun to watch the ships. Library telescopes often have decorative cabriole legs designed to harmonize with furniture styles of the day. They came in wooden storage cases for home assembly – the barrel and the pillar are separate, and the legs can be folded up.

◀ **Three-inch refracting telescope**
Made in France and signed by the American retailer, S. Thaxter & Son, Boston, *c.*1900. This powerful telescope was for celestial as well as terrestrial observation.
£1,000–2,000/ $2,000–3,000

◀ **Alvan Clark telescope**
Made by Alvan Clark & Sons, the most important American maker, *c.*1877, this 10cm (4in) brass astronomical telescope also has a starfinder attached to it.
£5,000–7,000/ $7,000–10,000

Library telescopes are highly collectable today because they are decorative pieces that still fit in well with modern furniture. However, fairly utilitarian telescopes are also very desirable. High quality instruments intended for serious scientific use were made in plainer designs but, being made of brass and hardwood, are attractive items too.

In the early 19th century, European instrument makers dominated the field, manufacturing telescopes and optical instruments. Until American manufacturing started to equal European quality, American instrument makers continued to import and retail telescopes from Britain, France and Germany. These imported instruments have survived well, and it's worth examining them closely. They will often have the maker's name engraved on the telescope itself, while the retailer's label is usually on the case. The more labelling an instrument has, the greater is its interest and value. The name of the retailer also makes a difference to the price, as some are better known than others.

Thaxter & Son was a leading Boston firm of instrument makers which retailed European instruments. They were costly objects at the time and were carefully looked after, so many of them are still in excellent condition today. These imported instruments were typically of much higher power than the library telescopes discussed earlier. In fact they are powerful enough for celestial observation (looking at the heavens) as well as for looking out to sea or land. Telescopes such as these appeal to serious scientific collectors both for their history and because they are mostly still usable today. If you look closely at the oak tripod above, you will see that the legs have pointed ends. This makes it possible to set the telescope up out of doors. The tripod is fully adjustable for uneven ground and even for height.

By the end of the 19th century, American manufacturing had improved, so fewer instruments were imported from Europe. Alvan Clark & Sons was the leading maker of astronomical telescopes in the United States and its work is highly sought after today. The distinguishing mark of a specifically astronomical telescope is the starfinder, or small telescope, that is used for sighting the great lens.

Collecting Telescopes

▲ English field binoculars
British-made binoculars dating from the
early 20th century. As this example shows,
the basic design of binoculars has not
changed for over a century.
£50–100/$100–150

▲ Telescopes in the home
Painting, possibly by the Canadian/American artist Wyatt
Eaton (1849–96), late 19th century, of Mrs Swift and her
sons. £10,000–13,500/$15,000–20,000

Anyone who has looked through binoculars will
know how hard it can be to find the object you want
to examine. The starfinder made it easier to pick out
one star from hundreds. Once the main telescope
was correctly sighted, the user could adjust the
focus. Astronomical telescopes also have tripods
for outdoor use. Clark's instruments are among
the most valuable, but it is possible to find more
affordable models.

Most people don't have the space for a large
collection of tripod telescopes, but, if you wish to
collect in this field, don't forget to look out for
binoculars. They were invented by a Viennese
named Voigtländer who, in 1823, came up with the
idea of fixing two individually focused telescopes
side by side. The central focusing ring was developed
by J. P. Lemaire two years later, but binoculars did
not replace the hand telescope until after 1859, when
A. A. Boulanger put prisms between the lenses of his
binoculars, which allowed them to be made with a
much shorter tube. Binoculars became widespread at
the end of the 19th century, so most of the examples
you find will be from the early 20th century.

This rare contemporary painting shows
us how telescopes were incorporated into
everyday life and also how they were seen as
symbols of wealth and learning. Captain W.C.N.
Swift of Massachusetts was the owner of a fleet
of China clippers in the second half of the 19th
century. In this picture we see Mrs Swift and
her two sons at their home, watching the
harbour anxiously for the Captain's return.
The boy on the balcony outside the window
is using a brass refracting telescope, similar to
the one illustrated on page 57, while his mother
holds a pair of binoculars in her lap. The
binoculars would obviously have been less
powerful but much easier to use.

The painting has been carefully posed, and
the two optical instruments have been given great
importance within it. Just as a skull would often
have been used as a prop in portraits of doctors to
denote their medical knowledge, so the telescope
on the balcony, when combined with the boy's
naval-style cap, immediately shows us that this
family has strong links with the sea. Mrs Swift's
binoculars reveal that she was a devoted wife,
concerned for her husband's welfare. Together
with the telescope, they also demonstrate that the
Swifts were a prosperous family who could
afford such expensive instruments.

Microscopes

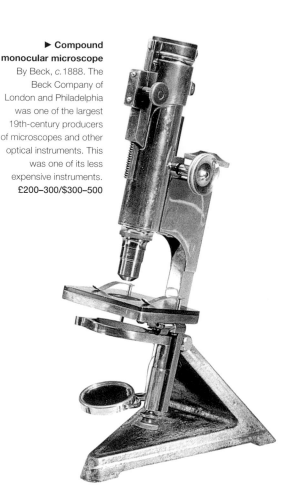

The invention of the microscope revealed the existence of a universe that had never before been imagined

The story of microscopes has many parallels with the story of telescopes (*see* pp.54–9). If telescopes revolutionized one end of mankind's universe, then microscopes transformed the other. The magnifying lens revealed a world of tiny life forms and changed the sciences of biology and medicine for ever.

Like telescopes, microscopes arrived more or less by accident. Good quality magnifying lenses have been around for a very long time indeed – archaeologists in Iraq have found magnifying lenses of rock crystal dating from about 700BC. Scientific writings from classical times noted the magnifying powers of a drop of water, and street traders in Victorian London used the same principle to make simple toys. Instead of putting a drop of water on a tiny object, they used a drop of amber. These little microscopes sold for a penny each.

Galileo is associated with the microscope as well as the telescope. Within months of making his first telescopic observations, the Italian astronomer had adapted his telescope to make a compound microscope.

However, the history of the microscope as a scientific instrument really begins in the 1660s, when a Dutchman named Antony van Leeuwenhoek (1632–1723) made a lens with the extraordinary magnification of 270 – a power that exceeded some later compound microscopes. His microscope was a very simple device, consisting of a bi-convex lens mounted between two plates of brass and held to the eye, but it turned the world of science on its head. Leeuwenhoek's microscope also revealed the existence of bacteria – but he kept the craft of making his astonishingly powerful lenses a secret, so bacteria were not seen again for another two centuries.

There are two main classes of optical microscope, simple and compound. The simple microscope consists of a single bi-convex lens positioned between the eye and the object to be viewed – like Leeuwenhoek's microscope. The compound microscope has

◄ Folding monocular microscope
By Smith & Beck of London, c.1856. Smith & Beck later became the Beck Company. This is a portable instrument designed for use in the field. It comes with a complete set of accessories.
£400–500/$600–800

▲ Specimen magnifier
This simple microscope is probably English, from the late 19th century. It would have been used for examining small specimens or for looking into liquids.
£15–20/$20–30

▲ Photographic metallurgical microscope
By Unitron, c.1935. This American instrument works in reverse, with the slide on top and the eyepiece in the base. It is made of black enamelled metal and has an internal electric illuminant.
£150–200/$200–300

two lenses, an objective lens and an ocular lens, mounted inside a tube. Both kinds were used from the 17th century. Advances in lens technology and production gradually brought the price of microscopes down, and production rose slowly. By the beginning of the 19th century, ownership of microscopes was becoming widespread.

Because microscopy was a fashionable hobby, microscopes were built to be decorative as well as functional. They were sold with all kinds of accessories, such as different eyepieces, pre-prepared slides, and forceps for holding specimens.

Developments and improvements occurred throughout the 17th, 18th and 19th centuries, and the microscope's shape gradually evolved into the design that we recognize today. Lens quality, focusing and illumination were all problems that had to be overcome before the microscope could become a truly useful scientific instrument. Today the varying designs throughout its

history are important factors in deciding the interest and value of any one piece.

There is a wealth of choice for collectors in this field. You may decide to focus your collection on one particular type, such as the simple microscope. It is also possible to specialize in a particular period or region – perhaps Georgian English, 19th-century Continental or even turn-of-the century American microscopes.

As you might expect, the older a microscope and the better its quality, the more expensive it will be. However, there are still some surprisingly affordable early instruments around, although they do represent the more simple designs. One essential point to remember is that people like to collect microscopes for their beauty as much as for their technical quality. Superior looks will always attract more interest, even in an inferior instrument. Interesting features, such as a novel way to adjust the stage or set the focus, are also important factors in value.

DIRECTIONS FOR USING THE PICTURES.
It will be noticed that the pictures are on one side of the glass, this side should be placed uppermost in the instrument, this will bring the numbers right.
Should there be particles of dust on the slides, they should be wiped off with a *Silk* handkerchief.
Should the lens need cleaning, use a silk handkerchief also. To clean the lens on the inside twist a portion of the handkerchief and press it into the tube, then by twisting the tube in the fingers the lens will be cleaned.

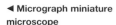

◄ **Micrograph miniature microscope**
American, *c.*1850–75. This simple, inexpensive microscope, marketed as a novelty item for viewing microscopic pictures of famous people and places, is part of a boxed kit including slides, tweezers and instructions. **£150–250/$250–350**

◄ **Group of six magnifiers**
(Front row) Three magnifiers, English, *c.*1835–50, for hanging on a watch or other kind of chain. **£50–85/$75–125 each**
(Back row, from left) Tripod magnifier, probably English, for looking at stones or papers; French pocket magnifier with spike for examining insects; English specimen magnifier (*see* p. 61). All late 19th/early 20th century. **£15–35/$25–50 each**

Simple Microscopes

The development of microscopes was underpinned by the development of lens technology. Although compound microscopes offered increased power and a wider field of range, they were severely hampered by the poor quality of early lenses. Air bubbles in the glass obscured the view, while chromatic and spherical aberrations made the specimen appear blurred and surrounded by a halo of colour. While this didn't matter so much in an astronomical telescope, it was a severe problem in an instrument designed for looking at tiny objects. Increasing the number of lenses tended to increase the difficulties, so simple microscopes remained the instrument of choice for some centuries. Research aimed at improving simple microscopes therefore continued for much longer than you might expect.

Leeuwenhoek's simple microscope remained the pattern for basic magnifiers for centuries. His device was held up to the eye while the specimen was held on a pin on the other side of the lens. This type of arrangement became known as the flea glass, since the device was often used to examine insects. Flea glasses were produced well into the 19th century. It is almost impossible to date them accurately, as the design did not change and most examples are unsigned.

Other versions of the basic magnifier were also very popular throughout the 19th century. Tiny glasses for hanging from a watch chain echoed the quizzing glasses of the previous century, but instead of peering at ladies through them, gentlemen would examine the cell structure of leaves, the crystalline structure of stones or anything else that took their scientific fancy. A more advanced version of the flea glass incorporated a barrel containing a spike on which the hapless insect could be impaled in order to aid closer observation. The quality of these instruments is not great but they are fun, novelty items and are adequate for amateur purposes. They are good additions to a microscope collection, since some simple magnifiers were also sold as accessories to a microscopes.

◀ **Ellis-pattern aquatic microscope**
By R. B. Bate, London, early 19th century. This is a classic example of the type used by amateur microscopists of the time – it is easily portable and could be carried in the pocket on walks. £400–535/$600–800

▲ **Group of English simple microscopes**
19th century. **(From bottom)** Folding naturalist's microscope, £150–200/$200–300; ivory-handled magnifiers, £15–50/$25–75; drum microscope £15–50/$25–75; Coddington magnifier, £15–50/$25–75; naturalist's microscope, £200–300/$300–500; compass microscope, £100–200/$200–300

The simple microscope became much more versatile towards the end of the 17th century when the compass microscope was introduced. This microscope was named for its resemblance to the drawing instrument. It had two hinged legs, one of which held the lens while the other held the object, either in forceps or impaled on a point. The compass microscope was hand-held, but it had a screw between the legs, which made it easy to find and hold the focus. And, most importantly, it was possible to use different lenses with varying powers of magnification in the same instrument.

The screw-barrel microscope took focusing a step further. It was invented by another Dutchman, Nicolaas Hartsoeker, at the end of the 17th century, and was introduced in England in 1700 by James Wilson, whose name is often used to describe this pattern of microscope. The lens was mounted in a threaded barrel so that its distance from the specimen could be adjusted. For the first time the microscope began to take on the form we recognize today.

In the mid-18th century John Ellis, an English naturalist and a Fellow of the Royal Society, developed the aquatic microscope. The idea for this had first been introduced by Leeuwenhoek, who built a microscope with a small glass container that could be used for examining liquids. With it he observed the transparent tail of a fish and was able to confirm the theory of blood circulation. Ellis's instrument used a watch glass to hold a small amount of pond water on the stage. The lens was held in an arm mounted on a pillar and could be moved from side to side as well as up and down. The microscope's case, small enough to fit in the palm of the hand, doubled as a stand.

Ellis's pattern was enormously popular. It was adopted by various different instrument makers and remained in production – with some slight improvements but basically unchanged – well into the 19th century. It was especially loved by amateur microscopists for use in the field. The most reliable way to date an Ellis-pattern microscope is by the

▲ **Group of naturalists' microscopes**
(Back left) Folding dissecting microscope by Ogden of Boston, *c.*1890; the iron base is also a dissecting table. £600–1,000/$1,000–1,500.
(Centre, from front to back) Agriculturist microscope by Bausch & Lomb, *c.*1880; Gould-pattern simple/compound microscope by R. Field & Son, Birmingham, *c.*1850. £150–250/$250–350 each. **(Front left, back right and front right)** These three show the varieties of design that were produced for the same instrument. Mid to late 19th century, £300–500/$500–800 each

maker. Should the instrument be unsigned, as many of them are, the case can be a good guide to the date. Cases covered in fish skin tend to be from the 18th and early 19th centuries, while mahogany cases are mostly from the 19th century.

Aquatic microscopes have often lost some of their pieces. The easiest way to spot missing pieces is by looking at the instrument when it is packed into its fitted case, when any empty compartments will be immediately obvious. Also, if a piece doesn't fit perfectly, it may be a replacement. However, it's not a major disaster if some minor parts are missing or are not the original ones.

During the first half of the 19th century several different types of lens were developed to replace the single bi-convex lens commonly used in the simple microscope. Doublet lenses (combinations of two lenses) had been tried since the 17th century, but had not been very satisfactory. In 1812, William Wollaston of London designed a very successful combination of two plano-convex lenses (plane, or flat, on one side and convex on the other). A diaphragm inserted between the two lenses

improved the resolution still further and helped to reduce distortion. These lenses are sometimes referred to as Wollaston doublets. The Coddington lens also appeared at this time – it was not especially powerful but was cheap to produce, so it was widely used for small magnifiers.

As lenses improved, work continued on the compound microscope (*see* pp.66–9), and some simple microscopes were adapted to compound lenses. The Cary- or Gould-pattern naturalist's microscope was one of these. Introduced in the 1820s, it was a development of the Ellis-pattern simple microscope. Cary sold it and often signed examples, although it was his employee Gould who made it popular, and rumour has it that Gould was in fact the designer too. It had a small tube that contained extra lenses and screwed onto the ring that held the simple lens, thus converting it to a compound lens.

Naturalists' microscopes were a new design of the mid-19th century and were very popular with the general public. They were made for many years, and still survive in good numbers. Many are signed

► **Pocket microscope**
French, c.1904. This example was sold as a souvenir piece at the 1904 World's Fair in St. Louis, Missouri. It gains its value from the accompanying sheet and original box. £100–150/$200–250

◄ **Simple/compound portable microscope**
French, mid-19th century. If the body tube is removed a simple objective lens may be substituted. A ball joint at the base of the pillar allows the user to select any angle for viewing. With leather case, £250–400/$400–600

Cary, London, but it's not unusual to find the names of other makers on them or no signature at all.

Microscope quality improved sharply during the middle of the 19th century, even as the price fell, which made them accessible to a wider range of people. For a farmer, an agriculturist's microscope was a very useful tool. Small, inexpensive and easily portable, it could be carried into the fields and used to diagnose blight on the crops.

That a farmer could buy and use such an instrument is an indication of the enormous impact that microscope technology had had on the advancement of the sciences. When 19th-century scientists rediscovered Leeuwenhoek's ability to see bacteria, biology was turned on its head. In the 1860s the French biologist Louis Pasteur finally exploded the long-lived theory of spontaneous generation when he showed that microbes did not arise from non-living matter but were introduced there from the environment. The German scientist Robert Koch built on the work of Leeuwenhoek and Pasteur when he isolated the anthrax bacillus in the 1870s, thereby demonstrating the germ theory of medicine. By the end of the 19th century every educational institution was supplied with microscopes and most students possessed their own. At the same time, microscopy remained popular among a vast number of amateurs.

Because so many were made, there are plenty of simple microscopes available for collectors today. There is a wealth of choice in designs, from the small portables to large models with dissecting tables. Best of all, they are not usually expensive, so it's possible to build a good-sized collection even on a limited budget. Specialist dealers are the most convenient places to look for simple microscopes, but of course you are unlikely to find bargains there. It is worth looking out for microscopes at general dealers, country auctions and house-clearance sales, as they quite often turn up in such places.

Small magnifiers appear everywhere, from junk shops to top microscope dealers. They are very affordable as they are not rated highly but they are, nevertheless, representative of the development of the microscope and certainly should have a place in your collection.

◀ **Culpeper-pattern compound microscope**
English, c.1780. This would originally have had a plinth with an accessories drawer and a mahogany pyramid-shaped case like a metronome's. Many of these microscopes are signed by leading makers of the time such as Adams, Martin or Jones. **£1,000–1,500/ $1,500–2,000** (perhaps double that if complete).

▲ **Nuremberg-pattern compound microscope**
German, early 19th century. Named after the town where it was made, this microscope is made of cardboard and wood. **£1,000–1,500/$1,500–2,000**

▲ **E. & J. Bausch compound microscope**
By E. & J. Bausch, forerunner of Bausch & Lomb, late 1850s. This is a simple, inexpensive microscope, similar to the French model on page 65. The value lies mainly in the interest of the maker's name. **£250–400/$400–600**

Compound Microscopes

The first compound microscopes were made in the early 1600s and consisted, like a telescope, of a body tube. They were also held in the same way as a telescope, and contained three lenses lined up one behind the other: the ocular lens of the eyepiece, the field lens (which made the field of vision much wider than was possible in a simple microscope) and finally the objective lens, which is nearest the object under examination. As with the simple microscope, illumination was a problem, and users had to stand near a light source in order to get enough light.

Microscope-making in the 17th and early 18th centuries was mostly based in London and Italy, with the London instruments dominating the market by the mid-1700s. Very few of these early microscopes have survived, probably because they were largely made out of fragile materials such as cardboard. Those that do exist are in public collections. Compound microscopes in particular were not made in great numbers, because the

quality of the view depended on the quality of the object lens. Any air bubbles, chromatic aberrations or spherical aberrations were magnified by the succeeding lenses and made viewing very difficult. Lens technology was limited at the time, and good quality lenses were both expensive and difficult to make.

Because the optics were unsatisfactory during this period, microscopes were mostly decorative objects built for amateurs rather than scientific instruments of discovery and learning. One English instrument maker, John Marshall, made a significant change in 1693 when he broke away from the Italian preference for keeping the barrel vertical and instead mounted it on a ball-and-socket-joint. He also attached the stage to the pillar so that when the user tilted the barrel the specimen would remain in focus. But Marshall's new design made his instruments expensive. In 1725, Edmund Culpeper, another English instrument maker, designed a vertical microscope mounted

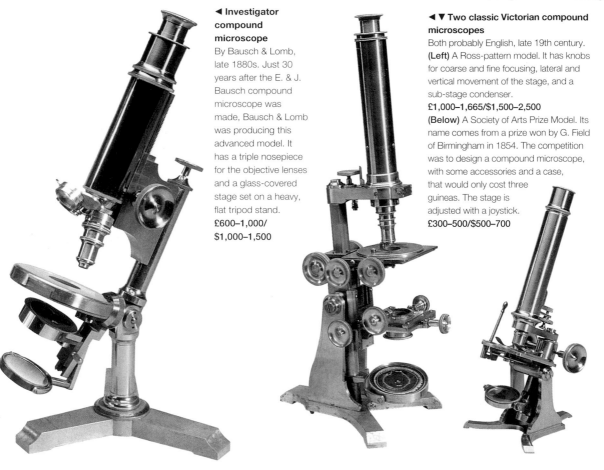

◄ **Investigator compound microscope**
By Bausch & Lomb, late 1880s. Just 30 years after the E. & J. Bausch compound microscope was made, Bausch & Lomb was producing this advanced model. It has a triple nosepiece for the objective lenses and a glass-covered stage set on a heavy, flat tripod stand.
£600–1,000/ $1,000–1,500

◄ ▼ **Two classic Victorian compound microscopes**
Both probably English, late 19th century. **(Left)** A Ross-pattern model. It has knobs for coarse and fine focusing, lateral and vertical movement of the stage, and a sub-stage condenser.
£1,000–1,665/$1,500–2,500
(Below) A Society of Arts Prize Model. Its name comes from a prize won by G. Field of Birmingham in 1854. The competition was to design a compound microscope, with some accessories and a case, that would only cost three guineas. The stage is adjusted with a joystick.
£300–500/$500–700

on a double tripod. It included a small mirror under the stage, which reflected light onto the specimen. The first Culpeper microscopes were made of wood and pasteboard or shagreen, but later models were of brass with wooden bases. They were the first really sturdy microscopes, and they are the earliest form that you are likely to find today.

You will probably also come across the Martin-pattern drum microscope. Benjamin Martin introduced this in 1738 – it's similar to the Culpeper design but the stage is partway up the body tube, which has a cut-out for access. The Martin-pattern drum microscope is one of the most widely copied and long-lasting forms, and was produced into the 20th century. It's not always easy to date examples, but as a rough guide the earlier ones are heavier and taller. Better quality is also a sign of an earlier date: those made in the first half of the 19th century often have sturdy mahogany cases. After about 1850 they were mostly sold in cases of lighter, cheaper wood.

The problem of lens quality continued to hold the compound microscope back throughout the 18th century. John Dollond's work on telescopes (*see* p.55) in the mid-18th century had not been applicable to microscopes because it wasn't possible to make the lenses small enough. However, by the 1820s, glass-making technology had advanced enough for instrument makers to return to work on improving the lenses for their microscopes.

It's a testament to the middle-class love affair with microscopes that the next great advance was made by a London wine merchant. John Joseph Lister, the father of the surgeon who discovered antisepsis (*see* p.127), invented a revolutionary microscope lens. In 1830 he presented a paper to the Royal Society on his design for an objective lens, which became the basis for the microscope lenses that are still made today. The compound microscope had at last come into its own. Its design evolved rapidly in the following decades, and soon the microscope was no longer an

◀ **Binocular/monocular compound microscope**
By Nachet et Fils, Paris, c.1890. The specimen may be viewed with either one or both eyes using this microscope. Nachet was one of the first makers to patent a binocular microscope, but his design was less convenient than the British models. However, his instruments are more decorative than their British rivals.
£2,500–3,000/ $4,000–5,000

▶ **Typical Victorian slide cabinet**
Probably English, late 19th century. These were used to store the fragile glass slides and are generally made of mahogany. Values depend on size and quality, but the slides they contain are often worth more than the cabinet itself.
£500–800/$800–1,200

expensive toy for middle-class adults but a fully functioning scientific instrument.

Lister set up a microscope-making business in the 1830s, assisted by an instrument maker named James Smith. Andrew Ross was another highly skilled maker who made some of the best microscopes ever. He worked alongside Lister too , and incorporated a lot of Lister's ideas into his instruments. Lister's nephews, Richard and Joseph Beck, also joined the firm, which became renowned for its innovative designs. In the 1850s it became the first British firm to produce a binocular microscope. Smith retired in 1864, but the firm continued under the Beck name. Its partnership with Queen & Co. of Philadelphia brought it considerable success in the United States, and many later instruments are signed "R. & J. Beck, London and Philadelphia". Beck microscopes were still being produced well into the 20th century.

By the end of the 19th century, interest in the microscope had spread well beyond just that of the amateur and production was huge. Every educational institution had a lab equipped with microscopes, and they had become an important industrial tool. The Edison Phonograph Company, for example, used hundreds of microscopes to examine the tens of thousands of diamond styluses it manufactured. And almost every instrument-making firm made microscopes.

If any one maker can be considered the finest, it has to be Powell & Lealand of London. From 1841 to 1912 the firm produced some of the finest microscopes. Its distinctive products, with their old-fashioned tripod stands, were said to have been made entirely by hand. Hugh Powell was reputed to have made every single objective lens himself, unaided and in secret. Today a Powell & Lealand instrument is the pride of any collection.

Abroad, mass production was the goal as much as quality. In France the firms of Chevalier and Nachet made excellent instruments, while notable names from Germany are the well-known Zeiss and Leitz of Leica fame (*see* pp.96–7). Their products sold internationally from the late 19th century until after World War II. There are plenty of Zeiss and Leitz microscopes available to

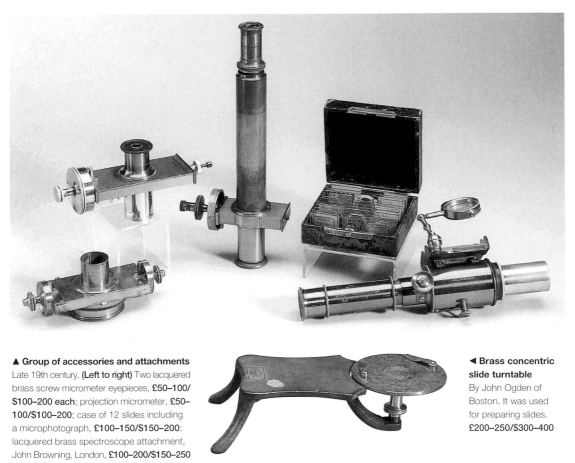

▲ **Group of accessories and attachments**
Late 19th century. **(Left to right)** Two lacquered
brass screw micrometer eyepieces, £50–100/
$100–200 each; projection micrometer, £50–
100/$100–200; case of 12 slides including
a microphotograph, £100–150/$150–200;
lacquered brass spectroscope attachment,
John Browning, London, £100–200/$150–250

◄ **Brass concentric
slide turntable**
By John Ogden of
Boston. It was used
for preparing slides.
£200–250/$300–400

collectors today, and they are of marvellous
quality. The only drawback is that they are
functional rather than decorative, so their value is
not as high as that of ornamental instruments
from the same period.

In the USA the New York firm of Bausch &
Lomb dominated the market, closely rivalled by
Spencer. Spencer microscopes did not vary much
in design and are not so collectable today, but
Bausch & Lomb produced a huge range of styles
from the 1850s onwards, and its work is much
sought after.

Most of the compound microscopes you will
find today are likely to date from after 1900. There
are plenty of earlier, more interesting pieces out
there, though, so it's worth visiting specialist
auctions and microscope dealers in order to track
them down.

Microscope accessories are also important. It's
always good to buy a microscope with as many of its
original accessories as possible. An instrument was
usually sold with a selection of eyepieces and
objective lenses, a bench condenser for help with

lighting and at least one device with which to hold
specimens. The overall price increased with the
number of accessories and this still holds true today.

Slides are a separate field in themselves. The
Royal Microscopic Society in London established
a standard size in 1840, and it quickly became the
standard everywhere. Earlier slides come in all
sizes; 18th-century instruments typically came
with multi-specimen slides of ivory and wood. In
the 1830s, small slides with individual specimens
were offered for sale. Many pre-Victorian kits
came with pre-prepared slides, but people liked to
make their own so you will find many amateur
slides too.

When you choose a microscope, always look for
condition and completeness first. Good condition is
particularly essential. Most of the 19th-century
microscopes were made of lacquered brass, but over
the years the lacquer has often worn off or been
deliberately removed. This loss can take away
as much as half the value of a piece. Check
all instruments for damage, and try to find a
microscope that still has its original case.

Weights and Measures

From moneychangers in ancient temples to village greengrocers, traders have depended on accurate methods for measuring goods

▲ **A standard 7-lb wool weight**
Issued in England under George III, late 18th/early 19th century. It is made of bronze and stamped with the royal arms.
£1,000–1,500/$1,500–2,250

The field of weights and measures is very broad and has an extensive history that involves every level of human society. Your own house is filled with instruments whose ancestry reaches back through millennia. Take a look at your ruler or tape measure – it represents a technology that was first developed thousands of years before Christ. The scales you use in your kitchen or stand on in your bathroom are likely to be a form of beam balance – the same technology moneychangers would have used. The fun of collecting these instruments lies in the sheer variety available and their affordability. Even with a tiny budget, you can build an intriguing and attractive collection in which every item will tell a story.

There were strict checks made by government departments to test the accuracy of weights and measures from very early times. If trade was to prosper, then it had to be fair, and each unit had to measure the same amount in every market place. Giving short measure has been a serious crime for centuries, and the systems we know today developed from the need for standardization. The seven-pound wool weight above is an excellent example of an early standardized weight. It was issued during the reign of George III to protect a vital sector of Britain's economy.

Today such weights are a monument to a system of weighing and measuring that used to dominate the world but was almost entirely overwhelmed by the French Revolutionaries' user-friendly metric system, introduced in 1793. Avoirdupois, as the system of pounds and ounces was named, began with the Romans, spread across much of the globe with the British Empire (thereby becoming known as Imperial measurement), and now only really survives in the USA, in a slightly variant form.

The other big attraction of this field is the huge variety of the instruments available. If you can think of anything that might need to

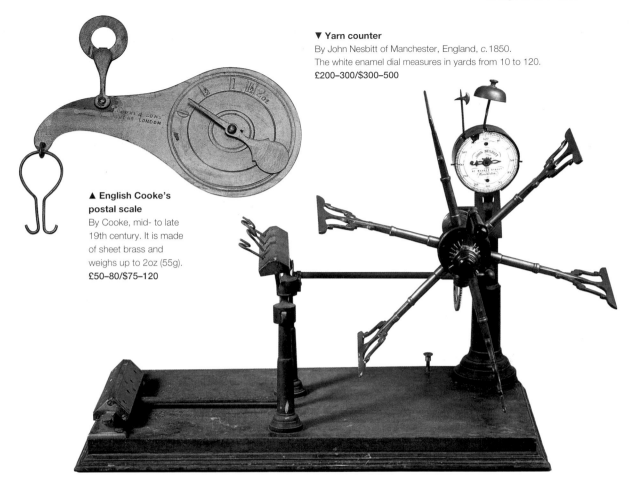

▼ **Yarn counter**
By John Nesbitt of Manchester, England, c.1850.
The white enamel dial measures in yards from 10 to 120.
£200–300/$300–500

▲ **English Cooke's
postal scale**
By Cooke, mid- to late
19th century. It is made
of sheet brass and
weighs up to 2oz (55g).
£50–80/$75–120

be weighed or measured out, someone will
have designed an instrument for it. As a rule
of thumb, the more specialist it is, the more
collectable it will be. Look for examples such
as the yarn counter above. It has a geared
six-armed wheel around which the merchant
would wind yarn. The dial reads off the
length and the bell rings every 120 yards.

Scales and balances are the most sought-
after of all weighing and measuring
instruments, and, again, those that weigh
specialist goods are the most desirable. For
instance, an egg scale will be of greater value
to collectors than an ordinary kitchen scale.
Postal scales are the most popular of all. The
Cooke's scale above is a simple but effective
design. Clip the letter on one side and read
off the weight from the dial on the other side.

Portable scales of all kinds are popular and
plentiful. Coin balances and coin testers for
checking currency are especially sought after.
They were most used from 1750 to 1820, and

it is possible to find boxed sets that include
a balance and standardized weights marked
"1 ducat", "½ a crown" and so on. They are
especially common in Britain, which had
busy ports and no doubt equally busy
counterfeiters and clippers.

British balances come in plain, canvas-
lined cases and tend to have loose weights,
either round or square. Continental weights
are square and come in fitted cases, often with
carved or punched decoration. The better
examples will have labels inside the lids,
extolling the accuracy of the weights or the
instrument in wonderfully flowery language.

If you find boxed sets of weights, check
that everything is there. If the case isn't fitted,
it's not always easy to tell. The amount and
quality of decoration will affect the value.
If it is by a well-known engraver, the value
will rise sharply. For example, anything by
Nathaniel Hurd (a Boston engraver) will
command a higher price.

▼ **Steel pocket balance**
By Samuel Read, 18th century. It comes
with brass pans and is in an oak case with
the maker's label on it.
£100–150/$150–200

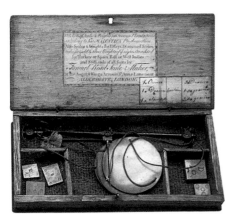

▶ **Complete set of US
standard weights**
c.1910, in their original
fitted oak case.
£100–200/$200–300

Scales, Weights and Rules

The reason that weights and measures are so popular with collectors is probably that standardized systems are so recent. It's hard to trace a logical course for their development, as the process was so gradual and was subject to many influences. From early times people used simple, arbitrary measures such as the length of an arm (the basis for the cubit of Biblical times) or the weight of a carob seed (the basis for the carat used by jewellers).

The scales and balances also developed over time in response to specific needs. From a collector's point of view, it makes more sense to sort scales and balances by their type and purpose rather than by chronological order. As a general guide, pick the area (pocket balances, industrial instruments or domestic scales, to mention just a few) that most interests you and focus your collection around that. Whatever you choose, you will find your collection reaffirms the importance of fair measure to all, whether buyers, sellers or laboratory experimenters.

The set of standard US weights pictured above offers an excellent example. This set would have been used by a US Trading Standards Officer at the start of the 20th century for checking commercial scales. The construction of the case shows us how seriously the government took the question of fair measure. It is compactly built of oak for portability (the officer would have travelled around to monitor traders) and has a lock for security.

Capacity measures were subject to the same checks – the officer's equipment included standard measures such as the pint, quart or gallon for liquid goods, and the bushel for grain and other dry goods. Traditional measures such as these are especially interesting. If you are doing a bit of detective work to trace a measure's country of origin, it's useful to remember that the Imperial (British) pint measures 20 fluid ounces while the American pint measures just 16 fluid ounces. The Americans also never used the stone (14lb). Thomas Jefferson proposed a decimal system of weights and measures as early as 1790, but Congress rejected it, and the system based on old English units remains today. Continental weights and measures use the metric system, which was one of the most significant contributions of the French Revolution and was first adopted in 1793.

▲ 19th-century beam balance
By Savage. This balance is of a particularly decorative design, and is made of brass on a mahogany base.
£300–500/$500–700

Collecting *Victorian Postal Balances*

▲ Victorian postal balance
A typical British postal balance, from the Victorian period. It has its complete set of original weights.
£100–150/$150–225

Bear in mind that, while standardized weights are relatively new, balances themselves are ancient indeed. The steelyard, for instance, is essentially the same as the beam balance that the moneychangers who famously aroused Christ's wrath would have used. Don't be misled by its name – it's not a linear measure, nor is it necessarily made from steel or even metal. A steelyard can be used to weigh absolutely anything from a beef carcass to a dose of salts. It consists of a long bar with a hook or pan for goods at one end and a sliding weight and a pointer at the other end. It has no fixed support – the user just hangs it up somewhere handy.

The miniature 18th-century steelyard shown on page 72 would have been hand held. It is made of ivory and is missing its pan, but this doesn't affect the value as much you might think because pocket balances are especially popular and this is a fairly rare type. It would have been used for measuring tiny amounts, perhaps of herbs, medicines or even precious stones. The user would have slid the cursor (on the right) along the calibrations on the beam until the balance was found.

The first general postal service with pre-paid adhesive stamps was introduced into Britain in 1840. After that, every letter-writer needed a pair of scales to calculate the weight and cost of sending a letter. As a result, a number of patents were granted for various designs of scales and balances.

Some were spring-loaded, rather like candlesticks in appearance, and they are quite collectable today. Other designs had captive (non-removable) weights, and some used twin swinging arms, with one arm measuring the first half ounce and the other weighing up to eight ounces. Postal scales and balances were produced in enormous quantities, and every middle-class home would have had one on the writing-desk.

The archetypal, traditional design for such balances is illustrated above. The user would have placed a letter on the right-hand pan and used the fitted weights on the left-hand pan to balance it. The most remarkable aspect of this balance to the modern collector's eye is that the postal rates are stamped in the right-hand pan. This was possible because, astonishingly enough, between about 1850 and 1920 there was no inflation in Britain. Wages rose but prices didn't, and postal rates may well have remained completely unchanged during the entire lifetime of the owner of this balance.

Victorian balances are very popular with collectors today, and there are plenty of examples around. Some are highly decorated with enamels and inlay and are likely to command a higher price than the plainer versions. However, the most important factor in their collectability is that the set of weights should be complete.

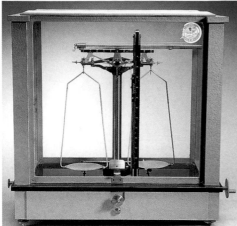

▶ **Micrometer scale**
By the Dodge Scale Co., New York, c.1905–10. It weighs quantities up to 5lb. The seal on the base indicates that a Standards Officer inspected it, and this detail adds further interest and value to the piece.
£100–200/$200–300

▲ **Analytical beam balance**
By W. Ainsworth & Sons Inc., Denver, Colorado, c.1950. It weighs up to 200 grams.
£100–150/$150–200

◀ **Pharmacist's half-ounce balance**
By Henry Tromner of Philadelphia, late 19th/early 20th century. It is made of oak with incised decoration and a marble top.
£100–150/$150–250

Keep an eye out for other kinds of portable scale. They are great fun and can be very specialist, which adds to their interest. Tea balances, for example, were used by merchants in the days when tea was still something of a luxury, and they often include tiny tasting cups.

Larger, fixed scales tend to be more expensive, particularly if they are ornate. Beam balances can be hard to date unless they are signed because the basic design hasn't changed for millennia. The example pictured on page 73 is 19th century, but its value is high because it is so decorative (the column is baluster-turned, the beam is a lattice design with a graceful lyre surround, and its base is made from mahogany). This type would have been used in a shop for weighing large amounts of almost any type of goods from foodstuffs to nails. The weights go on the left pan and the goods go in the right, which lifts out easily. Non-collectors often buy this kind of balance for its looks, so the market is much more competitive, which drives the price up.

Precision balances also come in varied designs, three of which are illustrated above. The typical analytical beam balance measures tiny amounts of substances, including gold dust. The difficulty of handling such goods dictates the design of the balance. The glass case prevents breeze, or even the user's breath, from disturbing powdered goods, and it keeps out dirt, which might otherwise get in and affect the measurement. These precision balances were often used in assay offices where miners would exchange their precious metals for cash. The glass case also meant that the miner could keep a close eye on the weighing process and make sure that the assay officer wasn't cheating him. There are plenty of 19th-century examples of this kind of balance available in the collectors' market today.

Pharmacists' balances are distinguished by their marble tops. It is an easy surface to keep clean, and any spilled medicines could be picked up without waste. The lid made it easy to carry around without damaging the balance, and the knob on the front raised the beam ready for weighing. Henry Tromner was the most prolific maker of precision balances in the United States. English names to keep an eye out for are Harrison, Ramsden and Fortin.

▼ Commercial brass beam balance
By Banfield of Brighton, England, late 19th century. Its base is made of oak, and the balance incorporates a baluster pillar.
£250–400/$400–600

▲ American counter-top Dayton scale
By The Computing Scale Company, early 20th century. It is named after the city in which the company was based – Dayton, Ohio. £100–200/$200–300

The micrometer scale was the Dodge Scale Company's attempt to improve on the beam balance. A dial in the centre shifted the weight from side to side instead of loose weights being used. Micrometer scales did work, but they were trickier to use. However, a micrometer will add authority to your collection as it demonstrates a rival design of great complexity that actually never seriously challenged the elegant simplicity of the beam balance. (It is interesting to include other versions of an instrument in a collection to compare the effectiveness of different designs.)

A less ambitious but equally ingenious improvement to the basic beam balance was the addition of a weight to the structure of the weighing side. If you look at the brass beam balance above, you will see that there is a weight suspended above the left pan. This weight was used to compensate for a heavy right pan or to allow for unwanted inclusions in the goods weighed – perhaps the wrapping for damp or sticky foodstuffs. This example is typical of the kinds of balance that were used by shopkeepers in the 19th century.

The early 20th century saw the development of the type of scale that dominated shops until the age of electronic measurement. In this type the pan was a combination scoop and weighing pan, and the two-sided dial meant that the weight was visible from both sides of the counter.

Brightly coloured and decorated examples such as the American Dayton scale shown above are especially sought after because they overlap with other collecting areas. In the United States, especially, village-shop items and items related to sweets and sweet shops are very popular. We can tell that these particular scales were probably used in a small village shop from the bright paintwork and the transfer decoration, and also because they only weigh up to a couple of pounds of goods. This example has the added interest of a paper label on the front that shows that it was last officially inspected in 1931. This raises the question of what happened after that date. Perhaps the owner took it home to use in the kitchen, or, more probably, the shop went out of business in the Great Depression, as so many others did.

◄ **Automatic micrometer**
By Louis Schopper, *c.*1900. Designed to measure paper thickness, it has a retailer's label with the name Foreign Paper Mills, New York.
£200–300/$300–400

▲ **American angle-measuring level**
By Davis Level & Tool Co, *c.*1875. Made of cast iron, with intricate scrolling decoration. The wholesale price at the time was $3 (£2).
£100–200/$200–300

British shop scales, on the other hand, were always stamped with the mark of the ruling monarch at the time of their manufacture, for example George V, to show that they had been checked. They may also have paper certificates.

If you find an item of interest, look for labels, signatures and decorations and, for a change, don't be too concerned about its condition. Scales and balances were everyday tools so wear and tear are inevitable. However, most were sturdily built to handle this kind of heavy usage, and it's unlikely that much damage will have been done. Remember that even relatively recent scales and balances are highly collectable. If you have an old set that your grandmother or aunt gave you when you first had your own home, don't throw them out without taking a good look at them first or getting an opinion from an expert.

Industrial weighing and measuring instruments represent the most esoteric group within this field and tend to be less collectable. This isn't necessarily a bad thing, though. If you are the collector, it means that you can obtain fascinating items for surprisingly little money. There are sophisticated instruments for measuring purity, heat, thickness – all sorts of qualities that don't immediately leap to mind as measurable. These instruments were mostly built for industrial or laboratory applications and therefore are not usually decorative items. The majority date from the 19th century and represent the growing involvement of engineers and other practical scientists in a field previously dominated by finance and commerce. It's really a market for the specialist collector.

One quality that all these esoteric items share is that they do not necessarily look like measuring instruments. The micrometer above has a large and obvious dial, but it is hard to see exactly what it is for – in fact it measures paper thickness. However, paper manufacturers around the world grade their product according to its weight. Thicker paper will obviously weigh more, so the thickness must be accurately measured. The user of the micrometer here would slide a piece of paper between the two rods under the dial and push down a lever. The thickness is read from the dial, which measures down to $\frac{1}{128}$th of an inch. Systems for measuring the size of paper for retail differ widely: Europe has the A system, where each successive number measures half the area of the preceding number. For example, the commonly used A4 is half the size of A3, and so on down to A1, which is the basic unit. Common sizes in the USA are the legal and letter, which have quite different measurements from the A sizes.

▶ **Dust counter**
By Bausch & Lomb, Rochester, NY, mid-20th century, it was used for measuring contamination levels.
£35–50/$50–75

▶ **US Bureau of Mines flash-point tester**
By the Taylor Instrument Company of Rochester, NY, early 20th century. This was used to measure the igniting temperatures of different substances.
£200–300/$300–400

A master carpenter or any other skilled craftsman would have used a level like the one shown on page 76. The dial in the centre measures an exact angle, not just a level plane. The level is made of cast iron, and the beautiful scrolled decorative work shows it is a professional's instrument, as such detail would not be found on a general contractor's tool.

The last two instruments that are illustrated are the most specialist of all, from a collecting point of view, and would probably attract interest from people working in industry today who might use modern versions of these items. The dust counter incorporates a microscope through which the user would have checked for contamination of samples. (The word "dust" is used here as a generic term for any contaminant.) The rubber ball was squeezed to spread the sample out under the lens. Obviously the dust counter would be an essential aid in checking, for instance, assay samples or medicinal chemicals for purity. This particular example comes with its case, instruction book and data sheets, which add to its interest.

The flash-point tester is particularly noteworthy because it was made by the famous instrument-making firm of Taylor of Rochester, New York, for the US Bureau of Mines. It is a prime piece of Industrial Revolution technology as it heats up substances and measures the temperature at which they will ignite. Necessity is the mother of invention, and this instrument was developed in response to the need for lubricants for newly developed machines. It could be used, for example, to measure the flash-point of engine oil in order to ensure that it exceeded an engine's peak running temperature. As industry developed so did the applications, as the instrument could also be used to test the temperature at which an acid might be stored in order to stop it heating up and escaping into the atmosphere.

Different measuring instruments tend to fall into fairly distinct categories, and, because this particular end of the field is so specialist, the market for such items will be much more restricted than that of the scales and balances discussed earlier. Linear measuring instruments such as rulers and yardsticks depend largely on their looks for their collectability. For example, a beautifully carved ivory measuring stick will command a higher value than a plain wooden example. And if a particular shop or firm's name appears on the item it will enhance the value. Capacity measures such as pints and litres are also dependent on their appearance, although non-metric measures are more collectable in the English-speaking world. Items with advertisements on them will also appeal to advertising collectors.

Communication

▲ Oak wall telephone
By Stromberg-Carlson, early 20th century. Unlike most phones of this period, this type did not have a magneto to signal the operator. £100–200/$200–300

If knowledge is power then communication instruments are the vehicles of power, for without them information cannot easily be exchanged

In 1999, American television's History Channel conducted a survey to find the most important person of the second millennium. The result was Johann Gutenberg of Mainz, Germany, for inventing printing with movable type in the 1450s. The survey concluded that this one invention had the greatest impact of any single technological device in the entire period.

Today we take it for granted that information can be easily, cheaply and, most of all, quickly disseminated. Of course it wasn't always so. For thousands of years the bulk of human knowledge has been passed on through the written word. Until Gutenberg's invention, words had to be slowly and painstakingly written out by hand. But afterwards, knowledge suddenly became much more easily available. People who hadn't been able to afford the beautiful manuscripts could suddenly afford printed books and so ideas could be exchanged and discussed within them.

From around the mid-19th century the telegraph carried information across countries and oceans almost instantaneously; then the typewriter brought a new and faster kind of writing into business, and then everyday, life. The telephone, on the other hand, gave importance back to the spoken word once again and laid the foundations for today's Internet.

It is important to emphasize how miraculous such items as the telephone were to our ancestors. Many people raise their eyebrows at the thought of collecting old telephones or radios, seeing them simply as older versions of something they already have. But an old telephone may have been the first one that its original owner ever used, or perhaps even the first one that someone ever saw. As for the early radios (that look clumsy and old fashioned to our modern eyes) – just think how it must have felt to a farmer in the American mid-West to hear the voice of his president coming into his home in 1924. It

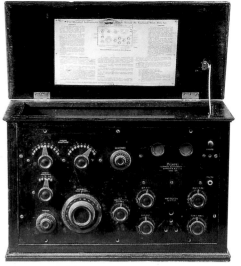

▶ **Franklin No. 7 typewriter**
By Franklin, c.1900. The curved keyboard makes it popular with collectors, but buyers at the time did not take to it. Few were made, and today such typewriters are rare items.
£450–700/$700–1,000

▲ **Federal Type 59 four-tube radio**
By Federal, mid-1920s. This radio is made of mahogany and ebonite, and it still has its instructions in the lid.
£300–500/$500–700

would have been a source of unimaginable pride, as exciting an event as it was for British people who heard the voice of their king, George V, in the same year when he made the first-ever radio broadcast by a reigning monarch. Today many of us feel that we know altogether too much about our politicians and rulers, but before the advent of radio most people went their whole lives without hearing or seeing the people who controlled their nation.

The instruments of communication are astonishing devices, though familiarity has dulled us to their wonder. If you still think that early models are not of interest, just look around your house. There is most likely a direct descendant of each item discussed in this chapter within your home. You almost certainly have at least one radio and one television in your household, quite possibly two or three or even more. Your computer uses technology that originated with the

typewriter and with movable-type printing. And the next time you pick up a newspaper, think about how it was produced and how long it took between the occurrence of the headline event to your reading about it. The huge technological advances that have been made in this area are truly fascinating.

A great attraction of this field is that the availability of most items is still reasonably good. As time passes, old typewriters, telephones, radios and televisions are naturally becoming scarcer, but by knowing where to look you can steadily build a collection. There is also still plenty to come across by pure luck or determination. Unlike most of the technological items in this book, communication instruments are often not recognized for what they are, so a keen eye is essential. For example, early telephones and radios often look like nothing in particular. And as far as value is concerned, the earliest examples are definitely the best.

► Hand printing press
c. 1930s. This is not a toy but was used by businesses for small work such as business cards or bill headings. **£50–100/$100–150**

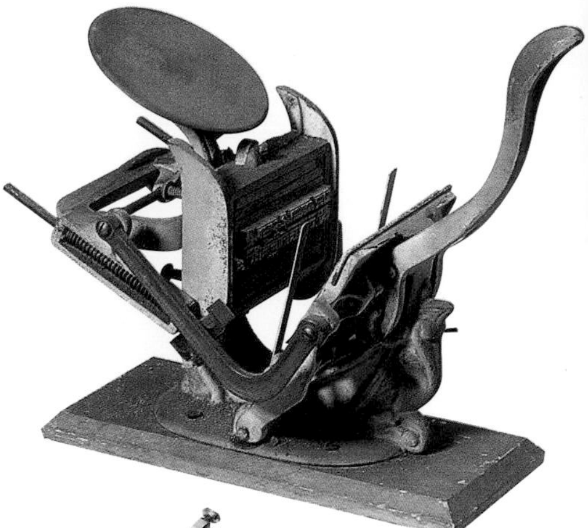

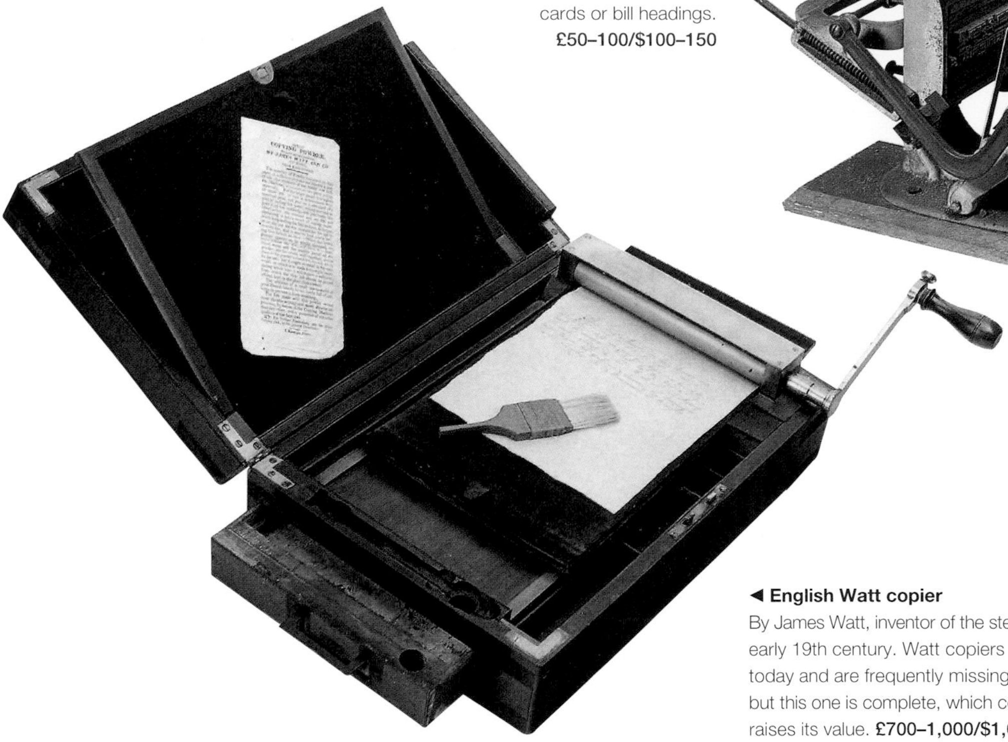

◄ English Watt copier
By James Watt, inventor of the steam engine, early 19th century. Watt copiers are rare today and are frequently missing pieces, but this one is complete, which considerably raises its value. **£700–1,000/$1,000–1,500**

The Written Word

As soon as people learned to write, it became clear that a device for making quick, legible copies of a written document would be a desirable invention. Until the 1440s most writing was done by hand, and communication and the dissemination of information were therefore extremely limited. A primitive form of printing using wooden blocks had been used, but the blocks, once carved, could not be adapted for different jobs. It was Gutenberg's invention of movable type in the 1450s that enabled copies of different documents to be run off from the same machine. And purchasers no longer had to wait months for a book to be carefully hand-copied. Once the type was set up, as many copies as were needed could be printed. The unit cost of books and papers was slashed as a result, and the ideas within them were able to circulate much more widely and swiftly. Without the innovation of printing, the Renaissance of the 15th and 16th centuries and the Enlightenment of the 18th century probably could not have taken place. The expansion of different governments, business and international trade also generated and maintained an enormous demand for quick printing and copying methods.

Most collectors today don't have the space or the inclination to collect full-sized printing presses, but fortunately there are plenty of alternatives. The small printing press illustrated above is typical of the kind used in the early part of the 20th century by small businesses. They would often have their own printing shops, especially if they were in rural areas without access to a commercial printer.

Toy printing presses were also very popular in the 1920s and 1930s. Children could print their own newspapers, posters, flyers and advertisements with their miniature presses. A whole set included type, ink and paper, and sets sold in huge numbers. Today they have survived well, although it is rare (and costly) to find a complete set. However, even an incomplete toy printing press makes a nice item for a collection as it works exactly like a full-sized press but is much more convenient to display.

▼ Graphotype typesetting machine
*c.*1930s–40s. It is 40cm (15¾in) high, has a 12.75-cm (5-in) diameter typesetting wheel and 35 alphanumeric and 9 character settings.
£50–85/$75–125

► Edison electric pen
By Thomas Edison, 1876. It is 15cm (5⅞in) long and is made of cast iron, brass and steel.
£10,000–13,000/ $15,000–20,000

Not all the smaller machines connected with printing are costly. This is because most of them are heavy and they also tend to have an industrial rather than a decorative appearance. The Graphotype typesetting machine above is rare but, owing to its functional looks and its impressive weight (45.5kg/100lb), it is an affordable piece.

All printing machines are much the same in principle, but copying machines vary enormously. There was a large and lucrative market for copiers in the early 19th century, so inventors fought to outdo each other without running foul of the patent laws. The patents are almost a collecting field in themselves – some are wonderfully practical while others are deeply flawed but still intriguing. The copier by James Watt illustrated on page 80 was used to make copies of manuscript documents. It worked by wetting the original document and pressing it onto the copy paper with the platen board. When the handle was turned, geared brass rollers squeezed the original and the copy paper together.

Other kinds of copier include the pleasingly named jellygraph, which used a plate of jelly, as well as the frequently overlooked carbon paper method. Much of the terminology from early methods still survives in modern printing and copying technology. One such example is the "cc" field in email forms. These two letters originally stood for "carbon copy".

Stencils were another popular way to make a document that required several copies, and the Edison pen was an early way of creating the stencil. It was invented in 1876 and worked rather like a sewing machine. The user wrote with it as with a normal pen, but onto paper made with paraffin wax. A tiny electric motor powered a steel stylus that perforated the paper as the user wrote to make thousands of tiny holes. The stencil was then put in a frame above a sheet of ordinary paper, and ink was rolled over it to make the copy. The Edison pen was quite successful but did not supersede the Sholes & Glidden Type Writer, and so today the Edison pen is a rare and highly prized piece.

▼ **Early typewritten letter and envelope**
Form letter from the Centennial Exposition of 1876. The
salutation, closing words and address were typed on a Sholes
& Glidden Type Writer at the exhibition. £50–100/$100–150

◀ **Hall Type Writer**
By the National Type
Writer Company,
Boston, *c.*1880s–90s.
It has a square index
and a hinged frame
in a mahogany case
(its character pad
is missing).
£300–700/$500–1,000
depending on
condition and model.

▲ **Fay-Sholes typewriter**
By Christopher Sholes, 1890s. This is
an affordable descendant of the rare
and much sought-after Sholes & Glidden.
£100–150/$150–200

Once the problem of making quick, accurate copies of documents had been solved, it was only a matter of time before attention turned to updating the method of writing the original. The market was wide open for a machine that would write faster than a pen but produce a document of print quality. The first successful typewriter, the Sholes & Glidden, appeared on the market in 1873–74. The very first patent, however, had been registered by the English engineer Henry Mill as early as 1714. At this time Mill specified "an artificial machine … for impressing … letters … one after another, as in writing … in paper or parchment, so neat and exact as not to be distinguished from print…".

It was the first of thousands of typewriter patents. Throughout the 19th century, inventors in Britain, Europe and the USA built a big variety of machines. Index typewriters were the first kind: each letter was selected by turning a pointer to it. The Hall Type Writer of the 1880s was the first commercially successful index typewriter. It sold in thousands in the United Kingdom and its native USA, though it was obsolete by the end of the century.

The intense competition meant that almost all the elements of the typewriter we recognize today were invented separately. By the 1860s it only remained for someone to put them all together in one machine. The person who did it was Christopher Sholes of Milwaukee, in the United States.

Sholes worked constantly to refine and improve his machines, and he eventually produced the dominant design. The Fay-Sholes typewriter above is a classic example, though its value today lies chiefly in its historical interest. When it was produced in the 1890s, patent wars were raging, and, interestingly, it is the designs that didn't catch on at the time that are now the most collectable. This is partly because they are rarer but mostly because they are idiosyncratic and unorthodox.

The typewriters that really caught on were to prove unexpected instruments of social change. Typing was deemed an acceptable way for a respectable woman to earn a living, and the typists, who were actually called typewriters themselves at first, were all women. For the first time, women could enter the office world as employees.

▼ Personal computer
Late 20th century/early 21st century. Today's update
of the typewriter deserves a place in the collection. It
still has the keyboard layout that Sholes invented.
Price depends on the model and capacity.

▲ People's Typewriter
c.1890s. It has a curved index (an
attempt to get around a patent) and
a circular type wheel with upper and
lower case characters on a mahogany
base (its lid is missing).
£450–700/$700–1,000 if it is in good
and complete condition.

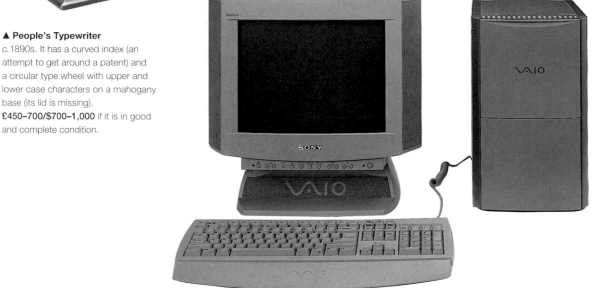

There are designs to please every collector in this field, whether you are interested in looks, engineering or history. For example, the Crandall machine of 1881 was a forerunner of IBM's golfball method: it had a sleeve with the letters on it that moved up and down and spun round when the keys were pressed. However, without electricity it wasn't quick enough, and the separate type bars overtook it in popularity. Some machines got around the keyboard patent by having plungers instead – these are popular with collectors today, but are quite rare.

Items associated with typewriters are also of great interest. A Sholes & Glidden typewriter was exhibited at the Centennial Exposition of 1876 in Philadelphia. For a small fee, visitors could send a personalized form letter from the Fair. The greeting, closing words and recipient's name and address were typed on the printed form letter with the Sholes & Glidden machine. Today these are much sought after, as are other early typewritten documents.

After the First World War, people began to look at harnessing electricity in their continuing search to speed up the process of writing. As far as

collectability goes, the story ends around here. Electric typewriters could do much that manual typewriters couldn't, and Crandall's sleeve became the cutting edge of typing thanks to IBM's rediscovery of his idea. But electric typewriters proved a dead end. The advent of computing swept all that clever engineering into history.

However, typewriters didn't sink without trace. They have left their mark right there on your QWERTY keyboard. The layout was invented by Christopher Sholes himself, and there is no logic in having it on a computer. Sholes chose it purely because it helped to overcome the problem of adjacent type bars tangling with each other. QWERTY is an anachronism on our hi-tech desks, but an alternative arrangement has yet to catch on.

Old typewriters are most valuable if they are as near-mint as possible in appearance. Thin machine oil aids cleaning and lubricating, but never try to repaint a battered machine. You will only reduce its value and spoil its looks. Serial numbers are helpful for dating machines and are usually engraved on the chassis underneath the right-hand end of the carriage.

▼ **Western Union Camel Back Key and Sounder**
By G.M. Phelps, mid to late 19th century. This is a rare example of a typical American telegraph transmitter that would have been used in small railroad stations or telegraph offices.
£450–700/$700–1,000

▲ **Western Union call boxes**
These were used to summon messenger boys to collect a telegram from a Western Union customer. When the handle is turned, the mechanism sends a signal to the Western Union office.
(Left) late 19th century, **£135–200/$200–300**
(Right) c.1920, **£65–100/$100–150**

Telegraphy

The telegraph we know today is technically called the electric telegraph. Before electricity was harnessed to send messages across long distances, people relied on visual telegraphy. Semaphore flags were the fastest method of communicating at a distance. On land, people could signal from hill to hill, but bad weather closed communications down. By the 1830s electric telegraphy had become a crowded field of research, and many systems were built and used.

Two systems appeared in the United States and England in the late 1930s. An engineer named Cooke and a physics professor called Wheatstone patented their five-needle telegraph in London. It was an alphabetical telegraph that spelled out messages letter by letter, using the needles as indicators. Across the Atlantic, a painter and amateur physicist named Samuel Morse demonstrated a system that used a simple code of dots and dashes. Morse code was the factor that made the telegraph really effective and it quickly became the standard operating code.

For a while in Britain the telegraph was limited to the railways. It took a murder to excite public interest in it. In 1842 a woman was killed in Slough, and the man responsible was seen boarding a train to Paddington. A full description of the murderer was telegraphed ahead; the man was arrested on arrival and was duly hanged for the crime. It was terrific publicity for the telegraph companies and they began to woo public custom, offering telegrams at sixpence a time. But people didn't understand the telegraph to begin with. One man thought that his writing on the telegram form would be sent down the wires as a liquid. A woman who lived near some telegraph wires believed they were transmitting voices (some 30 years before the telephone) and complained to the company about what they were saying.

The American telegraph penetrated daily life rather more quickly, especially after the outbreak of the Civil War in 1861 caused its use to become widespread. It was one of the first telegraphic wars;

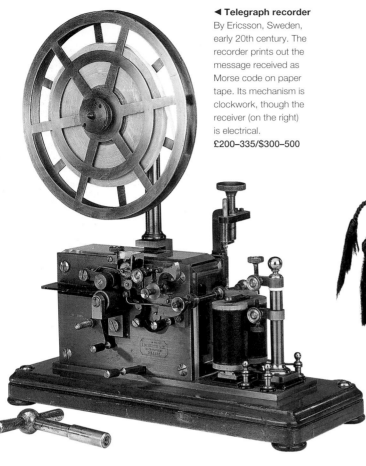

◀ **Telegraph recorder**
By Ericsson, Sweden, early 20th century. The recorder prints out the message received as Morse code on paper tape. Its mechanism is clockwork, though the receiver (on the right) is electrical.
£200–335/$300–500

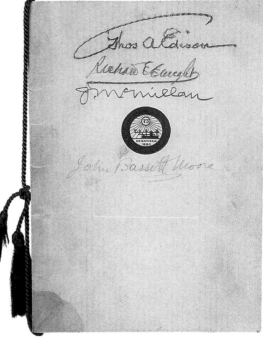

▲ **Signed menu**
From a banquet held for the Old Time Telegrapher and Historical Association/The Society of the United Military Telegraph Corps on board *Olympic* at New York on 17 September 1925. Note Edison's signature, which makes it particularly collectable.
£465–670/$700–1,000

journalists could wire their copy back to the newspapers for unprecedented speed in reporting. Every day President Lincoln would check the government receiver himself to stay abreast of events. After the war, the telegraph fuelled the expansion of railways and enabled communication across the continent. Businesses had call boxes in their offices so that if someone turned the handle a personalized number would alert the telegraph office, which would send over a messenger boy to collect the telegram.

Railway offices acted as message centres. The operator would have an outfit like the one shown on page 84 with which he could send telegrams, and then telegraph recorders picked up the message in the receiving office. They worked like tickertape machines, printing out the dots and dashes as words. The tape would then be cut into strips and glued onto the form, ready for delivery.

Telegraphy became a huge industry. Almost every boy wanted to be an operator, and many started out as messengers. They taught themselves Morse code and bought practice telegraph sets. There were even board games in which the players would begin as messenger boys and, by working hard, could become president of the company. Thomas Edison learned Morse code while he was selling newspapers and sweets on passenger trains, and succeeded in becoming an operator before inventing his multiplex telegraph.

There are not many real telegraph outfits around today as they were commercial equipment and companies didn't save them when they became obsolete. Good complete sets are therefore rare, and can be very valuable. However, there are plenty of telegraph keys around as operators often kept them as souvenirs. Practice outfits for boys have also survived in fair numbers, and you should be able to find them at affordable prices. Ephemera connected with the telegraph industry are also popular. Age and condition are important factors for all telegraphy collectables – the earlier the better, but poor condition will reduce value.

▲ Signed photograph of Bell
By Moffett. Alexander Graham Bell's signature is on the bottom, together with that of the photographer.
£200–300/$300–400

▶ Oak wall telephone
By the Chicago Telephone Supply Company, Elkhart, Indiana, c.1890. It is 105cm (42in) high, and still has its receiver, glazed magneto box and battery box. £300–500/$500–700

▼ "Butterstamp" telephone
c.1880–90. It is made of turned wood, with twin contacts and metal diaphragm. It is 14cm (5½in) high.
£300–500/$500–700

Telephones

The story of the telephone is one of chance and basic good luck. Its famous inventor, Alexander Graham Bell (1847–1922), was a Scotsman who came from a family with a great interest in speech and deafness. His mother was deaf, and his father and grandfather trained him in how to teach the deaf to speak. After the family had emigrated to Ontario, Canada, Bell eventually became a professor of vocal physiology at Boston University in the early 1870s. At this time he was already working on the idea of transmitting speech by electrical means. Bell tried to develop a harmonic telegraph at first, which would enable several messages to be sent over the same line, and in the process discovered that it was possible to convert sound into electricity and then back into sound again. He spent months experimenting with his discovery, with minimal financial backing provided by a man named Hubbard, his future father-in-law. Hubbard applied for a patent in 1876, without Bell's knowledge, and it was filed just hours before a rival

patent, thus assuring Bell of his place in history. On 10 March 1876, three days after the patent was granted, Bell made the first-ever telephone call, which was to his assistant. "Mr Watson, come here, I want you", he said.

However, the invention was only half the battle. Forming a company to market it and keeping the company afloat were to prove very difficult. The huge Western Union company tried to stop the Bell Telephone Company by any means it could as it didn't like the competition, even going so far as to cut Bell's wires. Eventually, however, Bell's company was integrated with the American Telephone and Telegraph Company.

The telephone has gone through many external changes in the past 125 years, but inside it has remained remarkably constant. The first phones had no dials, so users had to ask the operator to connect them to the people they wished to speak to. It is said that the dial was the idea of a Kansas undertaker named Almon Strowger when he found

▼ Candlestick telephone
From the 1920s. The original black lacquer has been removed from the base unit – this will reduce the value considerably.
£100–150/$150–200

▲ Swedish table telephone
By Ericsson, c.1910. This phone has a single handset, and is made of mahogany with ebonite and nickelled fittings.
£200–250/$300–375

▲ Bakelite telephone
American, c.1930s–40s. This example has an unusual colour combination that features a white base unit and black handset, still with its original cord.
£50–100/$100–150

that a rival mortician had suborned the local operator into diverting all Strowger's business calls to him.

There are plenty of different styles around for the collector today, and most of them are quite affordable. Very early telephones are rare and can turn up in odd places, often going unrecognized, especially if parts are missing. The "butterstamp" telephone is one of the earliest models you are likely to find. (It is so called because it resembled the stamps that transferred designs on to the tops of butter pats.) Many early phones used only one "butterstamp" unit for both transmitting and receiving; the design then changed to two separate units. Wall telephones are bulkier but have an attractive period feel to them. They were produced until the 1920s, but you can tell a 19th-century model by its design. Wall telephones of the 1890s followed the style illustrated on page 86, with a fiddle back and separate magneto and battery boxes.

Table phones reached their present form with the invention of the handset, which made using the phone much more convenient. Handsets appeared in Europe some time before they were popular in the USA, as it took a while for the new invention to cross the Atlantic. The candlestick phone shown here would originally have been painted black, but it has been stripped down to the brass. Some people prefer this appearance, but the phone has lost its original look and therefore much of its value.

Bakelite was developed in the early 20th century and made it possible to produce phones in different colours, although black remained the most popular. Later table models have been collectable for years as they only require simple rewiring to be usable. Rewiring will obviously lower the value of older telephones, but more recent types, such as the popular candlestick, should still retain their value. It's important that the rewiring should be carried out in a way that is still in harmony with the original.

Items connected with the telephone are also very collectable. For example, the photograph of Alexander Graham Bell on page 86 is a particularly desirable piece because it bears his signature.

◀ **Photograph of Marconi**
c. 1910. This signed photograph
dates from a time when Marconi
was not yet 40 but owned a company
that dominated the world.
£200–350/$300–500

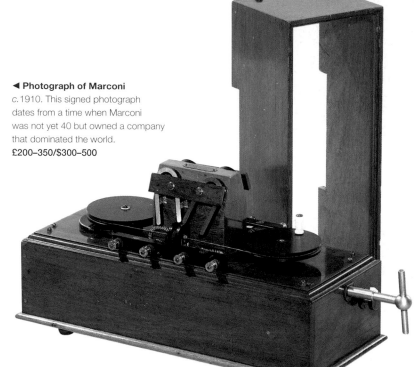

▶ **Magnetic detector**
By Marconi's Wireless Telegraph Co.,
London, *c.* 1910. It is made of mahogany
with a glazed lid and a clockwork motor.
£8,500–10,000/$12,500–15,000

Radio and Television

The idea of wireless communication was raised by the British physicist James Clerk Maxwell in a treatise in 1873. Fifteen years later a German named Heinrich Hertz demonstrated it in his laboratory. A number of scientists experimented with different ways of sending electrical signals through the atmosphere, but it was a young amateur who built the first practical system.

Guglielmo Marconi (1874–1937) was born to an Italian landowner and a member of the wealthy Irish Jameson whiskey family. He was self-educated in the field of science and made his first discoveries on his father's estates. Marconi had been interested in electrical phenomena from an early age; when he read of Hertz's experiments he was gripped by the idea that messages could be transmitted without conventional wires.

In 1894 Marconi repeated some of Hertz's experiments with a number of improvements. He offered his system to the Italian government, but it turned him down. Undaunted, Marconi moved to London and sought the help of his influential Jameson relatives. They provided financial backing and introduced him to William Preece, engineer-in-chief of the General Post Office.

Preece was a distinguished scientist who had built the UK's first phonograph and had also done a good deal of electrical experimentation – in fact he had just demonstrated a commercially promising system of wireless telegraphy himself when Marconi approached him. However, he recognized the possibilities of Marconi's system and gave the young man his full support. At the time Britain had the world's largest navy of military and merchant vessels, and both men saw the importance of wireless telegraphy for marine communications.

In 1896 Marconi registered the world's first patent for wireless telegraphy. He founded a private company and worked on improving the range of his system. In 1901 he transmitted the world's first transatlantic wireless message; a faint "S" in Morse code from Cornwall to Newfoundland.

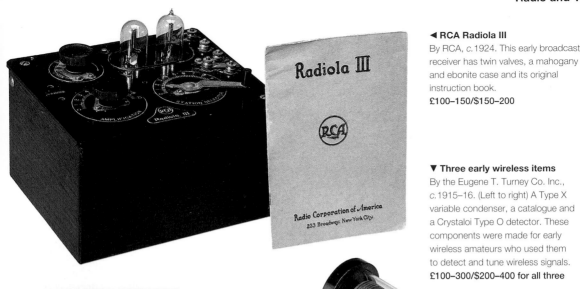

◄ RCA Radiola III

By RCA, *c*.1924. This early broadcast receiver has twin valves, a mahogany and ebonite case and its original instruction book.
£100–150/$150–200

▼ Three early wireless items

By the Eugene T. Turney Co. Inc., *c*.1915–16. (Left to right) A Type X variable condenser, a catalogue and a Crystaloi Type O detector. These components were made for early wireless amateurs who used them to detect and tune wireless signals.
£100–300/$200–400 for all three

◄ Round valves

By Marconi's Wireless Telegraph Co. Ltd, *c*.1920. The designer, Captain Round, was an engineer working for Marconi. **£1,000–2,000/ $1,500–3,000 each**

The earliest wireless instrument you are likely to find is the magnetic detector, which Marconi invented in 1902. It depends on the ability of radio waves to demagnetize a steel wire and pick up signals in much the same way that magnetized tape works in a tape recorder. Detectors were supplied to ships and land stations all over the world, and were still in use, although somewhat outdated, after World War I. With such heavy use, few have survived today, but keep an eye out – they have been known to appear at country auctions and other unexpected places and are worth quite a lot.

The next major breakthrough was the radio valve, or radio tube as it is called in the USA. It was invented by John Fleming, Marconi's scientific adviser. Fleming had worked for Edison and while with him had learned about the "Edison Effect" – the phenomenon that electricity only flows one way in a vacuum. Edison had discovered this while working on the light bulb but, while he found it interesting, couldn't think of an application for it.

Fleming's hearing was failing by the early 1900s, and he found it difficult to hear the buzzes from the magnetic detector. Remembering the Edison Effect, he tried amplifying the signal by running it through a glass bulb. It worked, and the radio valve was born.

Wireless items are hard to find because they were made usually for commercial rather than domestic use, but they are very collectable. Technology advanced quickly, and obsolete items were destroyed rather than kept in attics, as old radios often were later. Ephemera in this field are desirable too, especially anything related to Marconi.

The idea of radio as a household utility was first raised in 1916 by David Sarnoff, an employee of the Marconi Company. Sarnoff wrote a memo in which he raised the idea of a "Radio Music Box", or simple wireless receiver, such as the Radiola pictured above. Marconi had already successfully spread his operations into the USA in 1912; while Sarnoff's idea wasn't taken up until after World War I, it went on to completely transform American broadcasting.

◄ Federal Type 110 receiver
By Federal, *c.*1923. This three-tube wireless receiver has its instructions inside the lid and an RCA Type FH papier-mâché speaker horn. **£250–300/$400–500** if its horn is still intact.

▲ ► Two Fada radios
By Fada, *c.*1930s. Both have unusual butterscotch-coloured Catlin (Bakelite) cases. **(Above)** The model 652 Temple radio. **£200–300/$300–500** **(Right)** The Model 115 Bullet radio. **£450–600/$700–900**

Broadcasting in the United States was viewed as a commercial enterprise from the outset. After World War I, President Wilson decided that American radio could no longer be controlled by a foreign company, so in 1919 a consortium of General Electric and Westinghouse Electric bought the American division of the Marconi Company and formed the Radio Corporation of America, or RCA. By the early 1920s, Sarnoff's vision was a huge industry, and the former messenger boy was head of a new offshoot of RCA, the National Broadcasting Company, or NBC.

On the other side of the Atlantic, broadcasting developed along an educational, rather than a commercial, line. The British Broadcasting Company, or BBC, was formed in 1922 by three companies including Marconi. In Britain, radio was greeted as a miracle invention that would allow the dissemination of information across international borders to the detriment of warmongers. Indeed, engraved over the BBC's radio headquarters at Broadcasting House in London are the words "Nation shall speak peace unto nation".

Britain had been the birthplace of radio, but it was in the USA that it became a huge and powerful industry. The large and often isolated population there offered an enormous market for radios. RCA emerged as a giant of radio manufacture when it bought the nationwide Victor Talking Machine Company. Prices plummeted, and almost every household had at least one radio, even during the Depression. By 1920 the radio market was worth two million dollars, and by 1926 almost half a billion.

As a result, many of the wide variety of radios available to collectors today are American. Some people collect only the very earliest models, such as the Federal Type 110 (above), with its phonograph-like horn. The value of early radios will vary according to condition, rarity and the number of valves. As a rule of thumb, the more valves, the more powerful the radio and therefore the more it will be worth.

Radios from the 1930s are popular for their attractive designs. However, traditional walnut-cased radios are today much less desirable than the Bakelite radios, which have become very popular. Bakelite was usually black or brown, so a different

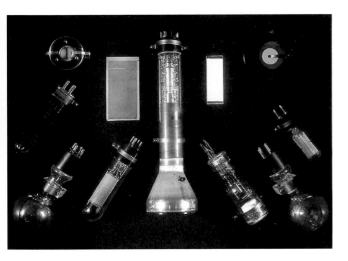

▲ Seven vacuum tubes
By Koller/GE, mid-20th century. A mahogany display case of vacuum tubes from the patents of Dr Lewis Koller, an American pioneer in early electronics and televisual technology.
£200–350/$300–500

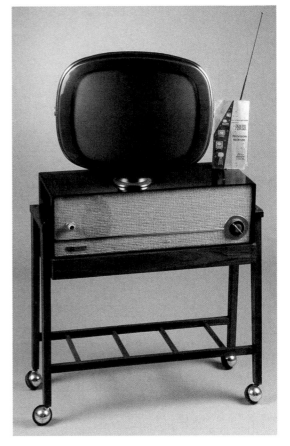

▶ Philco Predicta television
By Philco, 1960s. A classic television set with swivelling 40-cm (15-in) screen, base unit and teak stand.
£300–400/$500–600

colour will add value to a piece. Unusual shapes such as the Bullet shown on page 90 are also popular. The classic British Bakelite radio is one of the round EKCO models of the 1930s and 1940s. Check Bakelite radios carefully: minor damage such as missing knobs won't make much difference, but a cracked casing will lower the value a lot. Models from after World War II (eg transistor radios, which were developed by Bell Labs in the 1940s) are just starting to be collectable, so it could be worth hanging on to a nice model if you have one.

The next step in broadcasting was the invention of television. People had been working on the idea since the late 1800s, but it is credited to the Scotsman John Logie Baird. In 1925, after much experimentation, Baird transmitted the image of a ventriloquist's dummy from one end of his attic flat to the other. Because so many people were investigating the possibilities of television, there was more than one system available at first. Baird called his invention the Baird Televisor, and it was the first one used by the BBC, which transmitted programmes with it in 1929. However, by 1936 Marconi EMI had built a rival

system. Both systems broadcast images at a rate of 25 frames per second, but Marconi's system boasted 405 lines to Baird's 240. The following year Marconi's system was chosen as the standard for British broadcasting. Sets were sold commercially in the UK by several companies, and these now fetch high prices at auction, but pre-World War II television sets in the USA were still experimental and very few were made until the 1950s; they are not very collectable.

This field tends to attract two kinds of collector: those who go for visual appeal, and the "techie" collectors who are interested in original components and in anything associated with the great names of broadcasting technology. If you are concerned with the latter then look for unusually coloured Bakelite radios and don't bother with the mainstream products of the giant corporations. Go for unorthodox items such as the Stromberg-Carlson Breadboard, which had no case so you could see all its wiring. If you are attracted by the classic wooden 1930s models, then good condition is vital, as it is with all the cheaper radios. They were made in such great numbers, and so many survive, that you can afford to be choosy.

Photography and Optical Toys

The history of visual technology offers a wealth of different gadgets for making sophisticated images

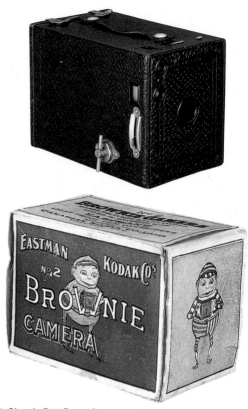

▲ **Classic Box Brownie camera**
Made by the Eastman Kodak Company, c.1900. These cameras are very common, but this example is especially desirable because it has its original box in good condition. **£50–100/$100–150**

People have always wanted to make pictures of the world they inhabit, and the story of this field reveals the search for ever better ways to make that visual record to show it to others.

While photography is a large branch of this field, it's by no means the only one. Optical toys – non-photographic instruments for looking at images – are fascinating to collect. The kaleidoscope is well known, but there are various other ingenious and decorative devices. The scioptic ball, for instance, projects the view just outside the window onto a wall inside the house, while the ceramic lithophane shows you an image with the illusion of three-dimensional depth. Those collectors who are particularly interested in photography will also find plenty of interesting gadgets. The stereoscope, for example, was first proposed in 1832 as a device to provide a three-dimensional view of a two-dimensional image. And by 1912 the science of moving pictures had developed to

the point where people could buy projectors to show short movies at home.

However, photography is the obvious place to start here as it has a rich and surprisingly long history. The camera obscura, which is the direct ancestor of the camera, had been around since the 1400s. The name means "dark room", and the device was used by painters to help them with their perspective. A camera obscura consisted of a box with a pinhole on one side and a glass screen on the other. Light coming through the pinhole projected an image onto the screen, where the artist could trace it by hand.

Like all good inventions, photography does not owe its existence to the efforts of one person. The three main names involved in its development are Joseph Niépce (1765–1833), Louis Jacques Mandé Daguerre (1789–1851) and William Henry Fox Talbot (1800–77). Niépce's contribution to photography came about while he was trying to improve the new printmaking technique of lithography. He

▶ Ikonograph Model D
By the Ikonograph Company of America. This home movie-picture projector is in perfect condition, and was originally bought from Macy's, New York, in December 1912. It is still in its shipping carton – perhaps it was an unwanted Christmas present.
£250–400/$400–600

◀ Holmes-pattern stereoscope with stereographs
Designed by Oliver Wendell Holmes (an American law scientist), mid-19th century. Viewer with stand.
£50–100/$100–150 (price halved if without a stand)
The stereographs depict "A Trip Through Sears, Roebuck & Co", the famous American mail-order firm. The set sold in 1908 for 35 cents (25p). **£15–35/$25–50**

discovered that he could copy lithographic engravings onto glass and pewter plates by using bitumen, which hardens when it is exposed to light. Using this process, he made the world's first fixed photographic image in 1826. He took the photo with a bitumen-coated plate in a camera obscura. The exposure time was eight hours.

Daguerre was a Parisian artist and theatrical designer. He owned a theatre, the Diorama, which presented a popular spectacle of large, painted scenes shown in succession. Like Niépce, Daguerre was interested in using the camera obscura to make images, but had his eye on the commercial aspect. The two joined forces in 1829, but it wasn't until 1835, two years after Niépce's death, that Daguerre discovered that silver iodide was much more light-sensitive than bitumen. He then tried coating a copper plate with it. The plate was put in the camera obscura, exposed for 20–30 minutes and developed with fumes of mercury. The process became

known as the daguerreotype, and when it was made public it caused a huge sensation.

Fox Talbot, an English amateur scientist from Lacock in Wiltshire, read an account of the daguerreotype and realized that it was similar to his own, as yet unpublished, work. He presented his "photogenic drawing", or calotype as his process came to be called, to the Royal Society in London. The difference with the calotype was that it produced a negative from which several positive prints could be made. However, the process was still to be perfected, and daguerreotypes dominated photography well into the 1850s.

You should find that you have a great deal of scope to pick and choose the items that most interest you. The devices are often very decorative, and many have survived in such good condition that they can still be used today. Early photographs and simple cameras can be acquired on a modest budget, while even the more sophisticated cameras and optical toys don't need to break the bank.

◄ **Two Kinnear-pattern mahogany cameras**
By Thomas Ross & Company, named for a design patented by C. G. H. Kinnear, a Scots photographer, c.1860. The design allows the camera to collapse into a compact case. The camera underneath is closed, the one on top is open.
£800–1,200/$1,200–1,800

► **Sliding box camera**
c.1840–60. The slide for the plate is on top. This rare type of camera is very popular with collectors.
£2,000–3,000/$3,000–4,500

Photography

Cameras from the mid-19th century are often made with wooden cases, usually mahogany, and have brass lens pieces. One early design was the sliding box camera, so called because it consisted of two mahogany boxes, one fitting inside the other. The two boxes were the focusing mechanism; by sliding one into the other, the user could change the focal length. Later cameras, such as the Kinnear-pattern model, used the classic mechanism of leather bellows to change the focal length. Cameras of this period (1840–60) are very rare and so can be valuable, but they don't often come up for sale.

Early photographs make an important addition to a collection of photographic technology, and they are easier to come by. Calotypes made according to Fox Talbot's process are very sought after. At the time they were not as popular as daguerreotypes because the process was difficult and the images were less clear. However, a few photographers stuck to them throughout the 1840s and 1850s, and today those calotypes are considered true works of art.

Daguerreotypes were especially popular in the United States, where the process was introduced by Samuel Morse after he visited Daguerre in Paris in 1839. By the beginning of the following year, photographers such as John Plumbe of New York City and the Langenheim brothers of Philadelphia had set up flourishing portrait studios. By the end of the 1850s, people could have their portraits taken for 25 cents (about a shilling), though the hinged leather cases in which the photographs were kept were extra. Not surprisingly, people flocked to acquire these "mirrors with a memory", and daguerreotypes survive in their thousands. The most valuable examples will be those that show well-known individuals (they were often copied and sold to the public), historical groups such as the Californian forty-niners (prospectors in the goldrush of 1849), occupational ones showing people plying their trade, and pictures of cities or landscapes.

In Europe, photographers had switched to an improved version of Fox Talbot's process by 1850.

◄ **Expo watch camera**
By the Expo Camera Company, United States, early 20th-century. A novelty camera, it was advertised as a "detective camera". This example has its original box and film cartridge, so its value is more than doubled.
£200–300/$300–500

► **Continental-pattern tailboard camera**
Early 20th century. It is made of walnut, with leather bellows for changing the focal length, and also has a Compur shutter and lens.
£120–180/$180–270

The big breakthrough came in 1851 when Frederick Scott Archer, another Englishman, invented the collodion, or wet-plate process. It was similar to the calotype but used glass rather than paper to make the negatives, so a much sharper image could be obtained. The glass also lasted longer, so more positive paper prints could be made from one glass negative. The disadvantage was that the whole process – coating the glass, exposing and developing it – had to be done at top speed, before any of the solutions dried. This wasn't a problem in a well-equipped studio, but it's astonishing that war photographers such as Roger Fenton in the Crimea or Matthew Brady in the American Civil War were able to produce work out in the field of a quality that has yet to be surpassed. There are not many wet-plate cameras around for collectors today as they were mostly owned by professionals who did not keep outdated equipment.

Collectable cameras mostly date from after 1879, when the dry-plate process was introduced.

Dry plates could be stored before use and didn't need to be developed immediately. This was the revolution that brought photography to amateurs, and it soon became an immensely popular middle-class hobby. Most of the classic mahogany cameras you will see today belonged to ordinary people, not professionals. Dry-plate cameras could be made fairly small, and they didn't need portable darkrooms so it was quite easy to use them out of doors.

As cameras became more affordable, more people bought them. Novelty "detective cameras" were especially popular – disguised as watches, hats, binoculars and even walking sticks, they were a great fad from the middle of the 19th century to its end. Today they are among the most hotly collected type of camera and sell for high prices.

Serious plate cameras of the early 1880s were still fairly cumbersome. The plate holders and focusing screens were unwieldy, and the exposure calculations could be tricky. A dour young American bank clerk named George Eastman decided that a better way

◄ **Graphic No. 0 camera**
By the Folmer & Schwing Company, New York
(the firm had been bought by the Eastman
Company), c.1915. This is a quality early roll-film
camera, which is actually unusually small for
a Folmer & Schwing product.
£200–300/$300–500

▼ ► **Luftwaffen Robot camera**
By the Berning Co, Düsseldorf, for the German Air Force,
c.1940. It was named for its clockwork film advance. It used
35mm film but produced a square image. The "Luftwaffen-
Eigentum" engraving on it doubles its value.
£100–300/$200–400

was needed. Eastman was a great innovator and a born businessman. He had already developed a faster and more sensitive dry plate, and formed the Eastman Dry Plate Company to produce and sell it,

In 1884 Eastman began experimenting with paper coated with gelatine instead of glass – and thereby invented roll film. The devices he built to hold the paper film rolls were adaptable to most dry-plate cameras, and his invention was an instant success. He changed the name of his company to the Eastman Dry Plate and Film Company, and started work on developing an affordable, portable camera.

By 1888 he had done it. It was priced at $25, and it held enough roll film for 100 exposures. When all the pictures had been taken the owner would send the camera back to the Eastman Company, which developed the film and returned the camera with a new film inside. When it came to naming the new camera, Eastman – who is said to have thought that the letter K was a strong, incisive sort of letter – played around with different letters until he came up with Kodak. The camera sold under the slogan "You press the button, we do the rest".

The next important introduction, in the mid-1890s, was the half-tone printing process, in which areas printed with large black dots appear as black while areas with smaller dots appear as various shades of grey. Half-tone printing was important because it enabled the economical, accurate and easy reproduction of photographs. For the first time ever, photographs were printed in newspapers, books and magazines. And so a new breed of photographer began to appear – the photo-journalist.

However, a reproduced photo depends on the quality of the original, and roll-film cameras still couldn't compete with plates. The famous Kodak Box Brownie sold in millions from 1900, when it was first made, until well after World War II, but it was definitely a camera for amateurs. Attempts to make better quality cameras for roll film were unsuccessful until after World War I, and serious photographers continued to use plate cameras into the 20th century, and in fact still do today.

The breakthrough came in 1921, when Oskar Barnack's 35mm Leica appeared. He had invented it in 1914 when he worked for the microscope

◀ **Leica IIIg camera**
By Leica, c.1950s. This is the final version of the screw-fit Leica (ie the lenses are screwed on instead of slotting in bayonet-style). It incorporates all the best features of the rangefinder Leica and is a favourite among collector photographers. Price with standard lens, £600–1,000/$1,000–1,500

▶ **Nikon F 35mm camera**
By Nikon, c.1960s. This was the classic photo-journalism camera of the time, and the one with which the Japanese toppled Leica's dominance. It is still used today. £300–500/$500–700

makers the Leitz company in Germany (the name Leica is a combination of "Leitz" and "camera"). Barnack chose 35mm film because that was the main size used in motion pictures, so it was readily available. By combining it with a top-quality lens in what was then a "miniature" camera he changed photography forever. For the first time the camera was truly portable, the lenses could be changed for wide-angle, telephoto or close-up shots, and the resulting image was the clearest and sharpest yet.

The invention of the Leica is something of a watershed for collectors. Classic photo-history collectors look for interesting, unusual cameras from 1840 to about 1920, while "modern-camera" buffs don't look at anything before about 1921. As a general rule, the better (and more expensive) a camera was at the time it was made, the more collectable it is today (with the notable exception of novelty cameras). For example, a Box Brownie is interesting because it was the first really cheap camera but, for the same reason, isn't valuable today.

Plate cameras continued to be made and used into the 20th century, even after roll film was invented. British plate cameras tend to be the best quality, but there are plenty of decorative American and Continental ones around. They are often made of walnut instead of mahogany, and the plates of Continental cameras are made with metric rather than imperial measurements. These models are very popular with collectors today, and are much more affordable than the earlier designs.

Don't worry too much if an older camera you wish to purchase isn't in working order. Leica and post-Leica cameras, however, should all be usable. Rarity can also be a big factor in value: the Leica Reporter, which had the capacity for 250 exposures, was made in small numbers and is very desirable today. Models with the Compur shutter on the front are also much sought after because Leica didn't make them for long. Leicas represent the high end of the collecting market, although their dominance was challenged after World War II by the Japanese manufacturers Nikon and Canon. Don't despair if Leicas are outside your budget. There were other firms producing 35mm cameras of great interest such as Alpa (Swiss), Agfa and Ihagee (both German).

▼ Scioptic ball
English, late 18th/early 19th century. This is an ebony scioptic ball, used for projecting external views through a shuttered window into a darkened room.
£500–800/$750–1,200

▶ Lithophane table burner
A German lithophane table stove, 19th century. It has a nickel frame and four panels. It would have been used to keep a teapot warm while entertaining the tea drinkers with views of rural scenes.
£200–300/$300–500

◀ An unusual kaleidoscope
Probably English, mid to late 19th century, this kaleidoscope is designed with the specimens in the base, rather than in the tube, where they are turned by a separate handle. The specimens here consist of an arrangement of various silk flowers.
£1,000–1,500/$1,500–2,000

Viewers and Optical Toys

Optical toys are immensely varied in size, purpose, decoration and price. They are not playthings for children; rather, they are beautifully made instruments that produce optical illusions or reproduce strange and wonderful images.

The newly created urban middle classes of the 19th century were experiencing leisure for the first time. Their entertainment was largely based in the home, and new diversions caught on and spread rapidly. It was a flourishing market for merchants who could ensure a regular supply of novelties, so thousands of optical toys were made. As a result there are plenty around today, and you have the choice of whether to specialize in one particular type or to hunt for as many different viewers as you can find.

Some optical toys were designed as pieces to accompany an instrument such as a microscope or, in the second half of the 19th century, a camera. The popular scioptic ball, for example, was often part of a microscopy kit. The borders of art and science were not so sharply distinguished then, and the

scioptic ball was of great use to middle-class young ladies who would use it as an aid to drawing. It normally came with a plain frame that fitted into a shutter over a window, and worked rather like a camera obscura. By turning the ball in the frame, the user could project the view immediately outside the window onto a wall in the darkened room.

Optical toys appeared well before photographic instruments became widespread. The kaleidoscope was invented by a Scottish scientist named Sir David Brewster in 1816. He patented his invention but made very little money from it because it is so easy to copy. Kaleidoscopes ranged in quality and price from cheap children's toys to highly crafted models. Brewster's original used brightly coloured beads to create the reflected patterns in the tube, but more expensive versions used re-creations of botanical or other scientific specimens. Today, basic low-quality kaleidoscopes cost about £65/$100.

Lithophane stoves or lamps were yet another popular early optical device. Instead of using

► **Label on cabinet**
This unusually well-preserved label adds to the value of the cabinet as without it it would only be worth around £500/$800

▼ **Lauer's Patent Revolving Photo Cabinet**
Made by Taft & Schwane, Chicago; patented by Lauer, c.1870. This rare invention allowed more than one person to view at a time.
£500–1,000/$1,000–1,500

▲ **Megalethoscope**
Made in Venice by Carlo Ponti, who both invented and produced it, c.1870. This walnut viewer is 1m (3ft) long and it is used for magnifying and illuminating large albumen print photographs.
£2,500–4,000/$4,000–6,000

mirrors to create a bright image, they relied on the translucency of bisque, a kind of unglazed white porcelain. The chosen image was moulded in relief and then mounted as panels in a burner or in a lamp-shade. The light glowing through the bisque gave the image a magical-looking depth. Lithophanes were mostly produced in Germany and often depict pastoral scenes or genre scenes, such as a couple in a wooded clearing or girls playing with a cat.

As the science of photography advanced and gained in popularity, people needed a good way to store and display their photographs. Where once families had owned one or two paintings, they could now afford photographs of all the members of the family. Inventors fell over each other to offer display systems. From the numbers of beautiful Victorian photo albums surviving today, we can deduce that the album was the most popular method.

Travellers had begun collecting photographs of exotic locations. Some would buy large-format photographs of cities and landmarks that they had

visited and mount them in albums. But others found this method flat and dull – for them the Megalethoscope was the answer. Entrancingly, it shows scenes in both day and evening light. A print is carefully treated on the back to let light through certain areas and then mounted on a curved wooden frame backed with a separate sheet of paper. When the back of the instrument is closed and the top opened, the light is directed onto the top of the print, giving a daylight view. Alternatively, if the top is closed and the back opened, the print is then backlit, giving an evening view. Some prints even have pinpricks in them to give the effect of starlight. The Megalethoscope was an Italian-made instrument, and most of the surviving prints show Italian scenes. There are quite a few examples around, and price will depend on the size of the stand and the quality and amount of carving. As a general rule, viewers are very popular and therefore rather pricey, especially the good ones. They are also rare and difficult to find.

▼ Table stereoscope
By Beckers, New York, c.1875. The eyepieces are on the side, and light enters from the top and back. The knob on the side is for advancing a belt of stereographs. The value depends on how ornate they are: this one is fairly plain.
£100–200/$200–300

▲ Table stereoscope
By J. W. Cadwell, North Reading, Massachusetts, c.1875. J. W. Cadwell was a small firm with a limited output. Owing to both this and its unusual shape, this particular viewer is a very desirable collector's piece.
£250–400/$400–600

▲ Brewster-pattern hand-held stereoscopic viewer
Probably English, c.1875. This viewer is made of mahogany with a shaped eyeshade and hinged top to allow light to enter. The handle has been replaced on this example, which may affect the price a little.
£100–150/$150–200

Stereoscopic Viewers

The stereoscopic viewer, or stereoscope, is a device that allows the user to see a photograph as a three-dimensional image. It works on the same principle as human vision – each eye sees the same thing from a slightly different angle, and when our brain combines the two images it gives depth to what we see. In order to make this principle work with photographs, an image was photographed through two lenses placed side by side and a few inches apart. The resulting pair of photographs was then mounted on a card to make a stereograph, which was then placed in the stereoscope.

The first stereoscopic viewer was invented by the British physicist Sir Charles Wheatstone in 1838. Wheatstone's instrument used mirrors to make the two images converge, and early stereographs were taken with two separate cameras. In 1849 the Scottish physicist and inventor of the kaleidoscope Sir David Brewster invented an improved viewer, which used refracting lenses. At the same time he built a twin camera that had both lenses mounted in the same case. The resulting

stereoscope was shown at the Great Exhibition in 1851, where it caught the fancy of Queen Victoria. Her approval assured its commercial success, and soon stereoscopic viewers were all the rage.

The viewers were made mostly of wood, usually mahogany, though some were produced in leather. The most expensive models were made from exotic woods, and were often intricately inlaid. Table or floor-standing stereoscopes were fashionable articles of drawing-room furniture in the mid-19th century and, like the hand-held viewers, were made from a range of different woods. The stereographs were mounted on a conveyor belt which was turned by a knob. Some of the larger viewers had two sets of eyepieces, so that two people could look at the stereographs at the same time.

It was an American who gave the device mass market appeal. Oliver Wendell Holmes, the famous law scientist, designed a cheap but effective stereoscope and deliberately didn't patent it. Anyone who wanted to build it could do so for nothing – and many manufacturers did. The Holmes-pattern

► **Stereograph storage rack**
American, late 19th century. A rack such as this was a convenient and decorative way to store stereographs. They are scarce today because the jigsaw construction is fairly delicate. The value increases with size and ornateness.
£100–200/$200–300

▲ **A Rowsell's-pattern stereo-graphoscope**
Probably English, c.1860s. The easel slides back and forth for focusing, and the base can be used for storage. The whole device folds flat and is made of walnut. £150–250/$250–350

stereoscope was still being made in the 20th century and is the most common type today. One versatile viewer was the stereo-graphoscope, which could be used for ordinary photographs as well as stereographs.

The stereographs themselves are also fun things to collect. The early ones were daguerreotypes, and some were sold already fitted into their own viewers. Not many of them were made, however, so they are fairly valuable today. But after wet collodion printing was invented in 1851, stereographs were produced in quantity at affordable prices.

At first, stereoscopic portraits of famous people were the most in demand, followed by generic views of Swiss mountains and so on. Today those views are not particularly collectable. Stereographs of historical places and people are of far more interest, for example those depicting the American Civil War – especially any taken by Matthew Brady. Carleton A. Watkins, a San Franciscan photographer famous for his pictures of Yosemite (now a national park) in the 1860s and 1870s, is another name to look out for.

Saucy stereographs were also produced in the mid-1800s. The demurely naked and semi-naked ladies were hot stuff then, and they are still beloved of collectors today. They don't often appear on the market, and always command a good price.

It is especially interesting to collect cards related to your local area. Town photographers would often sell stereographs of local places or events such as fires or floods. It was even possible to buy sets of cards depicting news events such as coronations, inaugurations and, of course, wars.

By the turn of the century, stereographs were so cheap to produce that big firms gave away sets of cards printed with their names as advertisements. The three main suppliers of viewers and cards were the American firms Keystone, White, and Underwood & Underwood, and the majority of early 20th-century stereographs will bear one of those names. All three firms sold improved viewers and millions of cards until as late as the 1930s, when stereographs and stereoscopes were overtaken by photo-journalism and the moving picture.

▼ A bi-unial magic lantern
Probably English, mid to late 19th century. Able to project two slides at once, these lanterns, now very rare, were used by professional lanternists for showing dissolving slides and creating other special effects. £2,000–3,500/$3,000–5,000

▲ Praxinoscope theatre
By Emile Reynauld, French, late 19th century. This is a more complex version of the popular zoetrope: the image is projected on mirrors in the centre of the wheel and viewed through the opening in the raised lid. Above the drum is a candle with a printed paper shade. £1,000–2,000/$2,000–3,000

Moving Pictures

As with still photography, if you want to collect devices related to moving pictures you do not need to be restricted to cameras. After all, the first successful motion-picture camera and viewer didn't appear until 1893, after George Eastman had made motion pictures possible by improving his roll film. He made it out of celluloid instead of paper, and that was the start of modern movies. But moving pictures had been around for a long time before Eastman. In fact, they can be traced back to the shadow theatre of Java. At 50,000 to 100,000 years old, it is thought to be the source of the oldest moving images in the world. Shadow puppets are beautiful and would make an intriguing addition to your collection. However, the main focus of this collecting area lies in America and Europe in the 19th and 20th centuries.

Before film, people relied on optical illusion to make images move. Optical toys based on the principle of the persistence of vision (that images remain on the eye for a split second after they have

gone) were popular from the middle of the 19th century onwards. The phenakistiscope, developed by the Belgian scientist Joseph Plateau in 1832, is the earliest of these. It uses a rotating disc printed with successive images, which are viewed through a slot. The zoetrope, invented in 1833, uses the same principle, but the images are printed on the inside of a hollow drum. The user looks at the images through slots in the cylinder, and spins the drum to produce the illusion of movement. These kinds of device have often lost their fragile shades or picture strips. If you are offered one, check first that all the pieces are there and that none of them has been replaced with a reproduction.

The earliest known reference to projection dates from the 17th century, when the magic lantern first made its appearance. These early slide projectors relied on the weak power of a candle, and not many people could watch them at once. However, the development of limelight in the early 19th century transformed the magic lantern into a

◄ **Child's tinplate magic lantern**
By Ernst Plank of Nuremberg, c.1890–1910. It is essential to their value that these be boxed and in good condition. Shape is also important: boxy, plain lanterns are the cheapest, and those in the shape of buildings are the most desirable. This cylindrical one is therefore mid-range in price. **£100–200/$200–300**

► **Kinora viewer**
English, c.1910. This was an inexpensive toy and is now very collectable. It is more common in Britain than in the USA. This is the most usual version: clockwork models are very rare. The reels should be present on all types as extras are expensive and hard to find.
£500–800/$800–1,200 with some reels.

sophisticated instrument. Limelight was a very bright light produced by heating a block of quick-lime with a blowpipe flame. It could project an image that was large enough and clear enough for a number of people to see. Soon magic-lantern shows were appearing all over Europe. The images were painted on glass slides and shown in succession to tell a story from the Bible, recount a historical tale or illustrate a lecture.

Before long, special effects began to appear. The dissolving screen so beloved of soap-opera directors has its roots in magic-lantern technology. By aiming two lanterns at the same spot, the lanternist could uncover one slide as the other was covered up. If you did this with, for example, a slide of a forest in winter in one lantern and a slide of the same forest in springtime in the other, you could create the illusion of the seasons changing. The lanternist could also use two or three specially painted slides to show simple animation. One of the most famous shows a snoring man with rats running up the bed

and into his mouth as it opens. Lanterns that could project two or three slides at once made it easier to perform these special effects, and bi-unial and tri-unial magic lanterns were at the cutting edge of mid-19th-century projection technology.

Smaller magic lanterns were also made for use at home. These tinplate toy lanterns were popular from the late 19th century into the first quarter of the 20th century, and they are very collectable today. The best ones were made by German toy companies, so look for names such as Ernst Plank of Nuremberg and Schoner & Carrette. The slides are usually of classic children's entertainment such as humorous stories and fairy tales.

All the optical toys discussed so far are highly collectable, which tends to mean that they are also quite expensive. But don't lose heart – toy magic lanterns can be much more affordable. They vary in value depending on their quality and condition, and can be found in an enormous range of different shapes and sizes.

◄ **Novitascope**
Made in Waltham, Massachusetts, c.1915. This was an attempt to revive the popular phenakistiscope of the mid-19th century. The box shows a delightful illustration of an early motion-picture theatre. **£100–200/$200–300**

▲ **Cinematographic camera**
By Ernemann of Dresden, 1910; now very scarce. It is expensively built, with a mahogany body for professional use, though a wealthy amateur might have bought one. Hand-operated by a crank (not visible), it uses 35mm film. **£2,000–3,000/$3,000–5,000** depending on condition.

With the coming of photography, people began trying to photograph movement. The most famous experiment was that of Eadweard Muybridge, an English photographer working in California. In 1877 he proved that a galloping horse does at some point in its gait have all four hooves off the ground at once. He did this by galloping the horse past a series of 40 cameras with tripwires attached to their shutters. In 1881 he designed and built a phenakistiscope-like projector that held a glass disc painted with images based on his photographs. With it Muybridge projected a realistic, although non-photographic, representation of a galloping horse.

Thomas Edison was fascinated by Muybridges's work, and after several experiments he produced the kinetoscope, which was exhibited in 1893. It was the first successful system of showing photographic motion pictures and used Eastman's celluloid film, taken with a separate camera called the kinetograph. Kinetoscope parlours were opened so that people could watch films for five cents a time, but their popularity didn't last long. This was because only one person at a time could use the kinetoscope, peering in through an opening in the top of the wooden cabinet. The other drawback was that the films only lasted about 30 seconds. They depicted a simple sequence such as a sneeze or a kiss, so the novelty wore off fairly quickly!

In France the brothers Auguste and Louis Lumière realized that the future of motion pictures lay in projecting films to a large audience, in the manner of the magic-lantern shows. In 1895 they built a combined camera and projector called the "cinématographe". The Lumières' work marked the birth of modern movie projection. Their films of people getting off a train or leaving a factory look dull to us now, but at the time they were miraculous; it's said that when the train came into view, the scared audience thought they were about to be hit.

By the early 20th century several organizations and individuals were making and showing motion pictures. In the USA and Britain, the Biograph and Mutoscope Company produced the bioscope, which showed films in theatres as part of vaudeville shows, and the mutoscope. The mutoscope was a viewer like the kinetoscope but used printed stills in a reel.

▼ **Carbon rod illuminant**

Made by Thompson & Co., Boston, 1910. This is the kind of carbon arc lamp that was used to light a magic lantern or an early motion-picture projector. This one is large, so was probably used on a projector.
£200–300/$300–400

▲ **Edison Home Kinetoscope**

Made by the Edison Company, c.1912. Not many of these were made, and fewer still have survived. Most have been well-used and are therefore in a battered condition. **£1,000–2,000/$1,500–2,500** (depending on condition and on which films or slides come with it. Slides alone will cost about £35/$50, while films cost about £100/$200 depending on their content.)

By 1900 it was possible to buy a complete projecting outfit for $100 or even less, and the makers of toy magic lanterns began selling toy cinematographs. Home movie cameras appeared on the market, but their nitrate film was expensive and highly flammable. The carbon arc lamps used for lighting the projection tended to set fire to the film easily, so these early cameras didn't catch on. Manufacturers tried other approaches, such as the Kinora. This was a viewer that got around the fire problem by producing a flip-book type of reel. It was a table-top mutoscope. People could also buy readymade films of subjects ranging from zoo animals to pillow fights or battleships at sea.

In 1912 both Edison and Pathé of Paris produced new domestic projectors. Edison's Home Kinetoscope offered both entertaining and educational films, and it also projected small magic-lantern slides. It was advertised as being simple enough for a child to operate, but it was actually a complicated device. In addition, its films were quite boring as they were either the outdated "shorts" of zoos from 10 or 15 years earlier, or dull educational

pieces. Edison's machine was also too expensive for most families: prices started at $72 – around a month's salary for most people – without the screen. Pathé's Kok "cinématographe" wasn't much cheaper, but its price included the projection screen, and it was easier to use. Instead of a carbon arc lamp, the Kok used a small electric bulb that was run from a dynamo cleverly connected to the film mechanism. By turning the handle, the user simultaneously ran the film and generated the electricity. The market for both projectors was small, but the Kok home "cinématographe" was the clear winner at the time. Today Edison's machine is the more valuable, partly because it is rarer but also owing to his name.

Early movie cameras had hard commercial use and were mostly thrown out when they became obsolete. As a result they are scarce today and so command quite high prices, even if in a battered condition. However, by the 1920s home cameras and projectors had become widespread. The first Kodak movie cameras ushered in mass production in 1923, and cameras from after this date are mostly very affordable, unless they have unusual formats.

Mechanical
Music

Charming musical machines are as popular today as they were in their heyday, more than a hundred years ago

▲ **Polyphon coin-operated disc musical box**
Made in Germany by Polyphon and retailed by William Russell, Leicester, *c.*1900. It takes 50-cm (19⅞-in) discs.
£2,000–3,500/$3,000–5,000

Today we take the artificial production of music as a matter of course. Almost every household in the Western world has a sophisticated music centre. We tend to look back fondly on the days when everybody made their own music, but those days never really existed. While music has always been a popular recreation, only wealthier people have had the resources to pay for musicians or musical training. But talent isn't needed to play mechanical instruments that have pre-programmed music, and maybe this was a factor in their development. They are also ingeniously crafted and great fun to watch, particularly the ones with bells or drums.

Most people are familiar with musical boxes and phonographs, but this field also includes singing mechanical birds, barrel organs and pianos, automatic pianos and the various rivals of the phonograph that fought for supremacy in the late 19th century.

The barrel organ is one of the oldest surviving instruments of mechanical music – one is listed in a 1598 inventory of the Duke of Modena. However, it was expensive and therefore mostly used in the realm of public entertainment. From the late 18th century onwards, barrel organs and barrel pianos were well known on the streets of London and other large European cities. Both incorporate the same principle of a revolving barrel set with pins. The pins in the organ operate keys that admit air to the pipes, while in the piano the pins move hammers that strike tuned wires. The simplest barrel organs were crude, portable instruments with 24 notes, but the top-of-the-range models were complex enough for Mozart to write music for them. The barrel piano had no such pretensions; strident and jangling, it was wheeled through London's poorest streets by Italian children who hired the instruments, with or without a monkey, from an entrepreneur in Clerkenwell.

▲ Fine grand-format (large-cylinder) musical box
By Nicole Frères, c.1870. It plays 12 operatic airs and has a silver tune list.
£4,000–5,000/$6,000–7,000

▼ Singing bird cage
By Bontems, Paris, c.1900. These were popular drawing-room ornaments.
£1,500–2,000/$2,000–3,000

◄ Type AP Graphophone
By Columbia, c.1905. Simple cylinder phonographs such as this were popular with children, or for travelling.
£200–300/$300–500

A few 18th-century examples of mechanical music survive today, but they are extremely valuable and tend to be museum pieces. Most of the examples now available to collectors date from the 19th century, when mechanical music reached its peak. There are also plenty of good examples around from the early 20th century.

Musical boxes, in particular, are widely available and affordable. Cylinder musical boxes were the next step up from barrel pianos and organs as they used a comb with tuned teeth instead of the wind pipes or strings. The louder disc musical box appeared toward the end of the 19th century and became the ancestor of today's jukebox.

The disc box looked as though it was here to stay, but within a couple of decades, it had vanished into the pages of history. By the time World War I broke out, the phonograph and its cousins had made a surprise appearance. They grew out of development work on the telephone and the telegraph, where the technology of "talking machines" had been developed as a business application (*see* pp. 114–15). By the early 20th century, home entertainment had left the realm of the craftsman and was now linked with industry.

When you are buying a machine don't just find out whether it plays: check that it plays well. Combs often have missing teeth, cylinders may have bent pins, and it could cost as much as the instrument is worth to have them replaced. This is because a comb's teeth have to be individually tuned and pins can't be replaced singly – the whole cylinder has to be repinned. Check any musical box over carefully and be sure to buy from a reputable source. Disc boxes are sturdier, and it's easier to see or hear any damage. Phonographs and gramophones are also easy to check, but bear in mind that the tone of early examples is not of particularly high quality anyway.

▶ **German Tanzbär
28-note automatic
accordion**
Made by Zuleger of
Leipzig, c.1920. It
comes with 13 rolls in
three original cartons.
£600–1,000/
$1,000–1,500

◀ **20-key barrel organ**
By W. Bruder & Son,
late 19th century. It
has a nine-tune barrel
and a tune selector.
£2,000–4,000/
$4,000–6,000

◀▲ **(Above) Silver
singing-bird box**
By Griesbaum, early 20th
century. It has a serpentine
front and sides.
**(Left) Tortoiseshell
singing-bird box**
French or German, late
19th-century. This box has
an engraved bronzed lid.
£600–1,000/$1,000–1,500 each

Pneumatic and Stringed

This class of mechanical music covers machines that had bellows or strings that were hit by keys. The barrel organ was hugely popular in the 19th century, when it was pushed through the streets of London and other large cities, taking music to the poorest classes. Bruder was one of the world's finest organ builders, and his machines are noted for their loud, clear sound. Barrel organs can be fairly small, but they are bulky and awkward to carry. The organ grinder would have pushed his instrument on a cart, or carried it on a pole or with a leather strap. The condition of the movement is always a vital factor when valuing a barrel organ; it was an expensive item, and the owner would need to have got a great deal of service from it in order to recover his capital outlay. Not surprisingly, many need thorough restoration today.

Mechanical musical instruments were very popular in wealthier households too. Musical ability was greatly valued, but not everyone had the talent required to play an instrument well. Automatic instruments were the answer. People could sit down in front of an automatic piano or organ and play away like a professional just by inserting a paper roll. By the early 20th century it was possible to choose from automatic pianos (or player pianos as they were often called), automatic organs or even automatic accordions. All of them work on the same basic principle – a perforated paper roll feeds through the mechanism and operates the keys of the instrument to produce the notes. However, automatic pianos and organs were very expensive and only wealthy families could afford one for domestic use. Some coin-operated models were built for use in public places, and these were very popular. Other affordable options were the organette and the automatic accordion.

The organette was an American invention and a cheaper form of the automatic organ. It operates from perforated paper rolls and has reeds instead of pipes. The organette's case is usually plain walnut with a little gold-coloured stencil decoration.

◄ **Coin-operated American Regina Mandolin Orchestro (automatic piano)**
By Regina, early 20th century. It has a 79-key piano mechanism.
£2,000–3,000/ $3,000–4,000

▲ **Orpheus 24-key disc-operated zither**
Late 19th century. It has 30 cardboard discs (not shown).
£1,000–2,000/ $1,500-2,500

Organettes were popular in clubs and churches, and in aspiring working-class households that didn't have real pianos or organs; as a result they are often referred to as the poor man's musical box. The paper rolls mostly contain dance numbers, marches or hymns. Player pianos and organettes are very affordable collectables today but are often in poor condition. Restoration can be very expensive so, unless you can do it yourself, check carefully before you buy.

The automatic accordion is held like a normal accordion. However, instead of having to play the notes yourself, you move the ratchet handle up and down. A perforated paper roll feeds through the movement and plays the keys for you. No musical ability required – but you will need strong muscles and good co-ordination. Again, condition is of paramount importance when buying these today.

Zither music was very popular in Europe in the late 19th century, and it wasn't long before the automatic zither appeared. Most used a perforated paper roll, but the one pictured above was operated

by a cardboard disc with holes in it. Zithers require regular tuning and are much less popular today, but ones like the Orpheus are collected for their shape.

At the more refined end of the scale is the exquisite singing bird. These birds were first produced in the 18th century and became extremely fashionable in the early 19th century. They required great skill to make, owing to the miniature mechanisms in the base that allow each bird to turn its head, flick its tail and move its wings. There are also tiny bellows and pistons to reproduce the bird's song. The bird-in-a-cage type is the more familiar, but tiny bird-in-a-box versions were made too.

These delightful pieces would have been extremely expensive – toys for the wealthy. They remained popular right into the 20th century, but the quality of their workmanship declined. The fine fusee movements gave way to simpler and cheaper spring movements, and the elaborate cases were replaced by plainer ones. Early examples are costly, but it is still possible to find attractive later ones.

◄ **Musical box**
By Nicole Frères,
c.1850. It plays
four nautical airs.
£1,000–1,500/
$1,500–2,000

► **"Gloria" piccolo-zither
interchangeable musical box**
By Paillard, late 19th century.
It comes with instruction sheet,
six cylinders and tune cards.
£3,000–4,000/$5,000–6,000

▲ **Expressif musical box**
c.1875. It plays eight airs (operatic
and dance) with mandolin expression.
£1,000–1,500/$1,500–2,000

Cylinder Musical Boxes

Musical boxes probably make up the richest field within mechanical music, purely because there are so many of them. Technologically they are interesting as it was a major advance to produce an instrument that could play music without any talent on the user's part, and to make it something that could be afforded by those below the aristocracy.

Cylinder musical boxes are the earliest kind of musical box, and they are also the most collectable examples of mechanical music. They developed in the 19th century from musical watches, which had small musical movements. Not surprisingly, given this history, nine out of ten of all cylinder movements were made in Switzerland. The Swiss firm of Nicole Frères is a particularly good name to look out for as its boxes are known for their consistently good programming and command a high value in today's market.

The cylinder musical box, however, suffered from two main disadvantages. First, it had a very small repertoire. By staggering the pins the makers could fit as many as 20 tunes on a single cylinder, but that significantly reduced the quality of each song. The other solution was to make interchangeable cylinders, but they were so expensive that only the very wealthy could afford them.

The second problem was that no matter how finely tuned a comb was, they all still had a similar sound. Clever craftsmen solved this by arranging the teeth to play the same note repeatedly. Sometimes this produced a mandolin effect, and sometimes a trill. There were other types of arrangements too, but the best way to produce "good" music was to concentrate on the quality of the programme. Features such as a zither attachment with tissue paper, a set of bells, drums or a castanet (a wood block struck by several hammers) were used to add interest, but just as often to cover up a less than satisfactory programme. As time went on these added extras became more common. Where the first musical boxes were built for quality of sound, later ones concentrated on fine casings and fancy sound

► **Full-orchestral interchangeable music box on stand**
By Paillard, c.1880. It has 16 six-air cylinders, a 20-key organ and optional six bells, drum and castanet.
£6,500–10,000/$10,000–15,000

▲ **Musical box**
By Billon-Haller, c.1880, with drum, six-bell, castanet and zither attachments. It plays eight airs.
£1,500–2,500/$2,500–3,500

effects that may not have sounded wonderful but were terrific fun to watch. The choice of music on the boxes is also a rough guide to aid dating – early ones generally contained operatic airs and pieces by fine composers. Popular songs didn't really make it into musical boxes until later in the 19th century.

Later boxes are still very collectable because they look more like our idea of a musical box, with polished cases and external decoration. They were made to suit all pockets: the Expressif represents the more accessible end of the scale, while the Paillard "Gloria" box is a high-end item. It would have been an expensive piece at the time it was made because it has interchangeable cylinders. This type was made in increasing numbers towards the end of the 19th century, in response to the competition from disc musical boxes that offered far wider repertoires. It's interesting to note that boxes for the American market tend to have the extra cylinders in drawers in the base, while those for the British market were sold with a matching table with cylinder drawers.

The reason for this is not known, but it may have been in order to keep the shipping charges down.

The cylinder musical box reached its peak around 1880. The last example shown above would be the high point of anyone's collection. It has everything: interchangeable cylinders, bells, drum, castanet and organ, all on a beautifully made matching table. Not surprisingly, pieces like this don't appear very often and are extremely costly.

There are several pointers to quality when choosing a cylinder musical box. First look at the length of the cylinder — as a rule of thumb, the longer it is, the better — then check the number of tunes it plays (few is best) and the maker. A well-known name will add value, but the boxes were mass-produced in such numbers that 90 per cent of them aren't signed, so this won't necessarily reduce the value. The sound it makes is also important, so you need to listen to a few in order to hear the range of quality. Finally, look at the condition of the case, inlay, tune card and other features before buying.

▼ Table disc box
By Symphonion, *c.*1900,
disc diam. 35cm (13¾in).
It has 30 discs.
**£1,200–1,600/
$2,000–2,500**

**▲ Capital "cuff"
musical box**
By F.G. Otto of New
Jersey, late 1890s. It
has a 10-cm (4-in) cuff.
**£2,000–2,600/
$3,000–4,000**

▲ Disc musical box
By Kalliope, *c.*1900, disc diam. 23.5cm
(9¼in). It comes with 12 discs and
optional six bells. The plain design
is typical of smaller boxes.
£1,000–1,500/$1,500–2,000

Disc Musical Boxes

The disc musical box was invented in 1886 by the German Paul Lochmann. Instead of a cylinder, a notched disc revolved on a spindle against tuned teeth. The first discs were made from cardboard, but they wore out too quickly so metal was used instead.

The advantages of the disc musical box over the cylinder one were many. The discs were cheap and easy to make and could be bought separately, so buyers were no longer restricted to whichever tunes came on the cylinder. This meant that a collection of discs was (theoretically) infinitely expandable. The boxes were also large and loud. The cylinder box had been a drawing-room piece, audible only to a few people gathered round the box itself, but the disc box was up to 3m (10ft) tall with a sound to match, and also an extremely sturdy piece.

The chief maker of disc boxes in Europe was Polyphon, so the boxes became known generically as polyphons. Symphonion, another German firm, was the other main European maker. In the USA, it was Regina who was the leading manufacturer.

Disc boxes reached the mass market in a way that the cylinder musical box had been unable to do. A big polyphon was a very expensive item, so only the rich could afford to buy one for themselves. In this respect they were a rich man's status symbol, just as the cylinder musical box had been. However, their great size and volume made them suitable for use in public spaces. Hotels, inns and clubs bought coin-operated versions and kept them supplied with the latest fashionable dance tunes and music-hall songs. Meanwhile, there were plenty of less expensive, table-top models that were popular in working-class and middle-class households.

Today disc boxes are very collectable items. Their life was short because of the unexpected development of the phonograph (*see* pp.114–15) but thousands of them were made, and they have survived well. Not all of them are huge – there are several table-top designs available. However, most small disc musical boxes did not have the additional features that were so popular in the cylinder boxes,

◀ **Coin-operated upright disc box**
By Symphonion, c.1900, disc diam. 54cm (21¼in). It has bells and eight discs.
£5,000–6,000/ $8,000–10,000

▶ **Corona Style 33 self-changing disc musical box**
By Regina, 1899–1900, disc diam. 70cm (27in). The box has 12 discs.
£13,000–16,000/ $20,000–25,000

so if you find one that has bells the value will be doubled. Cases are another thing to look for. The more handsome the case, the greater the value and appeal. Many boxes had the same size movement sold in a choice of cases, which were usually either plain or extravagantly decorated. The Symphonion box shown above has a case of polished walnut with engaged corner columns, an inner glass lid and a reverse print in the lid. It is an unusually elegant design, neither boringly plain nor overly ornate, and its value is increased because of this.

There is also an intriguing American table-top design known as the "cuff" because of the mechanism's resemblance to a shirt cuff. The "cuff" was manufactured by F.G. Otto. An employee of the firm, a pattern maker named Henry Lanfelder, patented it, probably to get around existing patents for disc boxes. It is just like a disc box except that the disc has been rolled up into a cone shape. The "cuff" examples are collectable more for their rarity than for their quality, and value increases with size.

One technological advance that helped the disc musical box's popularity was the invention of the automatic changer, which was first patented by Polyphon in 1896. Models such as the upright Symphonion had to have their discs changed manually, which meant that anyone within earshot of a coin-operated disc box was likely to hear the same tune over and over again. Self-changing disc musical boxes therefore attracted a lot of interest.

When buying a disc musical box look for names such as Polyphon, Symphonion, Regina, Mira, Stella and Kalliope. Then check the diameter of the disc (bigger is usually better) and the number of combs on the bedplate – two are better than one as they create a fuller sound. Finally, the more decorative the case, the higher the value. Large disc musical boxes can be very valuable, especially if they have extra features such as bells or percussion. Domestic machines are usually in better condition than commercial machines, but the coin-operated feature of the commercial examples is a great selling point.

Phonographs

Just as the disc musical box was getting into its stride, along came the talking machine and made it instantly obsolete. Thomas Edison invented the phonograph in 1877, but he was preoccupied with inventing the light bulb at the same time, so for more than 10 years the phonograph just remained a scientific curiosity. After that the story became one of outraged pride, patent battles and big business.

Edison's design was based on the revolving cylinder that had dominated mechanical music for so long. His phonograph had a grooved cylinder wrapped in tinfoil. There was a brief craze for it, but the tinfoil wore out very quickly and only 500 tinfoil Parlor Speaking Phonographs were produced. However, more were made by experimenters and machine shops for demonstrations, so there are quite a few tinfoil phonographs around today.

While Edison worked on his light bulb, Alexander Graham Bell picked up on Edison's phonograph idea and improved it. Together with his cousin Chichester Bell, a chemical engineer,

and an instrument-maker friend named Charles Tainter he built a phonograph with a wax-coated cardboard cylinder. This could be more closely grooved than tinfoil and therefore gave a longer playing time. The three men called their machine a Graphophone and got a patent for it in 1886. Their company eventually became Columbia, which is why Columbia products are called Graphophones, whether they are cylinder or disc machines.

Edison was furious when he learned of the new machine and immediately entered the field again, abandoning his electrical work and producing a phonograph with a solid wax cylinder. He persuaded eminent musicians to make recordings of serious music on it, but Tainter and Bell promptly sued him for patent infringement.

Meanwhile a German-American named Emile Berliner had built a talking machine that used a disc instead of a cylinder and called it a "gramophone" (*see* pp.116–17). The cylinder phonograph was actually the better machine of the two in terms of

▲ Edison Standard phonograph
c.1900. It has been placed in a Hawthorne & Sheble
cabinet with drawers to store the cylinders.
£600–1,000/$1,000–1,500 for the whole piece

Collecting
Edison Ephemera

▲ Signed photograph
A signed photograph of the American genius
Thomas Edison (1847–1931) taken c.1910.
£1,000–2,000/$2,000–3,000

sound quality, playing surface and engineering, but
the cylinders were more expensive and the selection
of music on them was poor.

Edison, Berliner (whose company eventually
became Victor) and Columbia battled for market
shares. Companies rose, merged and fell as everyone
tried to carve out a slice of this dynamic new market,
and patents changed hands in dizzying confusion.

There are so few early phonographs that you
will find it almost impossible to acquire one. Today
it is the phonographs with external horns that are
more sought after, while an example with an early
electric motor is worth about 10 times as much as a
spring-powered model. Phonographs were produced
in much larger quantities after 1900 and remained
in production until 1929. Examples from this era are
easily found, so it is worth holding out for the best.
Furniture companies also jumped on the band-
wagon by offering fitted cabinets for phonographs.
These can be great additions to a collection as they
are very handsome and not enormously expensive.

Thomas Alva Edison was born in Milan,
Ohio, in 1847. He was an inspired and
a prolific inventor who by the time he died in
1931 had patented more than a thousand devices
(although many of the patents under his name
were actually the inventions of his employees).

Edison is considered both a hero and a fool.
His genius lay in having the ideas, but he had
difficulty in keeping them going. He was also
unable to believe that others could improve
on his inventions and would cling to obsolete
modes. It was this conservatism, or rather
pigheadedness, that contributed to the failure
of his proudest invention, the phonograph,
against its inferior competitor, the gramophone.
Although his was the better machine, he insisted
on choosing all the music himself, in spite of
being totally deaf and without any musical taste.
He did put up a fight by adding various
improvements, such as longer-playing cylinders
and internal horn machines, and even produced
a disc phonograph, but to no avail.

His signature is very collectable today,
especially in the USA. The photograph shown
above is a particularly desirable piece because
portrait photos were popular gifts, and the sitter
normally inscribed them to the recipient.

▶ **Victor V gramophone**
By Victor, c.1910. It has a gooseneck tone arm and a wooden horn.
£2,000–3,000/ $3,000–4,000

◀ **Type AJ Disc Graphophone**
By Columbia, c.1903. It has a travelling arm and a soundbox connected directly to the horn.
£800–1,200/ $1,500–2,000

▶ **Victrola XVI internal horn gramophone**
By Victor, c.1910–12. This example has gilt fittings, and the Exhibition soundbox is in a mahogany cabinet.
£400–600/$700–1,000

Gramophones

Berliner's disc gramophone first appeared on the market around the same time as the Bell-Tainter Graphophone. It swiftly pulled ahead in popularity and influenced the development of electrical disc players and records in the 20th century. Even today's CDs and mini-discs have followed the disc pattern rather than the cylinder.

It is extraordinary that Berliner's design should have succeeded against the machines of Bell and Edison, for Berliner had none of the clout of those giants of telegraphy and telephony. It was the founding of Victor that made the difference, as the company was progressive and experimental. It recorded popular music and grabbed the public's imagination with its famous advertising campaign featuring the little dog Nipper listening to the record of his master's voice. (Nipper is perhaps best known as the logo of HMV, the British sister company of Victor.)

The spring motor made a huge difference to the price of the gramophone. Edison's electrical motors meant that his phonographs had to be sold for enormous sums. Berliner shrewdly avoided overpricing, and his first gramophone, the Seven-Inch Hand Gramophone, sold in 1893 for $12 (£8). But it had a direct drive that made it impossible to keep the speed consistent, and so not many were sold.

At this stage the gramophone was very much perceived as the poor relation of the phonograph, and Berliner had to overcome this prejudice. In 1896 his syndicate built a satisfactory spring motor, and a snappy advertising campaign was launched to promote "The Talking Machine That Talks Talk!". This was the "Improved Gramophone", which went on the market in 1897, and it is the earliest gramophone that survives today in any quantity. By the turn of the century the Improved Gramophone was down to $25. That brought it within reach of the mass market, and its success was assured.

Around the same time Columbia was making most of its money from records rather than machines. In 1903 shellac discs appeared, and the 12-inch disc

◄ **Bell gramophone**
By The Durable
Phonograph Company
Ltd., New York and
Cleveland, c. 1920. The
"bell" of the name refers
to its distinctive shape
£200–300/$300–500

► **Special Model L Portable**
By RCA Victor (designed
by John Vassos, a leading
designer of the time), in the
early 1930s. The piece
comes in an olive-green
leather-covered case with
chrome fittings.
£1,000–1,200/$1,500–2,000

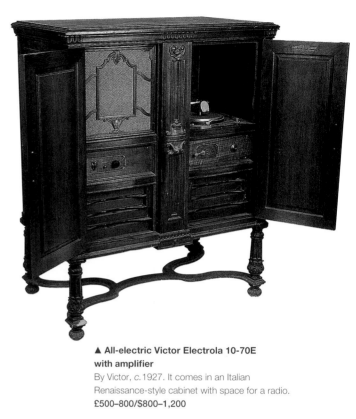

▲ **All-electric Victor Electrola 10-70E
with amplifier**
By Victor, c. 1927. It comes in an Italian
Renaissance-style cabinet with space for a radio.
£500–800/$800–1,200

with a playing time of four minutes was introduced. It remained popular until 1948, when Columbia introduced the vinyl "LP". There had been previous attempts to market long-playing discs but none had met with commercial success. Playing speed was an issue as many companies recommended playing their discs at speeds other than 78rpm. Fortunately, most machines came with a speed-adjust control. From about 1918 electric-powered models were reintroduced, but these were expensive, and few were sold. Studio recording machines continued to be weight-driven as this was more reliable than an electric motor.

Most of the major patents had expired by 1917–19, which meant that any company with half an idea could sell talking machines. Even the oddest ideas were put into production, such as the Durable Phonograph Company's Bell gramophone with its bell-shaped case. It looks very attractive, but the all-metal construction and small horn give it a pinched, tinny sound.

In pre-World War II Britain especially, portable wind-up gramophones became all the rage, and

production soared. At the same time, new recording techniques were being introduced as companies began using microphones instead of horns. The new electrical recordings, which began in 1925, were vastly superior to the earlier acoustic ones. This was the most important event of the 1920s, and it changed the sound of music for ever. However, it is at this point that talking machines begin to lose their popularity with collectors as they are no longer phonographs but record players. The all-electric RCA Victor Special Portable is one significant exception; this 1930s piece is very rare and much loved for its looks.

Wind-up gramophones with horns are the classic pieces for collectors. Wooden horns are highly sought after – they came as extras at the time and still add a great deal of value to a machine today. Cabinet gramophones are mostly too bulky to be of interest to collectors. There will only be substantial value if the cabinet is of very good quality, in peak condition and with all the portfolios (drawers for record storage) present, or if it is a re-entrant.

Calculating and Computing

The computer is a new invention, but it has transformed our lives so much that its predecessors are now valuable collectables

▲ **Gem pocket adding machine**
By Automatic Adding Machine Manufacturers, New York, *c.*1920. This machine is nickel-plated, in a fitted morocco case, and has the original stylus and instruction sheet. **£200–250/$300–400**

Before the 1940s there was no distinction between calculating and computing. In fact, "a computer" used to be the term that described a person who could operate a calculating machine. A wages computer, for instance, would use the machine to "compute" the standard calculations for the monthly pay-roll.

Today, people have rediscovered the joys of the mechanical instruments that preceded the PC and the Macintosh, and calculating devices have become one of the most popular fields of technology collecting. Almost any 19th-century device will be worth a fair amount, as are many early 20th-century instruments too. Prices do not really begin to fall until we get into living memory, but even then some are still surprisingly high.

As this is a relatively new field of collecting there is very little literature available on the subject. This means that you really need to know what to look for, while at the same time keeping your eyes peeled for the unusual machines. There are so many different kinds of mechanical calculator that you might not even recognize some of them for what they are. In the late 19th and early 20th centuries the fields of commerce and industry became more and more diverse, and people needed ever more specialized machines to help them with their calculations. Manufacturers hurried to fulfil the demand, so today this is a varied exciting field in which new discoveries are regularly made.

The first calculating machine was probably the abacus, which was invented many thousands of years ago in ancient Babylon. It is still in use in China, Japan and Korea today. We don't know who the inventor was, or even exactly when it was invented, but using a machine to do intellectual work was a groundbreaking idea. It didn't attain its final form overnight: the first abaci were simply lines drawn on the

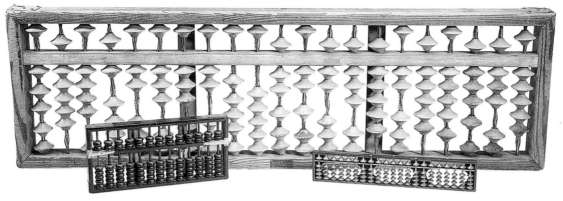

▲ **Group of three abaci**
Early 20th century. The largest is
35cm x 110cm (13¼in x 43in).
£100–200/$200–300; the other
two are **£50–85/$75–125** each.

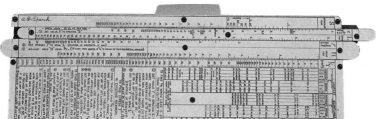

◄ **Otis King pocket
calculator**
c.1920s–30s. Its closed
length is 6in (15cm),
and it has spiral
logarithmic scales
as well as instructions.
This example also has its
original cardboard case.
£50–100/$100–200

▲ **Rare structural
beam slide rule**
By A. D. Stark,
c.1920–30. The rule is
made of celluloid and
mahogany with
six scales and
instructions.
£250–350/$400–500

ground to represent units, tens, hundreds and
so on. People would use pebbles laid on the
grooves to make their calculations. Then the
grooves were carved permanently on a tablet.
The next development brought the abacus to
its familiar form of beads strung on a frame
of vertical wires or columns. A similar system,
in use alongside the grooved tablet, was based
on squares. The chequered tablecloth was
originally an aid to calculation and gave us
the word Exchequer.

The slide rule is a classic example of the
more advanced machine. It was invented in
the 1600s by an English mathematician
named William Oughtred. His ingenious
device was used by engineers to make
advanced calculations right up until the 1970s,
when electronic calculators were introduced.

Of course slide rules are just one example
of the many types of pre-electronic calculator
available to collectors today. The French
mathematician and philosopher Blaise Pascal

is traditionally credited with the invention
of the calculating machine. In 1642 he built
a machine to help his father, a tax collector.
Pascal's machine used a system of numbered
wheels with complex gearing and could add
and subtract numbers up to nine digits long.

It is this mechanical complexity that is
the major attraction for collectors of science
and technology. The problems of building
a convenient, portable machine that could
handle lengthy numbers and complicated
mathematical calculations by purely
mechanical means led to the development of
some exquisite gems of engineering. Machines
related to specific professions or built to handle
specific tasks are also of interest, particularly
to people engaged in those professions or
tasks. Collecting does not necessarily stop
with the advent of electronics either – early
components from the first computers are
highly sought after, especially if they are
connected with the great names of computing.

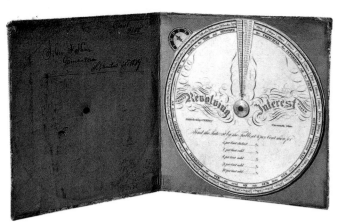

▼ A group of computing scales

By Aaron Palmer, c.1850. This shows four versions of the Palmer's Computing Scale/Fuller's Time Telegraph (including a pocket example). £300–600/$500–1,000 each, depending on their condition.

◄ Patent Revolving Interest Table

By C.M. Riley; published in Cincinnati, c.1839. It is made of card, with a thin metal split-pin to hold the discs together. This particular example is inscribed with the owner's name and town, the date 1839 and the information that it cost him $1 (65p) to buy. £200–400/$400–600

19th Century

During the 19th century more and more people took up work that required them to perform calculations. Manufacturing burst onto the economic scene too, elbowing agriculture aside to become the brash new job-providing industry. And it didn't just create the innovative engineering of the railways and smoke-belching factories that we associate with that era. Today we take our sophisticated system of credits and loans for granted, but this is a recent development that had its roots in financing the spread of industrialized society. Accounts departments followed hot on its heels, to guard investors' cash as it poured into the trains, ships and rumbling machines that carried the Industrial Revolution from Britain to the USA.

The market was there for affordable, easy-to-use calculating aids. For simple maths there were plenty of published books with tables for easy reference, and many small businesses used these. However, more complex calculations needed specialist instruments. There was no room for error

so the machines had to be completely dependable. They also had to stand up to heavy, repetitive use without breaking down or even losing accuracy. Hundreds of people designed calculators at this time, and the examples we see today are testaments to an age of practical ingenuity and intellectual brilliance.

The interest calculator is a good example. Interest obviously has many variable factors in its calculation, but the basic maths are not all that complex. The Patent Revolving Interest Table cleverly uses two printed discs, one on top of the other. The upper one has a cut-out section, and by turning the lower one to the required time period and reading down the table of values, the interest on a particular sum could be calculated. The Palmer's Computing Scale/Fuller's Time Telegraph is a much more complex version of the same thing. Again it is a revolving table, but this design deals with several different types of calculation, from the area of a circle to amounts in gallons. It was a very successful product in its day and went through a

▼ **Thatcher's calculator**
Made by Keuffel & Esser, *c.*1900. It is made of wood and paper, has instructions on the base and comes with its original box.
£500–1,000/ $1,000–1,500

▲ **Spalding Adding Machine**
By C. C. Spalding of Springfield, Massachusetts, patents dating to 1874 and 1884. The detail shows the sheet of printed operating instructions glued to the base.
£2,000–2,500/ $3,000–3,500

few updates and modifications in its lifetime. There are quite a few of these scales still around now, so you should be able to find one without difficulty. They are highly collectable items.

The slide rule is a complex form of computing scale, and the Thatcher's calculator is probably the most complex slide rule ever made. It was invented in 1881 and is still looked upon with awe today. The 10-cm (4-in) diameter cylinder has one scale on it and 20 angled scales above; the information within that distinctive design would fill an ordinary slide rule 10m (30ft) long. A Thatcher's calculator allowed the owner to quickly calculate figures to an accuracy of four or five places. The instruction book was 71 pages long and included several tables. Thatcher's calculators were made in the United States by Keuffel & Esser and in Britain by Stanley. They were produced well into the 1930s and aren't especially rare, but condition is paramount when collecting these items. And be sure to keep your eye out for the type with a magnifying glass built in.

These were made because the tables were produced in very small print, but examples are extremely rare today and are therefore worth a lot of money.

If your interest lies in mechanical aids, adding machines will probably attract your attention. The Spalding Adding Machine is an example of an early device and uses a system of finger-operated keys that move pointers. Machines like this are very rare today, and collectors snap them up quickly. This example is interesting because of the very American-looking instruction sheet on the back.

Calculators that have printing and illustrations typical of their time and place will always have added attraction for collectors. In general, condition is important for calculating scales but less so than for many collectables. This is because they were heavily used and relatively fragile, so you would expect them to show wear. However, do try to keep them in a stable environment where they will neither dry out nor grow mould. Keep them out of direct sunlight or the print will quickly fade and the value will be lost.

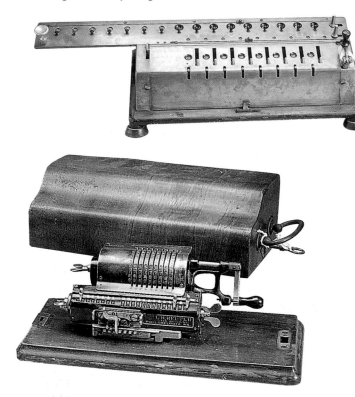

▼ The "Millionaire" electro-
mechanical calculator
By Hans W. Egli, Zurich, early 20th century. This one
still has its instructions and dividing schedule.
£500–1,500/$1,000–2,000 depending on condition.

▲ **(Top) TIM mechanical calculator** By Ludwig Spitz & Co.
of Berlin-Tempelhof, early 20th century. £400–535/$600–800
(Above) Brunsviga "Midget" mechanical calculator
By Grimme, Natalis & Co, Braunschweig, early 20th century.
£50–200/$200–300

20th Century

In the late 19th century two notable inventions
appeared in the field of mechanical calculators.
In 1885 a mechanic named Dorr E. Felt, who
worked for the Pullman Company in Chicago,
made a breakthrough with his "key-set" calculator.
It had a typewriter-style keyboard, which allowed
the user to enter numbers quickly. By the following
year Dorr had developed his prototype into the
Comptometer, a successful machine that dominated
the American market for the rest of the century. In
1892 yet another American inventor, William S.
Burroughs, added a patent keyboard adder-lister,
which produced a printed record of all the digits that
were entered, with the total at the end. Burroughs'
device was called the Burroughs Adding and Listing
Machine. As companies grew they found that they
needed rooms full of "computers" to work at great
banks of calculating machines. Visitors could identify
the accounts department in any company by the noise!

Today adding machines like the Comptometer
are fairly plentiful and not yet especially valuable.

However, it is the more complex, and in some cases,
earlier, machines that are of real interest to collectors.
Inventors and scientists were very keen to produce a
machine that could add, subtract, multiply and divide.
Although there were attempts at making these at least
as far back as the 18th century, the first really succesful
machine was designed in 1820 by Charles Xavier
Thomas de Colmar, using the step-cylinder principal.
His machine, the Arithmometere, sold in limited
but respectable numbers throughout the 19th century,
but it was very expensive and not that easy to use.

These machines were not made in huge numbers,
but their great size and expense meant they weren't
particularly disposable, and they are still found today
in store-rooms, company back offices or even in
scientists' basements. The three shown above are all
fairly well known among collectors. The TIM,
or Time Is Money, machine is a direct descendant of
de Colmar's Arithmometere and was espesially
popular with accountants. The Brunsviga is probably
the most common of the European-made machines.

◄ **Consul the Educated Monkey**
*c.*1920. This American toy calculator is made of tin plate, and comes with a sheet of tables for use in simple arithmetic.
£200–300/$300–500

◄ **The McCoy Golf Recorder**
Early 20th century. This is a pocket device for recording the score at each hole up to 18; it then calculates the total score.
£200–250/$300–400

▲ **Group of pocket calculators**
(clockwise from top) All early 20th century. Fowler's Calculator, £80–200/$200–300; McKee's Patent Pocket Century, £200–250/$300–400; Stephenson's Pocket Adder, £50–100/$100–150; money counter, American Register Co., £200–300/$400–500; Lord's Patent Pocket Calculator, £300–500/$500–800

The Swiss-made Millionaire calculator was another top-of-the-range machine from the early 20th century. It was usually a purely mechanical device, but the example illustrated here is electro-mechanical. The Millionaire was the Rolls-Royce of complex calculating machines, and its price today still reflects its quality.

As the cost of producing calculators fell, and more and more people became aware of them, a market for cheap and portable versions began to develop. Judging by the number of versions available, it seems that everyone had an idea for a miniature calculator of some kind. Many were made to look like the watches that people were already used to carrying in their pockets, and they caught on immediately. They were produced in their thousands, in a range of qualities, and are very collectable today.

Devices for purposes other than helping with calculations and adding up money were also invented at this time. The McCoy Golf Recorder is

a delightful early 20th-century example of just the kind of gadgetry that is still popular at the beginning of the 21st century. It helps you keep track of your score by individual holes (up to 18, naturally) and adds up your total score at the end. The original owner must have been the envy of the Country Club when he first nonchalantly pulled it out of his pocket.

Even children were catered for in this busy market. Consul the Educated Monkey is a classic example of the toy calculator, though it would be a lucky child who got to play with it nowadays. It is made out of tin plate, and, with the help of the sheet of tables, Consul would do all a child's arithmetic for him or her. The child would move the pointers on Consul's feet to the numbers that they wanted to add, subtract, divide or multiply, and Consul would move the window between his hands to the correct answer. Most of the surviving examples of Consul have lost the sheet of tables, and their value will be lower because of this.

▲▼**Eckert's slide rule**
By Keuffel & Esser, c.1943. The rule is inscribed "J. Presper Eckert, Jr". This is the slide rule used in building the first computer.
£2,335/$3,500 (owing to the provenance; otherwise £30–40/$45–60).

◄ **Alpina calculator**
West German, c.1961. This is an example of one of the last mechanical calculators made. It is in its original case with its instructions. **£50–100/$100–150**

▲ **Two Univac brochures and a letter**
c.1948–49. Early Univac leaflets and a form letter, which were sent in response to a customer enquiry. They are interesting because they represent the first marketing of the computer industry. **£1,000/$2,000**

In the 1930s, mechanical and electro-mechanical calculators were at the cutting edge of computing technology, and computers were still the people who operated the machines. However, as World War II progressed the need for still faster machines to handle more complex calculations became urgent. The science of ballistics (projectiles such as bullets, shells or rockets) was advancing at breakneck speed, and even machines that were state of the art simply couldn't handle the flow of information.

The United States Army turned to the University of Pennsylvania's Moore School of Engineering, and asked it to develop a new calculating machine. Two men, J. Presper Eckert and John Mauchly, led the design team. Eckert and Mauchly proposed using the fledgling science of electronics to improve the mechanical and electro-mechanical calculators. The US Army accepted their proposal, and Eckert and Mauchly began work on a machine to calculate ballistics tables in 1943. The fruit of their labour was ENIAC (Electronic Numerical Integrator and Computer) – the first machine that could truly be called a computer.

ENIAC was huge. It covered over 165 sq m (1,800 sq ft), weighed 30 tons and contained 18,000 vacuum tubes. Legend has it that when it was first turned on, the electrical drain dimmed lights all over Philadelphia. ENIAC had cost nearly half a million dollars to build but its performance was incredible. It could carry out 5,000 additions, 350 multiplications and 40 divisions in one second, which was a thousand times faster than any machine before it. This was a glimpse of the computer age that was to come.

Mechanical calculators did not die out straight away, however, as computers remained expensive, large machines for several decades. Probably the last mechanical calculator made was the Curta, produced in Lichtenstein until the 1970s. Small enough to hold in one hand, it could add, subtract, multiply and divide. These pieces are all highly collectable.

The next step in computing technology was the development of internal memory. Up until 1945 the data and instructions for calculating devices had always been stored outside the machine. In 1946, two British scientists found a way to create an electronic memory. Professors Frederick Williams and Tom

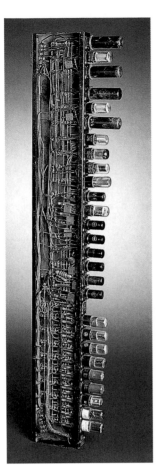

Collecting
Decade Ring Counters

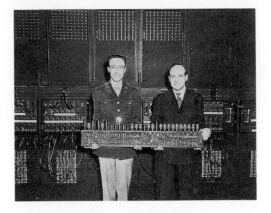

▲ **Photograph of the makers of ENIAC**
Corporal Herman Goldstine (US Army liaison officer, left) and J. Presper Eckert (right) holding a ring counter in front of ENIAC.

The vital building block from which ENIAC grew was the accumulator decade ring counter. This allowed electrical pulses to be turned into numbers. It could add and subtract and, most importantly, could carry a number higher than nine on to the next unit. Each ring counter was self-contained, and a bank of them were strung together to make up the accumulator of ENIAC. In other words, a ring counter acted rather like a wheel in a mechanical calculator. Today decade ring counters are extremely desirable collectables.

ENIAC contained 20 ring counters in all. A number of the features in Eckert and Mauchly's design proved influential to modern-day computer design. One example is the "plug-in" factor. Eckert designed the ring counters to be easily interchangeable, so that if one failed a replacement could be quickly inserted. Another interesting feature was the error-spotting system. If something went wrong, a light would blink. Ever since then, computers have been popularly depicted with banks of flashing lights.

ENIAC was not fully operational until after the end of the war. However, the US Army kept it in constant use, especially for its work on the hydrogen bomb. It has since been broken up and divided between the Smithsonian Institute and the University of Pennsylvania. Eckert and Mauchly left the University shortly after ENIAC was finished to found the world's first computer company. They built the Univac computer, and later sold the company to Remington Rand. The company is known today as Unisys.

Kilburn at Manchester University built a machine that stored information in cathode-ray tubes. Back in the USA, in 1951 Eckert and Mauchly developed the Univac I: the first computer to use magnetic tape to store data. It became the first commercially produced American computer.

Funding was crucial to the advancement of the computer industry. The high-speed IBM Stretch and the Univac LARC machines, produced around 1960, were both backed by the military. In 1963 the Manchester Atlas, another mainly military machine, became the fastest computer in the world. The crossover to commerce occurred in 1964, when IBM launched the System/360 range. For the first time buyers could select compatible hardware and software to suit their own needs and pockets. It's well worth learning more about the history of the computer, in order to train your eye for items that will become collectable. The first Apple computers are now attracting high prices, so don't be too quick to throw away a piece of hardware (or software) that you think is obsolete. In a few years' time it could be an important piece of computing history.

Medicine

The early physicians' tools are a graphic reminder of our good fortune in having been born since the discovery of antisepsis and anaesthesia

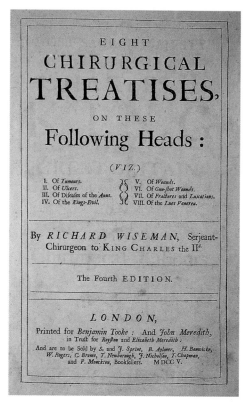

▲ **Book on surgical techniques**
By Richard Wiseman, 1705. The low price reflects the quantity in which this seminal textbook was printed – this is not a first edition, so it is affordable. £200–250/$300–400

The first thing to realize about collecting medical instruments is that the field is much wider than you might at first think. The frighteningly practical leg and finger saws and gruesome instruments for childbirth send many of us hastening to less threatening collectables, but don't be scared off. There are hundreds of fascinating and beautiful instruments related to healthcare that won't give you nightmares. For example, there are delicate blue-and-white china feeding cups for infants and invalids. If your interest is of a more scientific bent, then there are early stethoscopes, blood-pressure devices and eye-examining instruments too.

Some people like to collect instruments made from a particular material such as silver or ivory. Others prefer instruments related to quackery – see the phrenology head on page 130 as an example. Whatever attracts your interest, you will be able to assemble a representative collection without having to

take out a huge loan. Even the more sought-after items tend to be priced in three figures.

From the Greek physician Galen in the second century AD until the 18th century, medical practice remained virtually unchanged. Galen's philosophy rested on the four humours: melancholy, phlegm, blood and choler. These four had to be kept in balance, and the physician did this largely by prescribing certain foods thought to increase or suppress one humour or another. The other chief medical practice was bloodletting, which used cups, scalpels, leeches and highly decorated basins for catching the blood in.

Surgery in Europe was largely practised as a secondary trade by barbers, who had a useful stock of sharp instruments for letting blood and pulling teeth. In the 17th century a Royalist in the English Civil War named Richard Wiseman transformed the status of his profession. He was the personal medical attendant to Prince Charles (later Charles II) and became Master of the Barber Surgeons

▼ **American homeopathic medicine chest**
By Boericke and Tafel, Philadelphia, c.1875. There is a list of contents in the lid, and some of the bottles are missing from this example. However, sets of small bottles often have a few missing so this doesn't affect the price greatly.
£150–200/$250–300

◄ **Ebony-handled surgical instruments**
c.1850–1900. **(Left)** Large bone saw by Charrière à Paris, £100–150/$150–200; **(Centre)** Liston-pattern knife, £55–85/$80–130; **(Right)** metacarpal saw, £35–55/$50–80

Company in the City of London. Wiseman's authoritative texts on the practice of surgery were the standard handbooks for surgeons at that time. They were reissued a number of times, and today books like this are of great interest as they reveal the techniques of the period. They are not recommended for the squeamish, though, as the procedures are described and illustrated in lavish detail.

There's no getting away from the fact that goriness is a great attraction in this field for some people. Amputation instruments are hugely popular and have changed little over the centuries. The chief difference is the material from which they are made. Before people realized that dirt encouraged infection, the handles of saws and scalpels were made of wood and ivory. In 1865 the British surgeon Joseph Lister came across the germ theory propounded by the French bacteriologist Louis Pasteur. By applying carbolic acid to his surgical instruments Lister dramatically reduced the surgical mortality rate and so is

credited with the discovery of antiseptics. Because of his work, surgical instruments came to be made entirely out of metal, which could withstand boiling and soaking in carbolic lotion. Surgeons and instrument makers developed their own designs, and many instruments are named after their inventors.

Surgery was not the only answer, however, and most Victorian middle-class houses had well-stocked medicine chests. We wouldn't want to use them today – mercury, opium and arsenic were popular ingredients – but they are fascinating items for collectors.

If you find a medicine chest that interests you, make sure that it has as many of the original contents as possible. Check that bottles fit properly – replacement bottles are often too small. They may also be of a different height or colour, or carry a different label. This doesn't always matter, as the bottles were replaced once they were used up. For example, an 1850s chest may have a 1930s bottle in it, but it is still of interest.

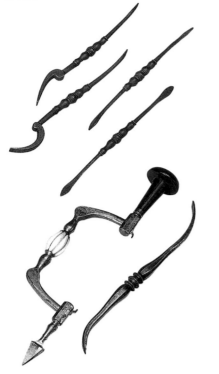

▼ **Complete set of field surgeon's instruments**
By Charles Lentz & Sons, Philadelphia, from the World War I era. It has its original steel case and canvas carrying case.
£200–250/$300–400

▲ **English étui covered in fish skin**
Late 18th century. The set contains three bleeding lancets.
£60–100/$100–150

▲ **Incomplete set of Continental trepanning instruments**
18th century. This set consists of a drill and five lenticulars.
£300–500/$500–700

Medical Instruments

Surgery has been practised since prehistoric times. Neolithic skulls show the marks of trepanning, or trephining as it is also known. This is the practice of cutting or drilling holes in the skull to relieve headaches or pressure from fractures. Trepanning drills and trephines (saws with circular blades) are popular with collectors, as are the accompanying lenticulars. These were used to lift the damaged section of a fractured skull away.

However, until the discovery of anaesthetics in the mid-19th century, surgical operations were not only rare but also incredibly fast. The surgeon operated as a last resort and worked at top speed in an effort to minimize the pain and shock suffered by the unanaesthetized patient. The record is held by Robert Liston (1794–1847), a Scottish surgeon who famously amputated a leg in less than two minutes. In the process he not only cut off his assistant's fingers but also sawed through the coat tails of a spectator. Although it may not seem like it, Liston was in fact a highly skilled surgeon, and he designed

a knife specifically for the dangerous procedure of amputation (*see* p.127). Complete sets of surgical instruments are much sought after today, and some fine examples from World War I can still be found. They typically include amputation instruments. Made of nickel steel and carried in a compact steel case, they were far more portable and hygienic than their Victorian predecessors.

Phlebotomy (vein-cutting, or bloodletting) remained a popular cure-all well into the 19th century, although it must have contributed to hundreds of deaths, most famously that of George Washington. He died of a sore throat in 1799 after physicians drained him of nine pints of blood in 24 hours. The procedure was usually practised by barbers, and today their traditional striped poles are still coloured red for blood and white for the tourniquet. The poles actually represent the sticks patients would squeeze to dilate the veins.

Leeches were often used to draw blood from a patient, and leech jars are very collectable, especially

▼ French lithotrite
By Charrière à Paris, 19th century. This
instrument was used in bladder surgery for
crushing stones or for removing foreign bodies
such as bone fragments. £100–200/$200–300

▼ Sphygmograph
By Charles Lentz & Sons, Philadelphia,
late 19th century. It runs from
a clockwork motor.
£200–250/$300–400

◄ ▲ Bloodletting set
Early 1800s. This set
comes with a 12-blade
brass scarificator, six
glass cupping jars and
a suction pump.
£300–400/$500–600

if they are labelled with the details of their purpose.
Otherwise, lancets or fleams (lancets with the blade
at right angles to the shaft) were used to make cuts
from which blood would be drawn. A set of lancets
in an étui (a pocket-sized fitted case) can be a very
attractive piece to collect.

It is also possible to find complete kits for
cupping, an ingenious and spectacular form of
bloodletting, in a fitted case. The barber-surgeon
would have made a cut, or several cuts, on the
patient's back and then burnt a match inside a glass
cup to create a vacuum. When he slapped the glass
down over the cut, the vacuum would have
"sucked" a good flow of blood from the wound.
Multi-bladed instruments called scarificators were
used to make several cuts at once. Dry cupping,
using heated glasses instead of cuts, was also used to
raise blisters and draw evil humours from the body.

Another surprisingly ancient surgical technique
is that of treating bladder stones. Instruments for
grasping and removing the stone through an

incision are centuries old, but before the days of
antisepsis, such operations were high risk. Clever
instruments called lithotrites were developed that
could crush the stone within the bladder so that the
fragments could be passed in the urine. If you are
wondering how this was accomplished, a look at the
lithotrite above will probably give you a vivid picture
of it! The curved end consists of two jaws that can be
opened and closed by turning a knob in the handle.
The surgeon would pinpoint the stone by feeling the
patient's abdomen, insert the lithotrite through the
patient's urethra, grasp the stone and tighten the
jaws to crush it.

If your eyes are starting to water at this point,
you may find that diagnostic instruments have
greater appeal. Stethoscopes were invented in the
mid-19th century and can form a whole collection
in themselves. They were made of wood until
rubber technology advanced sufficiently to make
reliable flexible tubing, and so early examples look
rather like ear trumpets. Some are very beautiful,

▼ **Dental forceps and tooth keys**
18th/19th century. **(Far left and far right)**
Forceps £35–50/$50–75 each; **(Centre)** tooth
keys £50–100/$100–200 (except first key from
the left, which has an unusual claw £250/$400)

► **Plaster
phrenology head**
By S. R. Wells &
Company, American
Institute of Phrenology,
late 19th century. The
divided cranium is
labelled with paper to
show where various
mental faculties were
thought to be located.
£100–200/$200–300

► **Fine mahogany
dental cabinet**
By The Ransom &
Randolph Co., Toledo,
late 19th/early 20th
century. This is the top-
of-the-range model
from the company's
catalogue.
£2,500–3,000/
$4,000–5,000

and are made of polished ebony or fruitwood. If you prefer something more technical, blood pressure monitors and pulse monitors (that are known as sphygmomanometers and sphygmographs) are intriguing. Sphygmographs date from around the 1860s; they draw a line that records the rate and pattern of the pulse, essential information for the diagnosis of many cardiovascular disorders.

Dentistry is a popular category of collecting that offers a surprisingly wide choice of items. Tooth-pulling was yet another string to the barber's bow, and he would often carry a selection of forceps for the purpose. It's painfully obvious how these items were used, and they are enormously popular today. They were made by blacksmiths for village or itinerant dentists who might request specific features, so there's a wide variety of designs – the more complex they are, the more valuable.

Dental cabinets represent the other end of the scale in terms of size and price, but they are very beautiful pieces of furniture. Top-of-the-range pieces were very skilfully made, with sophisticated designs incorporating differently sized drawers and

glazed cupboards with curved fronts. Today many collectors like to purchase these and use them to store and display their own collections.

The practice of medicine was transformed in the 19th century, when antisepsis and anaesthesia were discovered, but there were other innovations that didn't last the test of time. Phrenology, or "having one's bumps felt", was popular in its day. Phrenologists claimed to be able to determine a person's personality and abilities by feeling the shape of their skull. People could buy phrenology heads marked with the different qualities each area was meant to represent, and they sold in their thousands. This may seem laughable, but before you scoff just think of how many people now study their horoscopes. It's interesting to note that the National Socialist party in Germany used a similar pseudo-science to "prove" the superiority of the Aryan race.

Electricity was the great discovery of the 19th-century (*see* pp.134–5). It was so miraculous that people were convinced it must be a wonder cure for all sorts of ailments. The electro-medical machine was sold for domestic use, and the makers advertised

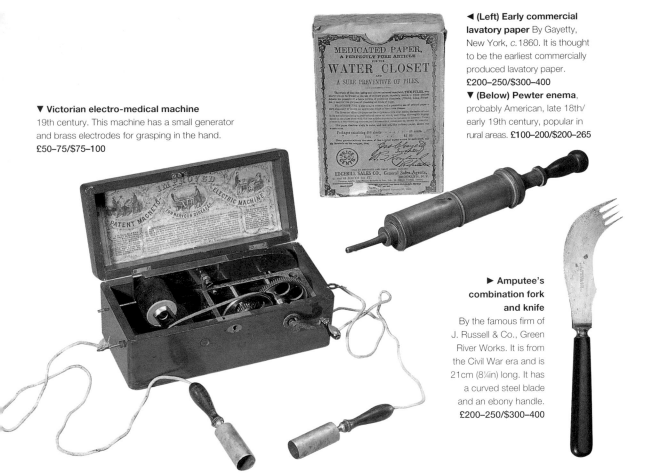

◄ **(Left) Early commercial lavatory paper** By Gayetty, New York, c.1860. It is thought to be the earliest commercially produced lavatory paper. £200–250/$300–400

▼ **(Below) Pewter enema**, probably American, late 18th/early 19th century, popular in rural areas. £100–200/$200–265

MEDICATED PAPER,
A PERFECTLY PURE ARTICLE
FOR THE
WATER CLOSET
AND
A SURE PREVENTIVE OF PILES.

▼ **Victorian electro-medical machine**
19th century. This machine has a small generator and brass electrodes for grasping in the hand.
£50–75/$75–100

► **Amputee's combination fork and knife**
By the famous firm of J. Russell & Co., Green River Works. It is from the Civil War era and is 21cm (8¼in) long. It has a curved steel blade and an ebony handle.
£200–250/$300–400

it as being helpful for pain or "nervousness and female complaints". It is in fact a simple magneto generator. The "patient" held the brass electrodes, and someone else turned the handle on the box quickly to produce a small charge. They must have been popular because hundreds have survived.

A discussion of domestic remedies would not be complete without mentioning the importance of bowel treatment. Colonic irrigation is by no means a modern invention. Louis XIV was lampooned for his fondness for enemas, and the Victorians were equally enthusiastic about keeping regular. The syringe type shown here requires a helper to use it properly, but it's otherwise fairly simple. Enemas like this one can often be found in collections of early American kitchen instruments as they are frequently mistaken for turkey basters. However, there are more complex ones available, with brass pumps and different-shaped inserts with hoses. The French even developed clockwork enemas.

The lavatory paper that people used was also important. The firm of Gayetty fought against the nefarious use of newspaper, announcing that it was

bad for the health, and offered its "Medicated Paper for the Water Closet". It is believed to be the earliest commercially produced lavatory paper.

Manufacturers in the 19th century also spotted a market among the war veterans who had assisted in the advancement of surgical practice. J. Russell & Company, the first and most famous firm of cutlers in America, developed what they called the "one-armed knife". A combination knife and fork, it was designed for amputees and was very popular during and after the American Civil War (1861–65). This thought-provoking instrument demonstrates the broad variety of items that are available in the field of medical collectables. They do not have to be gory, though it is true that the more an instrument makes you cringe, the more it is likely to be worth. Amputation sets remain the most valuable, and are a salutary reminder of how far the risk of surgery has fallen since Liston's day. Both his patient and his assistant in the two-minute amputation died later of gangrene, while the spectator died of fright on the spot, bringing the mortality rate for that operation to a spectacular 300 per cent.

Everyday Technology

The technology of the turn-of-the-century home shows us how much our everyday life has changed in just a few generations

▲ **Early chainstitch treadle sewing machine**
By Grover & Baker, a leading Boston company. This is a fairly plain model, but it is of an unusual design because the flywheel is not in the standard transverse position. £300–400/$500–600

Walk into a random selection of European or American households today and you are likely to see much the same equipment in each one. The brand names and styles might vary slightly according to individual taste or cost, but you would have no difficulty in turning on the lights, adjusting the central heating or air conditioning and identifying the refrigerator, vacuum cleaner and washing machine.

Such standardization has not existed since the Middle Ages, when home technology consisted of an open fire, a pot and a broom. Of course people have always needed light and temperature control in their homes, some way to store and cook food, and a means of cleaning. But new ideas didn't spread with the speed we're used to today. Household technology differed more between classes than between countries and, until recently, families either improvised or did without.

Since the end of the 19th century, domestic technology has advanced astonishingly quickly. It's quite possible for us to walk into a museum and fail to recognize objects that our grandparents or even parents might have used every day. For anyone interested in social history it's a fascinating field. These everyday objects show us how people who lived around 1900 had more in common with people of the 1700s than with us.

The humble sewing machine illustrated above is a charming piece, with elegant cast-iron tracery on the treadle. It's from the first period of sewing machines (pre-1875) and would have been very expensive to buy at the time. However, it would have transformed the life of any lady fortunate enough to own it. There was no off-the-peg buying of clothes then; almost everything a woman wore would have been stitched by hand. And, having made the costume, a woman would then need to keep it in order. Graceful ruffles at

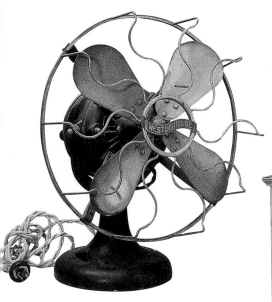

▲ Allwin gaming machine
Classic English coin-operated gaming machine, c. 1930, with a painted wooden case.
£100–250/$125–275

▲ Mrs Knox's fluting iron
American fluting iron (crimping machine) by Mrs Knox, c. 1870. It has a photograph of Mrs Knox herself in the base – an early marketing touch to emphasize the idea of something made by a woman for women to use.
£50–100/$100–200

▲ Westinghouse electric fan
American, patent dating from 1906. This is a typical 20th-century fan – its early date is revealed by the brass blades.
£50–85/$75–125

the neck and wrists were the height of fashion, and they were made with a fluting iron (crimping machine) such as the one that is shown above. The slug (the heavy metal rod inside the hollow rollers) would have been heated over a fire, and it took great skill to get it hot enough to shape the cloth without scorching it.

Electricity naturally transformed the design of household gadgets, and early electrical appliances are fast becoming collectable today. Be careful when collecting electrical items, though. Early safety standards were low to non-existent, and items can be lethal, so get an electrician to check yours over before you plug them in. If you need to replace worn or missing cord, do use reproduction cloth-covered flex. Nothing looks worse than modern plastic cord on an old appliance and it could lower the value.

Of course the new technology didn't just transform domestic life. The pattern of commerce changed forever as new industries

sprang up to deliver and utilize the new technology. Electricity was the most obvious advance, but don't overlook the less spectacular technology that developed then and that we still use as a matter of course. Coin-operated technology was used to sell all kinds of products, as well as for gambling, and the machines are wonderful pieces of late 19th-/early 20th-century advertising. It's also fun to look for early posters and print advertisements for all the new gadgets. People rushed to file patents for their inventions, and the models they had to supply form yet another area of interest.

This may seem an overwhelmingly varied field, but you will soon get a feel for what is collectable. There will always be more interest in a piece in its place of origin – for instance, the Allwin gaming machine will command a higher price in Britain than in the USA. When it comes to electrical items, bear in mind that only early ones are of value so far, though later ones are slowly becoming collectable.

▼ **Leclanché-pattern
wet cell**
Probably English,
c.1875. This cell is of
the type used to power
phonographs and
other early electrical
devices.
£200–400/$400–600

▲ **Wimshurst-pattern
electricity generator**
By the Central Scientific Company,
Chicago, early 20th century. This was a
demonstration piece for use in schools.
Two contra-rotating discs produce a
static charge and generate a spark
between the two balls.
£200–400/$400–600

▲ **One-sixth
horsepower
electric motor**
By Crocker-Wheeler,
1891. Crocker-Wheeler
was one of the most
famous American
manufacturers. This motor
is a very collectable piece.
£500–1,000/
$1,000–1,500

Electricity

When electricity was introduced to the public at the end of the 19th century it met with a mixed reception. Some people were fascinated, while others were terrified of the strange, invisible force. The fledgling electrical companies responded to this widespread fear with an astonishing campaign of reassuring propaganda. According to early advertising, electricity was the greatest boon to humanity ever. It was going to make life better and easier. It was going to light up the world, cure all known illnesses, let people communicate across the oceans, free them from drudgery, give them more leisure time and generally usher them into a new era. And of course it did most of those things.

The Greeks had observed that rubbing cloth on a piece of amber would produce static electricity. Queen Elizabeth I's physician, William Gilbert of Colchester, was the man who named the phenomenon in the late 16th century and he used the Greek word for amber: elektron. Until the early 19th century, electricity was little more than a scientific curiosity beloved of Enlightenment gentlemen. Many had small electricity-producing machines in their homes to show their scientific knowledge – it was considered the height of fashion among upper-class Americans and Europeans to invite guests round and give them an electric shock.

One major advance was the discovery of a way to store electricity. The first wet cell was invented around 1800 by Alessandro Volta of Italy. He used copper and zinc discs separated by paper discs moistened with acid or saline solution. The wet cell used acid to produce the charge when mixed with metal. Wet cells were very popular throughout the 19th century. They took over from clockwork and were eventually used to power almost everything, from phonographs, telephones and telegraphs to fire alarms.

Of course the problem with wet cells was the same as with the dry-cell batteries we use today. They run down and have to be replaced or recharged. In 1866 a German telegraph engineer

◄ **Ammeter**
By the Weston Electrical
Instrument Company,
1901. It is displayed
on an oak base with a
Boston retailer's label.
£100–200/$200–300

▲ **Chromolithographic
advertising poster**
From the Society of Electrical
Development, c.1920. This
poster was used to promote
the use of electricity. Most
major American cities had
annual shows to exhibit the
latest devices – sadly it is
not known which city this
Prosperity Week was held in.
£1,200–1,500/$2,000–2,500

► **Brass-and-
mahogany
electric bell**
c.1880. This handsome
piece is too large to be
a door bell but it could
be a demonstration
piece or part of a fire
alarm or telegraph.
£200–300/$300–500

named Werner Siemens discovered the principle of
the electric dynamo, which converts mechanical
energy to electricity. The dynamo produced a
constant flow of electricity, which meant that
electric motors could be put to general use. Early
motors were used in everything from large
mechanical musical instruments to small lighting
plants, and they are very collectable today. The tools
related to electricity and its production are equally
sought after. Unlike their modern counterparts,
some of these tools are beautiful handcrafted pieces
that exemplify the design ideals of their time.
Today these early electrical machines are of great
scientific and historic interest, and most of them are
very affordable for the collector.

Earliest is best where any electrical item,
whether domestic or commercial, is concerned.
This is still a new field of collecting, and practically
anything from the 19th century will be valuable.
Commercial electrical items from the 20th century,
such as machines or tools, are too similar to modern

machines to be collectable, although household
appliances from the first couple of decades of the
20th century are collected for their designs.

Electrical advertising is a particularly popular
area. Electricity was first generated for commercial
sale in the 1880s, shortly after Thomas Edison in
the United States and Joseph Swan in Britain
independently exhibited their electric-light bulbs in
1878 (see p.140). It did eventually take over from
gas, but it took a while to overcome the prejudice
of potential consumers. The huge – and extremely
successful – campaigns to persuade potential
consumers that electricity was a safe, clean and life-
transforming invention continued well into the
1930s and gave rise to some very attractive posters
and leaflets. However, the best examples tend to be
expensive because this area overlaps with other
areas of collecting, such as advertising and design.
Colour printing always raises the value, so
monochrome leaflets and newspaper advertisements
will be more affordable items to collect.

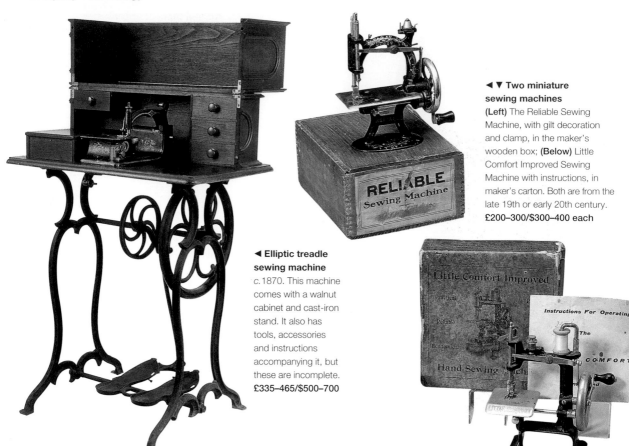

◄ **Elliptic treadle
sewing machine**
*c.*1870. This machine
comes with a walnut
cabinet and cast-iron
stand. It also has
tools, accessories
and instructions
accompanying it, but
these are incomplete.
£335–465/$500–700

◄ ▼ **Two miniature
sewing machines**
(Left) The Reliable Sewing
Machine, with gilt decoration
and clamp, in the maker's
wooden box; **(Below)** Little
Comfort Improved Sewing
Machine with instructions, in
maker's carton. Both are from the
late 19th or early 20th century.
£200–300/$300–400 each

Sewing and Laundry

Domestic work without machines was sheer
drudgery. One woman (yes, it was always a
woman) could not have run a household single-
handed. When labour was cheap and plentiful, only
the very poorest families in Britain had no help in
the home. However, the new factories soaked up
much of the labour pool, and servants became very
expensive – as they always had been in the United
States, which had a much smaller labour force.
Perhaps this was a motivation for the invention of
the many labour-saving gadgets that began to
appear in houses at the end of the 19th century.

Inventors and manufacturers were keen to cash
in on the new market, and many fortunes were
created. The methods industry used to meet its
demands laid the foundations for commerce today.
The sewing machine industry, for instance, was one
of the largest in the world. Singer, the leading name
in sewing machines, introduced such novelties
as female sales staff and the system of paying by
instalments to meet demand. The machines were

very expensive, but another way that Singer kept
costs down was with the innovative idea of overseas
factories, which reduced shipping and tariff costs.

Today many people like to furnish their houses
with early domestic gadgets. They are mostly
affordable, and the designs fit in well with modern
décor. Sewing-machine collectors appreciate the
combination of Victorian design and mechanical
ability. Product design was an important part of
any piece of technology. As is the case nowadays,
people wanted their machines to look nice and to
harmonize with their furnishings. The casting of
the iron on sewing machines was often sculptural,
incorporating classical pillars and serpentine sides
and imitating the carving normally found on
furniture. Treadle legs were modelled on the shape
of fine furniture, and the lid of the sewing machine
was often of fine wood with panelling or moulding,
to make the machine resemble a lady's writing desk.

The disadvantage of collecting sewing machines
is that they are large and very heavy, but there has

▼ **Electric iron with original cord**
By Edison/General Electric, c.1920s. The iron's original cord is still intact.
£35–50/$50–75

▼ **Anchor mangle**
By the Lovell Manufacturing Co., Erie, PA, early 20th century. The mangle is only 19cm (7½in) wide, so was possibly a salesman's sample or was used for cleaning small articles of clothing.
£100–200/$200–300

◄ **Patent model of a washing machine**
By H. Grandjean, New Berlin, Illinois, c.1874. It is not known if this model went on to be produced.
£500–800/$800–1,200

► **Advertising poster for the Star Washing Machine**
c.1850. Advertisements like this are highly collectable items in their own right.
£35–50/$50–75

been a surge of interest recently in miniature ones. These are not toys but inexpensive, simple machines that girls were given to learn to sew on. Millions of them were made, so there are plenty to choose from. The shape and finish are big factors in the value, and the presence of a box and instructions will double the worth.

A particularly interesting aspect of the machines for laundry is that they reveal "labour-saving" as a relative term. Today the hardest part of doing the laundry is deciding which programme to select on the washing machine. Not so very long ago, however, the average housewife would have been doing the family wash by hand. The mangle (or wringer, as it is known in the United States) was an early version of the spin cycle, and using one was hard work. Before the invention of synthetic fabrics, clothes were made of wool, cotton and linen, which held water like a sponge. Without a mangle it could take days for clothes to dry. However, even with a mangle it was still bicep-building work.

Not many people have the space or the desire to collect washing machines, but patent models like the one above are great fun. This machine may or may not have been mass-produced, but it illustrates the flourishing market for household technology. The advertisement for the Star washing machine is a fine example of how ephemera can broaden the scope of a collection. Often these advertisements are all that survive of a particular product, and the stories they tell are fascinating.

After the laundry had been washed and dried it had to be ironed. Old-fashioned flat-irons had to be heated in the fire and were horribly heavy and difficult to use. The electric iron was a godsend. Early ones had no thermostats, they just got hotter and hotter, but at least they heated evenly. Today these particular items still look good. If an item has its original cord, that will add about a third to its value. Just remember that you can't be too careful with early electrical appliances and must have them checked over before you use them.

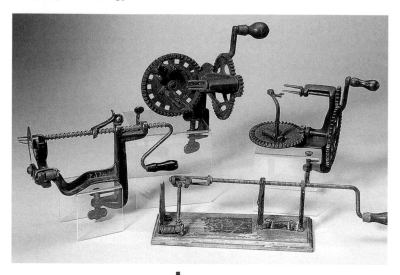

▼ **(Top) Butter churn**
American, 1878. It is made of wood with an iron handle and gear. **£65–135/$100–200**
(Bottom) Coffee-grinder
By the Enterprise Manufacturing Co., Philadelphia, c.1870s. It is made of cast iron and in a fair condition, **£100–150/$150–200**

▲ **Four apple corers of varying design**
From New England, c.1850–1920. This group shows the varying designs there were for corers. **£50–200/$50–300** (depending on the intricacy of the design).

◄ **Cast-iron candy-maker with chain-link and serrated designs**
By Thomas Mills & Brother, Philadelphia, 1875–1900. The maker stamps chain-link and chevron patterns onto the sweet mixture. **£200–300/$300–500**

Cooking and Cleaning

When people grew or otherwise processed most of their foodstuffs themselves, the work of maintaining household supplies was monumental. And before electricity reached into private homes, everything was done by hand or with mechanical help. The sheer labour involved inspired all kinds of specialist utensils, which have become popular collectables today.

The items available are fascinating clues to how life was lived in the very recent past. An early 20th-century housewife depended on a corer to prepare apples for drying, so that she had a supply of fruit for the winter. Today, with well-stocked supermarkets offering fresh fruit all year round, we are unlikely to use corers for this purpose, although they are still used when baking apples. The market for household gadgets was huge and untapped, so companies vied with each other to build ever better utensils, and of course to get round each others' patents. As a result of this there is enormous variety in this field – even the humble apple corer comes in many different designs.

"Country store" collectors, as they are known in the USA, are also very attracted to this area because it includes such items as coffee-grinders or candy-makers, which would have been used in local shops. Coffee-grinders are more common in the USA than in Britain; people who didn't own one could ask the shopkeeper to grind the beans for them on the shop grinder. The big cast-iron one shown here was almost certainly made for use in a shop – domestic coffee-grinders are smaller and lighter. The candy-maker is another very American item. Before candy (sweet) factories got going, candy-shop owners made their own stock. The basic sugar mix would be fed through a candy-maker. The rollers would mould it into a pretty shape, and then the length of candy could be cut into pieces with a special knife. Candy-makers are very rare and extremely desirable today.

Utensils from everyday rural life have been collectable for some years in the USA and they are beginning to attract more interest in Britain too.

▶ **Mechanical mousetrap**
German, early 20th-century. The box the mouse falls into is missing from this example. **£15–35/$25–50** (perhaps an extra £6/$10 if intact).

▲▼ **Two typical American electric toasters**
The top toaster is by Universal and the other by Hotpoint, both *c.*1920. They are still in good condition. **£15–35/$25–50 each**

◀ **Everybody's vacuum cleaner**
American, *c.*1920. Hand-pumped vacuum cleaners are not especially collectable, but this one has a fine transfer decoration, which gives it added interest. **£35–65/$50–100**

Mechanical butter churns can be found all over Europe and the USA. As with all other innovations of this time, there are lots of different designs. Some of them qualify as folk art, being handpainted with flowers and other patterns, and they will be the most valuable. However, on the whole, butter churns are affordable and fairly plentiful.

Electricity of course gave rise to a whole new range of domestic technology. From about 1915 on, cooking using electric appliances became very fashionable in the USA (it took another decade or two for the new inventions to become popular in Europe). There are lots of electrical cooking appliances from that period, but only the very earliest will be of value.

The electric vacuum cleaner was introduced in the 1920s but was very expensive until around the 1960s. Most people made do with mechanical carpet cleaners before then. The carpet sweeper was the design that worked best, but there were plenty of others, most of which didn't work at all. The hand-pumped vacuum cleaner was a short-lived idea but

sold, albeit briefly, in its thousands. Most of them have survived in very good condition because they were completely ineffectual, so nobody used them more than once. The labels are the most interesting part, so look for attractive graphics.

Overall, cooking and cleaning items tend to be bought for their decorative appeal rather than their technological interest. For example, very few people are going to collect old vacuum cleaners or any other device that takes up a great deal of space. They are more likely to buy single articles, such as one old coffee-grinder or one old kitchen range. One notable exception is old electric toasters. Collectors like toasters because they are small and easy to store, and, because they have always been fashionable items, they were made in a vast range of designs with delightful features. For instance, some have a grille on the top so that you can stand your coffee- or teapot on it to keep it warm. This is a whole collecting field in itself, and there is even a Toaster Collectors' Club for enthusiasts.

▼ Two early Edison Patent lamps
Made to an Edison patent, c.1900.
(Left) Brass table lamp in baluster form
with a marble base; **(Right)** wall lamp with
a gimbal yoke, made of nickelled brass.
£100–200/$200–300 each

**► Clockwork shoo-fly
pattern fan**
Late 19th century. This
fan has a painted
cast-iron base.
£250–400/$400–600

**▲ British mechanical
bellows**
Late 18th/early 19th
century. These bellows
are made of brass
and walnut.
£200–250/$300–400

Light and Heat

As the 19th century turned into the 20th century, domestic technology was transformed by the harnessing of electricity. In Britain and the United States most urban households and businesses were connected to the gas supply. Gas companies had grown huge because of the lack of competition, and by the middle of the 19th century every major city had a sophisticated network of gas pipes. However, the work of Thomas Edison was to sweep away all that went before it.

The first experiments in electric lighting were conducted by the famous British scientist Sir Humphry Davy (1778–1829) around 1807. From about 1840 a number of incandescent lamps were patented, but none of them was successful owing to the difficulty of creating a strong vacuum and the expense of obtaining electricity. After years of research and experimentation, Edison publicly demonstrated his incandescent light in 1878. Joseph Swan, a British scientist, simultaneously produced his own incandescent light, and so the two men

subsequently (and unusually, in a period notable for its patent wars) joined forces. At first electricity was expensive, and only the wealthier homes had electric light. The lamps were elaborately designed to please this affluent market, and they are collectable today not only because of their history but also because they fit in well with modern décor. Original shades rarely survive, but this does not affect the value much.

Interestingly, Edison himself realized the importance of a cheap supply of electricity. In fact, he can be said to have invented the industry. In the same year that he exhibited his light bulb he formed the Edison Electric Power and Light Company, and used it to finance research into an electricity supply that would undercut the gas companies.

Faced with the loss of their monopoly, the gas companies turned to heating and cooking, and they still hold a giant share of that market today. However, turn-of-the-century houses still relied on open fires for heat, while coolness was obtained by various kinds of fan. Mechanical hearth tools and

◄ **Luminaire**
Combination floor lamp and fan made by
the Cincinnati Victor Company, c.1920.
It was the only firm to make the Luminaire.
£500–800/$800–1,200

▲ **Early American electricity bills**
From the Edison Electric Power and Light Company, York, Pennsylvania,
c.1917–19. These are not common, as people didn't keep them any
more than we keep our bills today. They are collectable mainly for the
advertising on the back. **£35–50/$50–80 for the group**

fans are of interest to collectors today because there is a lot of variety and ingenuity in the designs. Hand bellows were actually perfectly efficient, but a mechanical version seemed more modern at the time and is a lot of fun to collect today.

In the USA high temperatures have always been a common problem, so a number of delightful mechanical fans were produced. Before electricity came into the home they often ran by clockwork. The Shoo-Fly is a typically American design and is as charming as its name. When this popular fan was wound up its sails would slowly revolve in a horizontal circle. Such fans were used on the table to keep flies away from food. Not all examples of this type of fan are labelled Shoo-Fly, but they were probably all made by the same firm. A shoo-fly pattern fan is surprisingly valuable, even in poor condition.

The Luminaire was a particularly inventive American piece that combined lights and a fan in one item of furniture. It is said to have been used in funeral parlours, or at the home of the deceased if a

wake was held there. Presumably, if you couldn't afford embalming, a Luminaire would have helped to keep the atmosphere pleasant. Whatever purpose it was used for, this is still a handsome piece of furniture for any room, and the fun, though rather macabre, background story makes it even more collectable. The example shown here has no shades, but they would probably have been the small tasselled type popular at the time. They are still made today, so it's easy to replace them if you wish.

Ephemera connected with the early electrical industry are interesting to collect, although there isn't very much of it. Old bills occasionally turn up in the back of desk drawers, and they are mainly collected for the advertising that was printed on the reverse. Any promotional literature related to items or the industry will attract interest from advertising collectors as much as from technological collectors. However, such ephemera shouldn't cost you much and they add interest to a collection, particularly if you can match an item to its advertisement.

▼ **Wizard
Fortune Teller**
By Mills, c.1925. This
machine was for
use on a counter
top. It has a choice
of six questions.
£450–600/$700–900

▶ **Globe Grip Test**
Early 20th century.
This example has fine
decoration. Grip the
handle and the ball
rises to show how
strong you are.
£2,500–3,000/
$4,000–5,000

▲ **Safety-match
vending machine**
Early 20th century. It is
made of glass and oak.
£450–600/$700–900

Coin-operated Machines

Coin-operated machines were as popular at the beginning of the 20th century as they are in the 21st. Today's teenagers in amusement arcades are, unknowingly, continuing a 100-year-old tradition, and some of the early games are very collectable today. Collectors tend to be very patriotic in their choice of machines. There are a few that have universal appeal, but, on the whole, British machines tend to attract more attention in Britain, American ones do better in the USA and so on.

Coin-operated machines have a surprisingly ancient, though discontinuous, history. In the first century AD Hero of Alexandria published plans for a coin-operated holy water dispenser. It relied on the coin landing on a plate that tipped and opened the water outlet, then the coin slid off to close it. It is not known whether the dispenser was actually ever used.

The first successful vending machines appeared in the 1880s. In the USA, Adams' Tutti-Frutti chewing-gum machine was installed in New York around 1890. There had been earlier attempts to

make vending machines (there are records of an 1850s stamp dispenser in England), but it was some time before anyone solved the problem of checking for false coins. An English inventor, Percival Everitt, noted that his machines worked until people tried to activate the mechanism by inserting paper or other small items, which gummed up the works.

By the beginning of the 20th century the difficulties had been overcome, and vending machines were everywhere. Hotels, restaurants and saloons had coin-operated machines that sold sweets and played music. Bars and clubs had the risqué kind with pictures of scantily clad ladies, while railway stations had vending machines for maps, tobacco and snacks.

People could buy almost anything from a machine, including fresh eggs, and it wasn't long before shrewd inventors realized that such machines could be used for entertainment too. Special arcades and parlours were built for these new machines, which were at their peak of popularity from 1890 to

▲ Stereoscope
By the American
Novelty Co., Cincinnati,
c.1915. It contains a
set of travel cards with
20 views of sights
around the world.
£3,000–5,000/
$5,000–8,000

**► Correct Weight coin-
operated scale**
By Jennings, 1920s–40s. It has a
central mirror and men's/women's
height/weight charts.
£300–500/$500–700

▼ Model 4 slot machine
By Pace, 1930s–40s. It is in a
cast-aluminium Art Deco case.
£500–800/$800–1,200

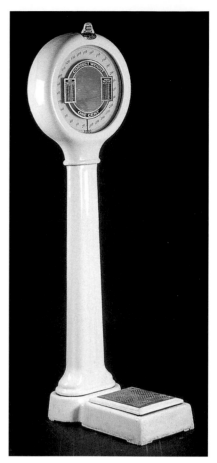

1930, when people flocked to gamble, test their
reactions, love or strength, have their fortunes told
and even receive electric shocks. Everitt also
patented the coin-operated weighing machine that
used to be found on almost every British railway
platform. The first ones showed the weight on a
dial; more sophisticated versions printed it discreetly
on a card, while the famous "I Speak Your Weight"
machines announced it to everyone.

The first successful gambling machines are
associated with two inventors in particular. Charles
Fey of San Francisco invented the "Liberty Bell" in
1889. It incorporates the familiar three-drum
design that is still in use today, and he put the
wholesome fruit pictures on it to appease anti-
gambling sentiment. The Liberty Bell motif gave
the fruit machine a fine, patriotic aspect, and it was
very popular indeed. The other name is H. S. Mills,
a Chicago newspaper boy and lemonade vendor.
He invented a simple machine that had a single slot
leading to three tubes. The gambler pushed a penny
into the slot; if it fell into one of the two "lucky"
tubes, two pennies were paid out. Mills went on to
found the huge Mills Novelty Company of Chicago
at the turn of the century, and by 1932 it was
manufacturing 70,000 machines a year.

Today coin-operated machines are one of the
most popular technical collectables. They are also
very expensive, and because they have been popular
for years it isn't easy to find them – you will almost
certainly need to go to a specialist auction or dealer.
Rare early machines are desirable, but collectors are
usually interested in the looks (showy is best) and the
complexity of the inner workings. Earlier examples
tend to be plain, so a later model with intricate works
and an ornate exterior may bring a higher price. The
machine type also affects its value: vending machines
are less desirable than gambling or skill games. The
one-armed bandits (or slot machines, as they are
known in the USA) are the most popular. Names to
look for apart from Mills are Jennings (a former Mills
employee), Pace, Bally, Caille Brothers and Watling.

▶ **Folding school desk**
By C. W. Sherwood, c.1870 80. This would have been a salesman's sample.
£450–600/$700–900

▲ **Patent model of a spring-bed bottom**
By Joshua S. Judson, of Austin, Minnesota, 1873. The label gives the patent information.
£100–200/$200–300

◀ **Early motor vehicle**
By George Hill, Milford, Ohio, c.1897. It is made of pine and metal.
£600–1,000/ $1,000–1,500

◀ **Model harvester**
c.1870. The model's height is fully adjustable, and it comes with moving parts.
£500–800/$800–1,200

Models

These delightful models are great fun to collect. They were made for a number of purposes: some were just for fun, others were salesmen's samples, and perhaps the most interesting were made for the US Patent Office.

During the mid to late 19th century the Patent Office required that every applicant for a patent included a model with their invention. In some cases the inventors simply sent an example of the item if it were small enough – such as a frying pan, a clothes pin or a hinge. If the invention was too big to be sent, the inventor would build a detailed miniature. In the 1920s the Patent Office sold off crate-loads of these 19th-century models and they have been collected ever since. It's important to remember that the only way you can be sure that an item really is a patent model is if it has the Patent Office's tag on it. This detail is vital to its value. There are plenty of models on the collectors' market today that probably are patent models, but without the tag they cannot be described as such.

Many patents were for simple improvements on common items and will therefore not have any great value. Likewise, patent models of items such as door hinges will not be worth a great deal. However, some, like the washing machine on page 137, are incredibly detailed miniatures of machines, with tiny reproductions of all the moving parts. Models of this quality can be very valuable indeed.

Travelling salesmen who couldn't fit their products into small suitcases required models of their wares to show to potential buyers. It isn't always possible to say for certain that a particular model is definitely a salesman's sample or whether it was a model to show investors or manufacturers. However, you can usually decide for yourself. The folding school desk illustrated above is a good example of a salesman's sample. It is the standard type of desk that was used in American schools for decades. The presence of the name of the company on the front adds still more to its interest, and it has a nostalgic feel that will raise its value.

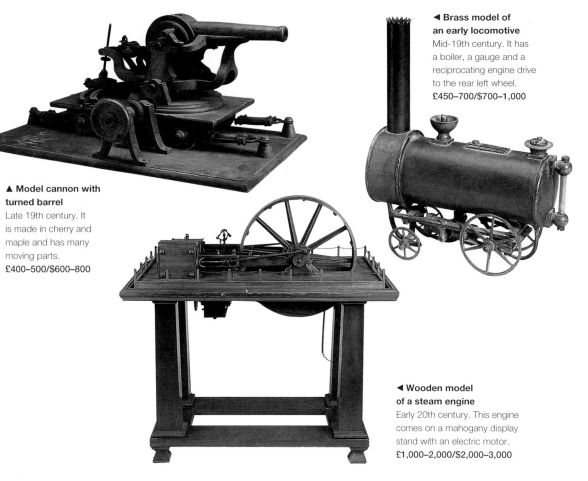

▲ Model cannon with turned barrel
Late 19th century. It is made in cherry and maple and has many moving parts.
£400–500/$600–800

◄ Brass model of an early locomotive
Mid-19th century. It has a boiler, a gauge and a reciprocating engine drive to the rear left wheel.
£450–700/$700–1,000

◄ Wooden model of a steam engine
Early 20th century. This engine comes on a mahogany display stand with an electric motor.
£1,000–2,000/$2,000–3,000

The little motor car was made either by or for George Hill of Milford, Ohio, after the Patent Office stopped requiring models, which was around 1880. It came with a number of papers from the inventor of the car, including the manuscript of his patent. It's a very rare example of what was probably a demonstration model from the dawn of the motor car industry. It is made of pine, and inside it has miniatures of some of the moving parts, including the differential gears to the front wheels – a very advanced piece of technology at the time. It is possible that this model was made to demonstrate the differential gearing to potential investors. Hill did advertise his cars, but it is doubtful whether any were manufactured.

All kinds of people made models. Professional model makers often had machine shops and would make items for clients – a new type of sprocket for a manufacturer to try out, perhaps, or a prototype for an inventor who was not a machinist. Thomas Edison himself started out as a machine-shop owner.

The model of the early locomotive could have been made by a professional model maker as a souvenir of England's first locomotive, or by an amateur for fun. The large model of the steam engine, on the other hand, was built for a display at a Massachusetts steel mill, to show how its power plant operated. The tiny wooden cannon is more of a mystery. It might be a patent model, could be an apprentice woodworker's piece, or perhaps was just made for fun. Whichever it is, it was beautifully made and has many working parts.

Models are collectable owing to their fine workmanship, and it is this that will determine their value. You can accustom your eye to quality by visiting museums such as the Science Museum in London or the Smithsonian Museum in Washington D.C. to see their examples (*see* pp153–54 for details). When you are looking at a model to buy, examine it closely to see if it has working parts. The best models are perfect replicas of the real thing – almost works of art in their fine detail and craftsmanship.

Fakes and Reproductions

The first thing that a collector needs to be aware of is the difference between a fake and a reproduction: a reproduction is simply a copy, while a fake is deliberately intended to deceive. You can't always rely on what the seller tells you, and it can be hard to know what to look for when trying to determine whether a piece you are interested in buying is a fake or not.

A good place to begin is to find out which items are most often faked. Some are just too difficult or costly to fake – musical boxes, for example. However, India seems to be doing a brisk trade in fake brass theodolites and compasses. They are of low quality and high polish, often signed "Stanley, London", and are appearing in flea markets all over Europe. India has also been making fake horn gramophones for the last decade or so. Fortunately their quality is so poor that, after you have seen a few real machines, the Indian fakes are easy to spot.

Even top-quality fakes and reproductions have telltale signs. For instance, if every single screw in a supposedly early-18th-century piece is machine-made, your alarm bells should go off. One or two screws might have been replaced in an original, but

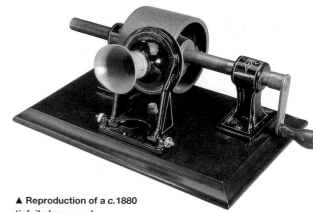

▲ **Reproduction of a c.1880 tinfoil phonograph**
Produced c.1970. Its excellent condition points to the fact that it is not an original. However, this piece is very well made (from casts of an original) and is of value to collectors because the originals are so rare and costly. **£200–300/$300–500**

if all of them are of a much later date, something is wrong. A piece that looks like new but which the seller claims is unrestored also gives cause for concern. Anything that is more than a couple of years old is going to show signs of wear – and the older it is, the more wear you should expect.

The place where you find an item can also give clues to its authenticity. Astonishing items do occasionally show up in out-of-the-way places, but it doesn't happen very often. A genuine medieval French quadrant is really most unlikely to have found its way to an antiques fair in Little Rock, Arkansas. Of course, if the seller is willing to attest it in writing, then you don't need to worry. But if the seller isn't as forthcoming as you would wish, you should walk away. Good sellers should always be able to tell you something about pieces. If they honestly don't know, and even the experts don't always have all the answers, then they should say so.

The key to spotting fakes is practice. Get to know what items should look like. Handle as many as you can, open them up, look underneath, even smell them. It doesn't take long to train your instinct. And use other people's expertise: get to know fellow collectors and dealers and ask their advice.

More experienced collectors may come across something they didn't know existed. Occasionally this is something to get excited about. More often it is something to be suspicious of. For instance, a brass kaleidoscope was recently advertised online as being signed "Ross, London". Ross was a very fine instrument maker but he's not associated with kaleidoscopes. A check through his original catalogues confirms that indeed he never listed them. The moral is, if a piece doesn't seem to fit with what you know, be very wary.

▶ **Fake Renaissance portable globe/sundial**
From c.1980. The globe is of stained resin instead of ivory and is moulded instead of engraved. Portable dials usually have adjustable gnomons but this one is fixed at 90 degrees, which is of very limited usefulness. The pillar is attached to the base by a machine-made thread. This piece is of no value at all.

Collectables of the Future

If we look at what makes objects from the past collectable, we can make a good guess as to which items from our own time will become sought after in the future. Quality and rarity are two key factors. And an item that was top of the range for its time is likely to retain its value far better than a piece from lower down the scale.

The numbers in which a particular item was sold is also important. Designs that were only produced for a year will be rarer, and hence more valuable, than designs that sold for a decade. And if a machine was withdrawn because, for example, the type of record it played became suddenly obsolete, then it will mark a specific phase of that technology's development. Such historical interest will add further value to it.

A third consideration is the extent to which an item is typical of its time. Look at its appearance and the technology behind it. A piece that immediately evokes its era will always attract interest.

One example of a future collectable might be the MiniDisc. In the early 1990s the big recording

▲ MiniDisc player
By Sony, c. 1992. If you are interested in collecting items for the future, then keep them as pristine as you can. This example is unused and is still in its original box with all its accessories and leaflets. It was first released in 1992 and cost **£365/$550**

companies noticed that vinyl records and cassette tapes were going out of favour; they tried to replace both at once with the MiniDisc. Initially it flopped because hardly anything was available on the format at that time, but it was relaunched a few years later as an easier and cheaper alternative to a CD burner and the MiniDisc became more widely used. However, music technology has moved on yet again and the MP3 is the latest development, using the internet as the principal source of music. A MiniDisc player could become desirable as an example of one, perhaps short-lived, direction that technology took in the late 20th century.

Prototypes of important inventions are very often extremely collectable. Not many people know the name of Dr Arthur Schawlow, but he was a co-inventor of the laser. One of the applications he saw for it was as an eraser, and this oddity could turn out to be a very good investment for the future. Similarly, anything associated with a famous scientist or inventor will always have value.

It's worth thinking about future collectors too. Who will have the money to collect and what is likely to appeal to them? Try to cast your mind forwards 30 years and think about what will define our era and what people will miss from it. Early computer and internet technology could be one area – the first Apple Macs and Texas Instruments calculators have already become design icons. Music technology is changing fast, too. Perhaps people will want to collect shortlived items such as the eight-track tape player.

Whatever you decide to put aside for the future, apply the same rules that you use to guide your collecting now. Look for quality, rarity and, above all, interest. Don't just do it for the money. Pick out things that either have historical importance or are simply fun to have.

▼ Prototype laser eraser
By Dr Arthur Schawlow, c. 1967. This is for erasing mistakes from typewritten and manuscript documents. The fitted carrying case is marked Arthur Schawlow, Dept of Physics, Stanford University. It was purchased in 2000 for **£435/$650**

Care and Restoration

Once you own an antique it is important to care for it properly. Many pieces suffer badly from well-meaning attempts to put existing damage right. The golden rule is always: if in doubt, do nothing. Some "restoration" can never be put right.

First of all, think carefully about whether your new acquisition even needs any work. A lot of items arrive on the market straight from a dusty attic or a damp barn. While some damage may have been caused by the environment they have been stored in, they usually need nothing more than a simple clean. If you do clean an item, stay away from solvents and use mild soap and water applied with a soft cloth. Old cotton T-shirts work very well. Do be careful

not to get paper labels wet or to let soapy water drip into a mechanism. For wooden pieces, use top-quality furniture cleaners and polish (ask your dealer for recommendations) rather than supermarket brands. Some polishes are very good for covering scratches. If the damage is extensive, read up on refinishing – there are great books available. Small pieces that have fallen off are easy to glue back, but use animal glues. Avoid epoxies or other instant adhesives as they are irremovable once used.

One of the worst mistakes made with brass pieces is to polish them. Most brass was originally lacquered, and it is this finish that gives it its soft, warm glow. Polishing removes the lacquer, which makes the brass vulnerable to tarnish and gives it a hard shine. You can have brass re-lacquered but go carefully. A musical box cylinder is almost always lacquered when it is cleaned and restored (although originally they weren't lacquered as the technology was not so good then) and this is acceptable as it keeps the cylinder from tarnishing. However, re-lacquering a microscope would be much less acceptable. It is always a very good idea to read up on restoration before you touch any piece. You will find advice on what to do and, most importantly, what not to do.

It can't be stressed enough that keeping a piece in its original condition is best. Some wear and ageing are only to be expected in an antique, after all, and patina can't be faked. If you do decide to go for restoration, choose a restorer whose work you have seen. Don't aim for a brand-new look, go for something its first owner might have expected after five or ten years' use.

If you wish to store a collectable it's best not to wrap it up too much, as that can hold in damp. Cloth is better than paper for wrapping purposes, though. Plastic isn't good if the item is going to be placed in a warm/hot area like an attic as, if it gets warm, the finish can get soft and stick to the plastic. A closed box is often the most sensible packing, and of course if you buy a piece with its original packing-cases then always use those.

Preserving good condition is easier than restoring it. Keep your displayed pieces out of direct sunlight, especially if they are made of wood or paper. Dampness and humidity are very damaging to metal and will harm wood finishes too. However, an overly dry environment can cause wood to split. Avoid extremes in humidity, and keep your pieces away from heat sources. Protect the mechanism of phonographs and gramophones with a light oil, but use it sparingly so as not to clog up the works. Finally, don't dust your pieces too often, and never use modern-day products. Use a feather duster or a static duster that won't cause wear to the surface.

▼ Two examples of a Cooke & Sons postal balance
Both from the mid to late 19th century. **(Top)** This postal scale has suffered severe corrosion and discolouration from a combination of dampness held in the paper in which it was stored and the chemicals within the paper. It could be cleaned to improve its look but this would probably cost more than its actual value so is not worth doing. **(Bottom)** This one has its original lacquered-brass finish.

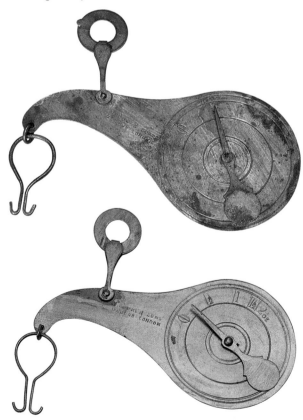

Display

A well-planned display not only helps to preserve the historical and financial integrity of your items but will also show them off to their best advantage. Before you start, think carefully about where your collection will be. Will it just be concentrated in certain areas or will you have pieces spread throughout the house? Unless your collection is small and consists of tiny objects, you'll probably find that the answer is both.

Look at the concentrated parts of your collection first and consider your storage options. Don't make the common mistake of putting carefully chosen pieces on cheap mass-produced shelving – it will ruin the effect of your hard work. It's easy to keep an eye open for possible storage units while you're out and about tracking down new items. Victorian and early 20th-century cabinets have useful features such as drawers (very good for small items), high shelves (excellent for keeping fragile pieces out of harm's way) and slide-out work surfaces (convenient for showing off individual pieces). Free-standing book-cases work well too. This kind of furniture may cost a good bit more than modern high-street pieces but it will make a world of difference. Many such pieces are also collectors' items in themselves.

If the museum effect is not your style, or doesn't suit your collection, think about combining antique with modern. Many antique instruments can be displayed in the manner in which you would show a piece of sculpture, and so modern quality furniture with a plain finish and clean lines will show them off very well. For example, put a softly glowing brass sextant on a plant stand of plain, pale wood, or a selection of sundials on glass and

▲ **Secretary-bookcase**
French Provincial, from the mid-18th century. An attractive oak bookcase makes a good curio cabinet for a varied collection of scientific and technical instruments. The pale wood is an excellent background for brass pieces.
£1,000–1,665/$1,500–2,500 for the bookcase

metal shelving. One immense advantage of modern furniture over older pieces is that you can adjust the height of the shelves to suit your pieces.

Larger pieces such as gramophones are items of furniture in themselves. A horn phonograph placed next to your CD player will attract interest and demonstrate the evolution of recorded sound.

Another common mistake is to let your smaller items get lost or overlooked. Everyone picks up odds and ends over the years, and it's a shame to lose them in the back of a drawer. Look out for little display cases. The initial outlay for an old unit will be worth it as your collection will be properly visible.

Finally, give some thought to relating your items to specific rooms when deciding where to display them. Pharmaceutical items can fit well in the bathroom, and irons or apple corers can look very attractive in the kitchen. Don't overdo it, though, or you could make visitors uncomfortable. Some of those medical and surgical items are probably best suited to a museum-style display in an innocuous room such as an office.

◄ **Small shop-display case**
Probably American. This unusual turn-of-the-century display case has been pressed into service to store phonograph accessories such as rare cylinder-record boxes, needle tins and advertising items. Added together they are worth more than most entire phonographs, but the individual items are so small that they often get lost. **£135–200/$200–300 for the case**

Glossary

Alidade A revolving index for reading the graduations of an astrolabe, a quadrant or a similar instrument.

Artificial horizon A reference used to measure azimuth angles when the weather or darkness obscures the actual horizon.

Binnacle The box in which a ship's compass is kept to protect it from the elements.

Bisque White unglazed porcelain.

Bi-convex lens A lens that is convex on both sides. It was very difficult to grind these accurately, so often two plano-convex lenses were used back to back, forming a doublet lens.

Bubble level A small tube filled with liquid but with just enough air left to form a small bubble. When the tube is placed on its side, the position of the air bubble indicates when the level is precisely horizontal.

Calotype The method of photography devised by Henry Fox Talbot in the 1830s. Importantly, it was the first method that produced a negative from which multiple positives could be taken.

Camera obscura A box with a pinhole on one side and a glass screen on the other. Light entering the pinhole projected an image of the exterior onto the screen, where an artist could trace it.

Celestial globe A globe that shows the relative positions of the stars as seen from the earth's surface. Owing to the spherical shape, the resulting map is inside out.

Chromatic aberration A phenomenon of refracted light that causes the image of an object seen through a refracting telescope to be surrounded by rings of different colours.

Chronometer A very precisely built mechanical timepiece used by navigators to determine their longitude at sea, and also by astronomers to calibrate their measuring devices.

Clock A timepiece that signals the time by striking a bell.

Compass rose The assembly of a magnetized needle, cap and bearings along with the card on which the relative directions are printed.

Copernican system A model of the universe in which the sun lies at the centre and the earth revolves around it.

Cupping The application of cups from which the air has been exhausted to a cut in the skin in order to draw blood. This method was used in bloodletting.

Daguerreotype Early method of photography invented by Louis Jacques Mandé Daguerre in 1835. It relied on silver iodide as the light-sensitive coating.

Diorama An exhibition of pictures seen through an opening, with lighting effects to make the scenes change rapidly.

Doublet lens A bi-convex lens made from two plano-convex lenses placed back to back.

Draw The parts of the body of a telescope that can be extended and retracted into each other to change the length, and therefore the focus, of the instrument. The draws also helped the instrument to be closed up to a smaller and more portable device.

Enlightenment, the Age of A term used to describe the trends in thought and writing in Europe and the USA during the 18th century. It was used by writers at the time, who considered they were emerging from centuries of darkness and ignorance into a new age enlightened by reason and science.

Escapement The part of a timepiece that connects the wheelwork with the pendulum, allowing a tooth of a cogwheel to escape at each vibration. Too much friction in the escapement will slow or stop the clock.

Etui A pocket case for holding small or fragile items, such as medical instruments.

Gimbal A device for keeping a hanging object level, as with a compass, a transit or a telescope.

Gnomon
1. An upright rod for taking the sun's altitude by its shadow.
2. The pin on a sundial whose shadow points to the hour.

Gores Elliptical sections of paper pasted onto a globe to make up a spherical map of the earth's surface.

Lancet A small, sharp medical instrument used for piercing the skin.

Leyden jar This jar is a simple form of capacitor or electrical condenser, used for storing an electric charge. It was named after the University of Leyden in The Netherlands, where it was invented in 1745.

Limelight A bright light produced by heating a block of calcium oxide (lime) with a flame fuelled by hydrogen and oxygen.

Lithophane An optical toy that consisted of a burner with ceramic panels. Relief images on the panels gained a three-dimensional effect from the backlighting of the burner's flame.

Lithotrite A medical instrument used for removing calcifications or stones from the bladder.

Megalethoscope An Italian optical toy that allowed the user to see photographs of the same view as if it were daylight or night-time.

Objective lens The lens (or combination of lenses) in a microscope or telescope that is nearest the object of examination.

Ocular lens The lens (or combination of lenses) in a microscope or telescope that is nearest the user's eye.

Orrery A mechanical model that demonstrates the relative positions and movements of bodies in the solar system. The simplest orreries show the earth, moon and sun. More complex examples show the entire solar system, or at least those planets that had been discovered at the time when a particular orrery was built.

Patina A film or surface appearance that develops on objects over time. It is used by experts to help date many items, particularly those made of wood, ivory, stone and certain metals.

Phenakistiscope An optical device designed to give the illusion of moving pictures. It consisted of a disc with a series of successive images printed on it. A slot revealed one image at a time. When the user looked through the slot and spun the disc, the images appeared to move. The name means "deceiver of sight".

Phlebotomy The practice of medical treatment through bloodletting to remove the "bad humours."

Phrenology The theory that mental faculties were located in various parts of the brain and could be investigated by feeling the bumps on the outside of the head.

Planetarium The name used by Benjamin Martin for his improved orrery. Today, a building inside which you can see a representation of the night sky projected onto the inside of a hemispherical roof.

Plano-convex lens A lens that is convex on one side and flat on the other.

Provenance The history and background of an object, which serves to prove its authenticity.

Ptolemaic system A model of the universe dating from the second century BC in which the earth lies still at the centre of the universe and the sun, stars and planets move around it.

Reflecting telescope A telescope that uses a curved mirror or mirrors in concert with additional lenses to magnify an object.

Refracting telescope One that uses a lens or lenses only to magnify an object.

Rhumb Any of the 32 points (magnetic headings) on a ship's compass.

Rhumb line A navigational course consisting of a steady and unchanging magnetic compass heading. Owing to the constant

change of the earth's magnetic field (variation), this will appear as a curve when plotted on a map or navigational chart.

Royal Society A scientific association founded in London in 1660 and granted a royal charter by Charles II in 1662. Since then it has advised the British government on scientific matters in a semi-official capacity. It conducts and supports scientific research, and awards medals such as the Copley Medal (dating from 1731) and the Royal Medals (dating from 1825 and 1965).

Scarificator A medical instrument consisting of up to 12 spring-driven blades designed to break the surface of the skin for the purposes of bloodletting.

Scioptic ball A spherical optical toy that fitted into a window shutter. A lens inside the ball projected the exterior view into the darkened room.

Shagreen A granular leather made from shark or ray skin, occasionally from horse or donkey skin.

Spherical aberration Non-convergence of light rays due to a difference in focus of the marginal and central parts of a lens. An object seen through a lens with spherical aberration will appear blurred.

Spontaneous generation, theory of The theory that minute organisms and simple forms of life are produced from dead matter or interaction with inorganic substances. It was prevalent before microscopic observations became possible. Antony van Leeuwenhoek was the first to challenge the theory in the 1660s, when he used his microscope to demonstrate that weevils hatched from tiny eggs and were not created from the combination of wheat grains and sand.

Stage The part of a microscope that supports the object to be examined.

Steelyard A weighing machine consisting of a lever with a short arm for the item weighed and a long, graduated arm along which a single weight can slide.

Stereograph A card with paired photographs of the same object taken from slightly different angles. When viewed through a stereoscope, the stereograph image appears to be three dimensional.

Stereoscope A viewer for looking at stereographs.

Sub-stage Apparatus under the stage of a microscope.

Tellurium A specialist term referring to a mechanical model that demonstrates the relative position and movement of the earth, sun and moon.

Terrestrial globe A globe showing the surface features of the earth. They may also include the tracks of voyages of discovery, shipping lanes or undersea cables.

Transom A cross beam or cross-piece used on early latitude-measuring devices.

Trepanning The medical practice of using a small cylindrical saw to remove a piece from the skull in order to relieve pressure on the brain. The saw itself was called a trepan.

Trephine An improved version of the trepan.

Tribrach A device used for levelling an instrument. It consists of three individually adjustable supports.

Triplet lens Three simple lens shapes combined to form a lens that would be difficult or impossible to grind from a single piece of glass.

Zoetrope An optical device designed to give the illusion of moving pictures. A series of successive images was printed on a card lining the inside of a hollow drum. When the drum was spun, the images appeared to move.

Further Reading

Adler, Michael,
Antique Typewriters,
Schiffer 1997

Bailly, Christian,
*Automata The Golden Age
1848–1914*, Sotheby's 1987

Baumbach, Robert,
*Columbia Disc Phonograph
Companion*, Stationary
X-Press 1996

Baumbach, Robert,
*Look For The Dog:
An Illustrated Guide
to Victor Talking Machines*,
Stationary X-Press 1995

Bedini, S.,
Thinkers and Tinkers,
Smithsonian 1975

Bennett, J.A.,
*The Divided Circle: A
History of Instruments
for Astronomy,
Navigation and Surveying*,
1987

Bennion, Elisabeth,
Antique Dental Instruments,
Sotheby's 1986

Bennion, Elisabeth,
Antique Medical Instruments,
Sotheby's 1979

Bolle, Bert,
Barometers,
Argus Books Ltd, 1978
(reprinted 1982 & 1984)

Bulleid, H. A. V.,
Musical Box Tune Sheets,
Musical Box Society of
Great Britain 1999

Emmins, Colin,
*Automatic Vending
Machines*,
Shire Publications Ltd 1995

Fabrizio, Timothy and Paul,
George,
*The Talking Machine:
An Illustrated Compendium*,
Schiffer 1997

Fearn, Jacqueline,
Domestic Bygones,
Shire Publications Ltd 1977

Feldman, Anthony & Ford, Peter,
Scientists and Inventors,
Bloomsbury 1989

Frow, George,
*Edison Cylinder Phonograph
Compendium*,
Stationary X-Press 1994

Frow, George,
The Edison Disc Phonograph,
George Frow 1983

Gordon, Bob,
Early Electrical Appliances,
Shire Publications Ltd 1984

*The Grolier 1996 Multimedia
Encyclopedia*
Grolier Electronic Publishing

Hambly, Maya,
*Drawing Instruments
1580–1980*,
Sotheby's 1988

Harley, Basil,
Optical Toys,
Shire Publications Ltd 1988

Head, Carol,
Old Sewing Machines,
Shire Publications Ltd 1982

Hopp, P.M.,
*Slide Rules: Their
History, Models and Makers*,
Astragal Press 1999

Hudson, Graham,
The Victorian Printer,
Shire Publications Ltd 1996

James, Duncan,
Old Typewriters,
Shire Publications Ltd 1993

Jewel, Brian,
Antique Sewing Machines,
Costello 1985

Lloyd, Steven,
*Ivory Diptych Sundials
1570–1750*,
Harvard University Press 1992

McKeown, James & Joan (eds),
*McKeown's Price Guide to
Antique and Classic Cameras*,
Centenial Photo 2001

Ord-Hume, Arthur W. J. G.,
*The Musical Box: A Guide for
Collectors*, Schiffer 1995

Pearsall, Ronald,
*Collecting and Restoring
Scientific Instruments*,
David & Charles 1974

Pearsall, Ronald,
*Collecting Mechanical
Antiques*,
David & Charles 1973

Pearson, Lynn F.,
Amusement Machines,
Shire Publications Ltd 1992

Scott-Scott, Michael,
*Drawing Instruments
1850–1950*, Shire
Publications Ltd 1986

Turner, Anthony,
*Early Scientific Instruments,
Europe 1400–1800*,
Sotheby's 1987

Turner, Gerard L'E.,
Collecting Microscopes,
Studio Vista 1981

Turner, Gerard L'E.,
*Scientific Instruments
1500–1900: An Introduction*,
University of California
Press 1998

Tweedale, Geoffrey,
*Calculating Machines
and Computers*,
Shire Publications Ltd 1990

Warren, David J.,
*Old Medical and
Dental Instruments*,
Shire Publications Ltd 1994

Watson, Fred,
*Binoculars, Opera
Glasses and Field Glasses*,
Shire Publications Ltd 1995

Wilbur, Keith,
Antique Medical Instruments,
Schiffer 1987

Wynter, Harriet & Turner,
Anthony,
Scientific Instruments,
Charles Scribner's Sons,
New York 1975

Young, Anne Mortimer,
Antique Medicine Chests,
Vernier 1994

Useful Addresses

Below is a list of clubs, societies and museums related to science and technology. This is not a fully comprehensive list by any means; most clubs are fairly small and too specialized to list here (such as the toaster collectors' club), and are often specific to certain regions or countries. However, the clubs that are listed are all very active and are a good starting point for finding other ones.

A lot of museums have displays of some kind for science and technology, and many focus on their local regions or special fields of interest. Listed here are the larger museums that are internationally known by collectors. Also included are the three main auction houses that deal in science and technology collectables, namely Christie's, Sotheby's and Skinner.

There are no specialist dealers listed here simply because there would not be room to list them all, and the author does not want to include some and not others. The relevant clubs and internet websites will provide you with the names of dealers in your area of interest.

MUSEUMS

United Kingdom
Museum of the History of Science,
Old Ashmolean Building,
Broad St,
Oxford OX1 3AZ
Tel: (0044) 1865 277280
Fax: (0044) 1865 277288
www.mhs.ox.ac.uk

National Maritime Museum,
Greenwich,
London SE10 9NF
Tel: (0044) 20 8312 6608
Fax: (0044) 20 8312 6522
www.nmm.ac.uk

National Museum of Photography,
Film and Television,
Bradford,
West Yorkshire BD1 1NQ
Tel: (0044) 1274 202030
Fax: (0044) 1274 723155
www.nmpft.org.uk

Royal Museum,
National Museums of Scotland,
Chambers St,
Edinburgh EH1 1JF
Tel: (0044) 131 225 7534
Fax: (0044) 131 220 4819
(Good collection of basic scientific instruments, especially Scottish-made ones; also a fine collection of phonographs and gramophones)

Science Museum, National
Museum of Science and Industry,
Exhibition Rd,
South Kensington,
London SW7 2DD
Tel: (0044) 20 7938 8000
Fax: (0044) 20 7942 4124
www.nmsi.ac.uk

Whipple Museum of the
History of Science,
Free School Lane,
Cambridge CB2 3RH
Fax: (0044) 1223 334554
www.hps.cam.ac.uk/whipple

United States of America
Adler Planetarium and
Astronomy Museum,
1300 South Lake Shore Drive,
Chicago, Illinois 60605
Tel: (001) 312 322 0304
Fax: (001) 312 322 2257
www.adlerplanetarium.org
(Large collection of early instruments, especially timekeeping and astronomy)

Dittrick Museum of Medical History,
11000 Euclid Ave,
Cleveland, Ohio 44106
Tel: (001) 216 368 3648
Fax: (001) 216 368 0165
www.ohwy.com/OH/d/ditmusmh.htm

Edison National Historic Site,
Main St and Lakeside Ave,
West Orange, New Jersey 07052
Tel: (001) 973 736 0550
Fax: (001) 973 736 8496
www.nps.gov/edis
(Edison's "invention factory" – a wonderful place to visit. Most factory buildings are gone, but his original library and labroratory remain.)

George Eastman House,
International Museum of
Photography and Film,
900 East Ave,
Rochester, New York 14607
Tel: (001) 716 271 3361
Fax: (001) 716 271 3970
www.eastman.org

Harvard University Science Center,
1 Oxford St,
Cambridge, Massachusetts 02138
Tel: (001) 617 495 2779
www.peabody.harvard.edu/museum_scientific.html
(An important collection of scientific instruments, especially good quality and early pieces, both European and American)

Henry Ford Museum and
Greenfield Village,
20900 Oakwood Boulevard,
Dearborn, Michigan 48124
Tel: (001) 313 271 1620
Fax: (001) 313 982 6244
www.hfmgv.org

Museum of Science and Industry,
57th St and Lake Shore Drive,
Chicago, Illinois 60637-2093
Tel: (001) 773 684 1414
Fax: (001) 773 684 7141
www.msichicago.org

National Museum of American History,
Smithsonian Institute,
14th St and Constitution Ave NW,
Washington DC 20560
Tel: (001) 202 357 2700
www.americanhistory.si.edu
(A wonderful collection of all forms of US science & technology; strong on photography, commu-nications, transport and maritime).

Australia
Powerhouse Museum of
    Applied Arts and Sciences,
500 Harris St,
Ultimo,
Sydney,
New South Wales 2007
Tel: (0061) 2 9217 0111
Fax: (0061) 2 9211 0333
www.phm.gov.au

Canada
National Museum of Science
    and Technology Corporation,
P.O. Box 9724,
Ottawa Station T,
Ottawa,
Ontario K1G 5A3
Tel: (001) 613 991 3044
Fax: (001) 613 990 3654
www.nmstc.ca

Germany
Deutsches Museum,
Postfach,
Munich D-80306
Tel: (0049) 89 2179-1
Fax: (0049) 89 2179-324
www.deutsches-museum.de
(The national museum, with a large
collection of all types of science &
technology instruments)

The Netherlands
Museum Boerhaave,
Lange St,
Agnietenstraat 10,
2312 WC Leiden
Tel: (0031) 71 521 4224
Fax: (0031) 71 512 0344
www.museumboerhaave.nl
(A major museum with an
important collection of scientific
instruments).

The National Museum from
    Musical Clock to Street Organ
    (Mech Mus Museum),
Buurkerkhof 100,
Utrecht 3511 KC
(A collection of musical
instruments of all shapes
and sizes)

CLUBS AND SOCIETIES
The City of London Phonograph
    and Gramophone Society,
Mrs Suzanne Coleman
(Membership Secretary)
51 Brockhurst Rd,
Chesham, Bucks HP5 3JB
England
www.musicweb.force9.co.uk/music
/frms/clpgs.htm
(Founded 1919, subscription £15 UK
& Europe, $28.50 USA, £17 elsewhere)

Magic Lantern Society of the
    United States and Canada,
Secretary/Treasurer Sharon Koch,
13540 Seabeck Hwy NW,
Seabeck,
Washington 98380 USA
www.magiclanternsociety.org
(Founded 1977, subscription $25)

Musical Box Society International,
Box 297,
Marietta,
Ohio 45750
USA
Fax: (001) 304 428 5587
www.mbsi.org
(Founded 1949, subscription $45
USA, $55 in Canada and Mexico,
$70 elsewhere)

Photographic Collectors Club
    of Great Britain,
Membership Office,
Church St Industrial Estate,
Haydon Bridge, Hexham,
Northumberland NE47 6JG
England
Tel/Fax: (0044) 1920 821611
www.pccgb.org
(Founded 1977, subscription £22 UK
and EU countries, £30 elsewhere)

Photographic Historical Society
    of New England,
PO Box 189,
West Newton Station,
Boston, Massachusetts 02165
USA
Tel: (001) 617 731 6603
Fax: (001) 617 277 7878

*Rittenhouse: Journal of the American
Scientific Instrument Enterprise,*
PO Box 151,
Hastings-on-Hudson,
New York 10706
USA
(not a club as such, but a very
good and informative journal)

Scientific Instrument Society,
31 Stanford in the Vale,
Faringdon,
Oxon SN7 8LH
England
www.sis.org.uk
(Founded 1983, subscription £35
in UK, £40 elsewhere)

AUCTION HOUSES

United Kingdom
Christie's South Kensington,
85 Old Brompton Road,
London SW7 3LD
Tel: (0044) 20 7581 7611
Fax: (0044) 20 7321 3321
www.christies.com

Sotheby's,
34–5 New Bond St,
London W1A 2AA
Tel: (0044) 20 7293 5000
Fax: (0044) 20 7293 5989
www.sothebys.com

United States of America
Skinner Inc. Auctioneers and
    Appraisers of Fine Art,
357 Main St,
Bolton,
Massachusetts 01740
Tel (001) 978 779 6241
Fax: (001) 978 779 5144
www. skinnerinc.com

and

The Heritage on the Garden,
63 Park Plaza,
Boston,
Massachusetts 02116
Te:l (001) 617 350 5400
Fax: (001) 617 350 5429

Index

Page numbers in **bold** refer
to main entries; those in *italic*
refer to illustrations

abacus 118–19, *119*
accordions, automatic *108*, 109
Adams, Dudley 46
Adams, George 18, 23, 46
adding machines 118–19, *118*,
  121–2, *121*
advertising 52–3, 135, *135*, 141, *141*
Agfa 97
agriculturist's microscopes *64*, 65
Ainsworth, W. & Sons 74
albums, photo 99
Allbrit planimeters *33*
Allwin *9*, *133*
Alpa 97
Alpina 124, *124*
American Civil War 84–5,
  101, 131
American Novelty Co. *143*
American Telephone and Telegraph
  Company 86
amputation sets 127, *127*,
  128, 131
analytical beam balances 74, *74*
Andrews, A.H. *46*
anemometers 53, *53*
aneroid barometers 50, 51–2, *51*
angle-measuring levels *76*, 77
Ansonia Clock Co. *19*
Apple computers 125, 147
apple corers 138, *138*
aquatic microscopes 63–4, *63*
Archer, Frederick Scott 95
architect's drawing instruments *35*
Aristophanes 10
armillary spheres 48, 49, *49*
Armstrong, Thomas & Brothers *35*
artificial horizon, sextants
  40–1, *40*
astronomy:
  armillary spheres 48, *49*
  celestial globes 44, 45, *46*, 47
  clocks 18, 20
  orreries 48–9
  telescopes 58–9, *58*
auctions 7, **8**, 9
Augsburg 16, 18
Automatic Adding Machine
  Manufacturers *118*
automatic musical instruments 108

back staff 36–7, *37*, 38, 39
Bacon, Roger 54
bacteria 60, 65
Baird, John Logie 91
balances 71, 72–6, *72–5*, *148*
Banfield of Brighton *75*
banjo barometers 45, 51

Bardin of London *47*
Barmack, Oskar 96–7
barometers 44, *44*, 45, **50–2**,
  50–2, 53, *53*
barrel organs 106, 108, *108*
barrel pianos 106
Bate, R.B. *63*
Batson sketching case *32*, 33
batteries 134–5, *134*
Bausch, E. & J. *66*
Bausch & Lomb *64*, *67*, 69, *77*
Bavaria 16, *18*
beam balances 73, *73–5*, *74–5*
Beaulieu 23
Beck, Joseph 68
Beck, Richard 68
Beck Company 60, *61*
Beckers *100*
Beckmann Co. *27*
Belgium, surveying instruments 23
Bell, Alexander Graham 86, *86*, 87,
  114, 116
Bell, Chichester 114
Bell Laboratoriess 91
Bell Telephone Company 86
bellows *140*, 141
bells, electric *135*
Ben Gershon, Levi 36
Berg of Stockholm *49*
Beringer, D. *17*
Berliner, Emile 13, 114–15, 116
Berning Co. *96*
Bett *48*
Billon-Haller *111*
binnacles 43
binocular microscopes 68, *68*
binoculars 55, 59, *59*
Biograph and Mutoscope
  Company 104
bioscopes 104
Biram *53*
Bird, John 40
birds, clockwork 106, *107*, *108*,
  109
blood-letting sets 129, *129*
Bloud, Charles *15*, 18
Blunt & Co *21*
Board of Longitude 23, 40
Boericke and Tafel *127*
Bontems *107*
Boston 48
Bostwick, J.H. *16*
Boulanger, A.A. 59
Box Brownie cameras *92*, 96, 97
box cameras 11
Brady, Matthew 95, 101
brass, care of 148
Breithaupt, F.W. & Sohn 23
Brewster, Sir David 98, 100
Brewster-pattern stereoscopic
  viewers *100*

British Broadcasting Company
  (BBC) 90, 91
Broadhurst, Clarkson Co. 55
Browning, John *69*
Bruder, W. & Son 108, *108*
Brunel, Isambard Kingdom 32
Brunsviga 122, *122*
bubble levels, theodolites 30
bubble sextants 41
Burroughs, William S. 122
Burt, William Austin 30–1
butter churns *138*, 139
Butterfield of Paris *14*, 16–17
"butterstamp" telephones *86*, 87
buying antiques **8–9**

cabinets:
  dental 130, *130*
  slide 68
Cadwell, J.W. *100*
calculating machines **118–24**,
  118–24, 147
calotypes 93, 94
camera obscura 11, 92, 93
cameras 11–12, *11*, **92–7**,
  92–7, 105
candles, timekeeping 14
candy makers 138, *138*
Canon 97
capacity measures 72, 77
Cape Verde islands 42
carbon arc lamps 12, 105, *105*
care and restoration **148**
Cary, William 23, 46
Cary of London *6*
Cary-pattern naturalist's
  microscopes 64, 65
catalogues, auctions 8
celestial globes 44, 45, *46*, 47, 49
Celsius, Anders 52
Celsius scale, thermometers 52
Centennial Exposition, Philadelphia
  (1876) *82*, 83
Centigrade scale, thermometers 52
Central Scientific Company *134*
Charrière à Paris *127*, *129*
chartometers 34
Chevalier 68
Chicago Telephone Supply
  Company *86*
chronometers 14, 15, *15*, **20–1**,
  20–1, 39, *39*
circuits, electrical 13
Clark, Alvan & Sons 54, 55, 58,
  58, 59
cleaning collectables 148
cleaning equipment **139**, *139*
clepsydras 14–15
clocks 14, 15, 16, 18, 21
clockwork birds 106, *107*, *108*, 109
clubs, collecting 7–8

Coddington magnifiers *63*, 64
coffee grinders 138, *138*
coin balances 71
coin-operated machines 133, *133*,
   142–3, *142–3*
coins 7
collections, building **9**
collectors' clubs 7–8
collodion process, photography 95
Columbia *107*, 114, *114*, 115,
   116–17, *116*
Columbus, Christopher 36, 42, 44
communication **78–91**, *78–91*
compass microscopes 63, *63*
compass roses 42
compasses:
   drawing instruments 33,
      34, *34–5*
   marine compasses **42–3**, *42–3*
   surveying instruments 23,
      24–5, *24–5*, 146
compound microscopes 60–1, *60*,
   64, **66–9**, *66–9*
Comptometers 122
computers 79, 83, *83*, 118, **124–5**,
   124–5, 147
Computing Scale Company 75
condition 8
Cook, Captain James 41
Cooke 84
Cooke, T. & Sons 23
Cooke, Troughton & Simms 29
Cooke's postal scales 71, *71*, *148*
cooking **138–9**, *138–9*
Copernicus, Nicolaus 46, 54–5
copying machines *80*, 81
Crandall 83
Crates 44
Crocker-Wheeler *134*
cross staffs 36, *36*
Ctesibius of Alexandria 15
Culpeper, Edmund 66–7
Culpeper-pattern compound
   microscopes 66–7, *66*
Currier & Simpson 53
Cuthbert, John *56*, 57
cylinder musical boxes 107, *107*,
   110–11, *110–11*

Daguerre, Louis Jacques Mandé
   92, 93, 94
daguerreotypes 93, 94, 101
Danfrie, Philippe 25
Davis, John 36–7, *37*
Davis Level & Tool Co. *76*
Davis quadrant 37
Davy, Sir Humphry 140
Dayton scales 75, *75*
dealers 7, **8**
Dellatour & Co. 55
dentistry 130, *130*
"detective cameras" 95
Dieppe 16
disc musical boxes 107, **112–13**,
   112–13

displaying collectables **149**, *149*
dividers 33, 34, *34*
dividing engines 23
Dodge Scale Co. *74*, 75
Dollond 18, 23
Dollond, John 55, 56, 67
domestic technology **132–41**,
   132–41
doublet lenses, microscopes 64
drainage levels 26, *26–7*
Drake, Sir Francis 36
draughtsmen's pens 35
drawing instruments **32–5**, *32–5*
Drown, Solomon Junior *31*
dumpy levels 27, *27*
Durable Phonograph Company
   117, *117*
Duren, H. *38*, *39*
dust counters 77, *77*
Dutch Estates General 54
Dutch navy 39

East India Company 40
Eastman, George 95–6, 102
Eastman Kodak *92*, 96
Eaton, Wyatt *59*
Eckert, J. Presper 124, *124*, 125,
   125
Edison, Thomas 89, **115**,
   115, 145
   kinetoscopes 104, 105, *105*
   light bulbs 6, 135, 140, *140*
   phonographs 12, 13, 114,
      114–15, 115, 116
   telegraph 85, *85*
Edison electric pens 81, *81*
Edison/General Electric *137*
Edison Phonograph Company 68
Egli, Hans W. *122*
Egypt, sundials 16
Einson-Freeman *41*
Ekco 91
electricity 13, *13*, 133, **134–5**,
   134–5, 139, 140
electro-medical machines 130–1,
   131
Elgin National Watch Co. *21*
Elliot *85*
Elliot & Sons *34*
Elliott Brothers 23
Ellis, John 63
Ellis-pattern aquatic microscopes
   63–4, *63*
enemas 131
English quadrant 37
ENIAC 9, 124, 125, *125*
Enlightenment 80, 134
Enterprise Manufacturing Co. *138*
Ericsson *87*
Ernemann of Dresden *104*
Everitt, Percival 142, 143
Expo Camera Company 95
Expressif *110*, 111

Fada *90*

Fahrenheit, Gabriel 52
Fahrenheit scale, thermometers 52
fakes **146**, *146*
fans *133*, *140–1*, 141
Faraday, Michael 6, 13
Fay-Sholes typewriters 82, *82*
Federal *79*, *90*
Felt, Dorr E. 122
Fenton, Roger 95
Fey, Charles 143
Field, G. *67*
Field, R. & Son *64*
film 96, 102, 104, 105
Fitz globes *47*
flash-point testers 77, *77*
flea glasses 62
Fleming, John 89
Flinders, Commander Matthew 43
Flinders bars 43
fluting irons 133, *133*
Folmer & Schwing Company 96
Fortin 74
Fortin-pattern barometers *50*, 51
Fox Talbot, William Henry 92, 93,
   94
France:
   armillary spheres *49*
   medical instruments *127*,
      129, 131
   microscopes *62*, *65*, 68, *68*
   moving pictures *102*
   sundials *16*, *19*
   surveying instruments *22*,
      23, 25, *25*, *26*, 29
   telescopes 58, *58*
Franklin *79*
Franklin, Benjamin 13
French Revolution 70, 72
future collectables **147**, *147*

Gale, James *42*
Galen 126
Galileo Galilei 52, 54, 55, 60
gaming machines 9, *133*, 143
garden sundials 16, *16*, 17, 19
Garrison, John 40
Gayetty 131, *131*
General Electric 90
generators *134*
geography **44–9**, *44–9*
George V, King of England 79
Germany:
   barometers *51*
   calculating machines 122,
      122, 124, *124*
   chronometers *20*
   magic lanterns 103, *103*
   mechanical music *106*,
      108, 112
   microscopes 68–9
   photography 96
   sundials 17, *18*
   surveying instruments 23, *27*
   telescopes 57, 58
Gilbert, William 134

gimbals, marine compasses *42, 43, 43*
Ginn & Heath *47*
globes 44–5, *45*, **46–8**, *46–8, 49, 146*
gnomon, sundials 14, 16, 17
Godfrey, Thomas 38
Goldstine, Herman *125*
Gould-pattern naturalist's microscopes 64, *64*
Graham, George 48, 49
gramophones 12, *12*, 13, 107, 114–15, **116–17**, *116–17*, 146, 148, 149
Grandjean, H. *137*
graphometers 23, 25, *25*
graphophones *107*, 114, 116
Graphotype typesetting machines 81, *81*
Gravatt, William 27
Greece, ancient 48, 134
Green, Henry J. *50*
Griesbaum *108*
Grimm, Natalis & Co. *122*
Grover & Baker *132*
gunner's levels 26, *26*
Gurley, W. & L.E. 30, *30, 31, 32*, 33
Gutenberg, Johann 78, 80

Hadley, John 38
Hadley quadrant 38
half-tone printing 96
Hall Type Writer 82, *82*
Hamilton Watch Co. *21, 39*
hand telescopes 55, *55*
Harris & Company *44*
Harrison 74
Harrison, John 14, 20–1, 36
Hartsoeker, Nicolaas 63
heating **140–1**
Hero of Alexandria 22, 142
Hertz, Heinrich 88
Hewett *72*
Hicks, John Joseph 50
Hill, George *144*, 145
Hill, Nathaniel 46
HMV 116
Holmes, Oliver Wendell *93*, 100–1
Hooke, Robert 51
Hotpoint *139*
hourglasses 14
household technology **132–41**, *132–41*
humidity, hygrometers 53
Hurd, Nathaniel 71
Huygens, Christiaan 56
hygrodeliks *51*, 53
hygrometers 53

IBM 83, 125
Ihagee 97
Ikonograph Company *93*
Indonesia 42

Industrial Revolution 6, 7, 22, 32, 44, 77, 120
interest calculators 120–1, *120*
Internet **8–9**, 147
Iraq 54, 60
irons 137, *137*
Italy:
    microscopes 66
    spectacles 54
    sundials *16, 18*
    viewers 99, *99*

Janzoons, Zacharias 54
Java 102
Jefferson, Thomas 72
jellygraphs 81
Jennings 143, *143*
Jerome, Chauncey 18
Jones, A.W. & S. *23*
Jones, Thomas 23
Jones, W. & S. *28*
Josling, Gilman *45*, 47
Judson, Joshua S. *144*

kaleidoscopes 92, 98, *98*, 146
Kalliope *112*, 113
Kassel 23
Kelvin scale, thermometers 52
Kennard, P. *24*
Keuffel & Esser *40, 43*, 121, *121, 124*
Keystone 101
Kilburn, Tom 124–5
kinetoscopes 104, 105, *105*
King, Benjamin *37*
Kinnear-pattern cameras 94, *94*
kinora viewers *103*, 105
Knox, Mrs *133*
Koch, Robert 65
Kodak 96, 105
Koller/GE *91*

Lanfelder, Henry 113
Langenheim brothers 94
Langlois, Claude 23, 34
latitude 20, 36, 46
Lauer *99*
laundry **137**, *137*
lavatory paper 131, *131*
leech jars 128–9
Leeuwenhoek, Antony van 60, 62, 63, 65
Leica 96–7, *97*
Leitz 68–9, 97
Lemaire, J.P. 59
Lenoir, Etienne 23
lenses 10–11, *11*
    cameras 11, 97
    microscopes 60–1, 62, 66, 67
    projectors 12
    telescopes 54, 55, 56
Lentz, Charles & Son *128, 129*
Leonardo da Vinci 32
levels, surveying 23, **26–7**, *26–7*
library telescopes 57–8, *57*

light, pinhole cameras 11, *11*
lighting 135, **140**, *140–1*
lightning 13
limelight 102–3
Lincoln, Abraham 85
Lippershey, Hans 54
liquid compasses *42*, 43
Lister, John Joseph 67–8
Lister, Joseph 127
Liston, Robert 128, 131
lithophanes 92, 98–9, *98*
lithotrites 129, *129*
Lloyd, Andrew *51*
Lochmann, Paul 112
London 46, 60, 66, 106, 108
longitude 20–1, 36, 38, 39, 40, 41, 46
Loring, Josiah *45, 46*, 47
Loring & Churchill *25*
Lovell Manufacturing Co. *137*
Luftwaffen Robot cameras *96*
Lumière, Auguste and Louis 104
Luminaires 141, *141*
lunar method, calculating longitude 40, 41
Lynch *27*

McCoy Golf Recorders 123, *123*
magic lanterns 102–3, *102–3*, 105
magnetic compasses 42
magnetic detectors *88*, 89
magnifiers *61–3*, 62, 65
mangles 137, *137*
manuscript globes 46
map-making 10
Marconi, Guglielmo 6, 88–9, *88*
Marconi EMI 91
marine compasses **42–3**, *42–3*
marine telescopes 57, *57*
Marshall, John 66
Martin, Benjamin 49, 67
Mauchly, John 124, 125
maximum/minimum thermometers *45*, 52
Maxwell, James Clerk 88
measuring instruments 22, **70–7**, *70–7*
medicine **126–31**, *126–31*
medicine chests 127, *127*
Megalethoscopes 99, *99*
Merrill, P. *24*
Merrill, Robert *38*
meteorology *44–5*, **45**, **50–3**, *50–3*
micrograph miniature microscopes *62*
micrometer scales *74*, 75
micrometers *69*, 76, *76*
microscopes **60–9**, *60–9*, 98
Mill, Henry 82
Millionaire calculators *122*, 123
Mills, H.S. *142*, 143
Mills, Thomas & Brother *138*
miners' compasses 25
MiniDiscs 147, *147*
Mira 113

models **144–5**, *144–5*
Molleneux of London *20*
Morin, H. *29*
Morse, Samuel 84, 94
Morse code 84, 85, *85*, 88
motors, electric *134*, 135
mousetraps *139*
movie cameras 105
moving pictures 12, 92, *93*, **102–5**, *102–5*
Moxton, John 46
Mozart, Wolfgang Amadeus 106
music, mechanical **106–17**, *106–17*, 147
musical boxes 8, 106, *106–7*, 107, **110–13**, *110–13*, 146
mutoscopes 104
Muybridge, Eadweard 104

Nachet et Fils 68, *68*
National Broadcasting Company (NBC) 90
National Type Writer Company *82*
naturalist's microscopes 64–5, *64*
navigation 14, 20–1, **36–43**, *36–43*
Neckham, Alexander 42
Negretti & Zambra 23, *45*, 50, *52*
Nesbitt, John *71*
Netherlands, telescopes 54
New York 48
New Zealand 41
Newton, Isaac 55, 56
Newton, John 46
nibs 35
Nicole Frères *107*, 110, *110*
Niépce, Joseph 92–3
Nikon 97, *97*
Nineveh 54
noonday cannon sundials *15*
Norman, Matthew *15*
Norris & Campbell *40*
North Pole 43
novitascopes *104*
Nuremberg 16
Nuremberg-pattern compound microscopes *66*

octants 37, **38–9**, *38–9*, 40
Ogden of Boston *64, 69*
opisometers 34
optical toys 92, **98–9**, *98–9*, 102–3
optics 10–11, 54
organettes 108–9
Orpheus *109*
orreries 48–9
Orrery, Charles Boyle, 4th Earl of 48
Otis *119*
Otto, F.G. *112*, 113
Oughtred, William 119

Pace 143, *143*
Paillard *110*, 111, *111*
paintings 7
Palmer, Aaron *120*

pantographs 34
parallel rulers 33
Paris 54
Pascal, Blaise 119
Pasteur, Louis 65, 127
patent models 144, 145
Pathé 105
pedometers *22*
pens 35
People's Typewriter *83*
Pepys, Samuel 7
pharmacists' balances 74, *74*
phenakistoscopes 102, 104
Philco *91*
phlebotomy 128
phonographs 12, *12*, 106, 107, *107*, **114–15**, *114–15*, *146*, 148, 149
photochemistry 11–12
photography 11–12, **92–7**, *92–7*, 99, **104–5**
phrenology 130, *130*
pianos, automatic 106, 108, 109, *109*
pinhole cameras 11, *11*
Pistor & Martins *57*
planetariums 49
planimeters 33, *33*
Plank, Ernst 103, *103*
plate cameras 95–6, 97
Plateau, Joseph 102
plumb lines 22
Plumbe, John 94
pneumatic musical instruments **108–9**, *108*
pocket barometers 52, *52*
pocket globes 47
pocket microscopes 65
Polyphon *106*, 112, 113
Ponti, Carlo *99*
postal scales 71, *71*, 73, *73, 148*
Powell, Hugh 68
Powell & Leland 68
praxinoscope theatres *102*
Preece, William 88
printing 78, **80–1**, *80–1*
projectors *11*, 12, 92, *93*, 102–3, 105
proportional compasses 33–4, *33*
protractors 32, 33
psychrometers 53
Ptolemy of Alexandria 46, 54

quadrants 24–5, *24*
Queen & Co. *53*, 68

Radio Corporation of America (RCA) 89, 90
radios 78–9, *79*, **88–91**, *88–91*
Ramsden, Jesse 23, 27, 28, 40, *57*, 74
Rand McNally 48
Ransom & Randolph Co. *130*
RCA Victor 117, *117*
Read, Samuel *72*

recording equipment 12–13, *12*
reflecting telescopes 55, *56*
refracting telescopes 55, 56, *58*
Regina *109*, 112, 113, *113*
regulators 21, *21*
Renaissance 44, 80
reproductions **146**, *146*
restoration **148**
Reynauld, Emile *102*
Riley, C.M. *120*
Ritchie, E.S. *42*, *43*
Rittenhouse Brothers 23
Roman Catholic Church 55
Romans 16, 70
Ross, Andrew 68
Ross, Thomas & Company *94*
Ross-pattern compound microscopes *67*
Round valves 89
Rowley, John 48
Rowsells-patent stereographoscopes *101*
Royal Microscopic Society 69
Royal Society 6, 38, 63, 67, 93
rulers 32, 33, 70, 77
Russell, J. & Co. 131, *131*

Sarnoff, David 89, 90
Savage *73*
scales 70, 71, **72–7**, *73–7*, 143, *143*
Schawlow, Dr Arthur 147, *147*
Scheiner, Christoph 34
Schenk, W. & Co. 23, *28*
Schoner & Carrette 103
Schopper, Louis *76*
scioptic balls 92, 98, *98*
Scott, Captain Robert 29
screw-barrel microscopes 63
sectors 34, 35
semicircumferentors 23, 24, *24*, 25
set squares 32, 33
sewing machines 8, 132, *132*, **136–7**, *136*
sextants 23, 37, **40–1**, *40–1*
Sherwood, C.W. *144*
Sholes, Christopher 82, *82*, 83
Sholes & Glidden 81, *82*, 83
Shoo-Fly fans *140*, 141
shop scales 75–6, *75*
Short, James 55, 56
Siemens *85*
Siemens, Werner 135
Sierra Leone 42
simple microscopes 60, 61, 62–5, *62–5*
Singer 136
Sisson, Jonathan 23, 27, 28
slide cabinets *68*
slide rules 119, *119*, 121, *124*
slides, microscopes 69
Smith, James 68
Smith & Beck *61*
Society of Arts *67*
solar compasses 30–1, *30*

Sony *147*
sound recording 12–13, *12*
Spalding Adding Machine 121, *121*
specimen magnifiers *61*, *62*
spectacles 54
spectroscopes *69*
Spencer 69
Spencer, Browning & Co. *50*
Spencer, Browning & Rust *40*, *57*
sphygmographs *129*, 130
spirit levels 53
Spitz, Ludwig & Co. *122*
Stackpole and Brother *29*
Stanley 121, 146
Stanley, W.F. 23
Star Washing Machine *137*
starfinders, telescopes 58–9, *58*
Stark, A.D. *119*
steelyards *72*, 73
Stella 113
stencils 81
stereoscopes 92, *93*, **100–1**, *100–1, 143*
stethoscopes 129–30
Steward, J.H. 23
stick barometers *44*, 45, 50–1, *50*
Stockert of Bavaria *18*
storing collectables 148
stringed musical instruments **108–9**, *109*
Stromberg-Carlson 78
Strowger, Almon 86–7
styluses, phonographs and gramophones 12–13, *12*
sundials 14, *14–19*, 15, **16–19**, 20, *146*
surgery 126–7, *126–9*, 128
surveying 10, **22–35**, *22–35*
Swan, Joseph 135, 140
Swift, Mrs *59*
Swift, Captain W.C.N. 59
Switzerland:
    calculating machines 122, *122*, 123
    musical boxes 110
    surveying instruments 23, *28, 35*
Symphonion 112, *112*, 113, *113*
sympioesometers 52

Taft & Schwane *99*
Tainter, Charles 114
tape measures 70
Taylor of Rochester *51*, 77, *77*
tea balances 74
telegraphy 78, **84–5**, *84–5*, 107
telephones 78, *78*, 79, **86–7**, *86–7*, 107
telescopes **54–9**, *54–9*
    levels 27, *27*
    theodolites 30
television 79, **91**, *91*

telluriums 49, *49*
Temple, J.H. 50, *50*
terrestrial globes 44–5, *45*, **46–8**, *46–8*, 49
Texas Instruments 147
Thatcher's calculators 121, *121*
Thaxter, S. & Son *40*, 58, *58*
theodolites 10, *10*, 22, 23, 24, **28–31**, *28–31*, 146
thermometers 45, *45*, 50, *51*, 52–3, *53*
Thompson & Co. *105*
TIM mechanical calculators 122, *122*
timekeeping **14–21**, *14–21*
timepieces 14
toasters 139, *139*
Tompion, Thomas 48, 49
Torricelli, Evangelista 50
toys:
    calculators 123, *123*
    optical toys 92, **98–9**, *98–9*, 102–3
trepanning 128, *128*
triangular dividers 34, *34*
tripod telescopes 55
Tromner, Henry 74, *74*
Troughton 23
Troughton, Edward 40
Troughton & Simms *30*, 33
Turney, Eugene T. Co. *89*
typesetting machines 81, *81*
typewriters 78, 79, *79*, 82–3, *82–3*

Underwood & Underwood 101
United States of America:
    barometers *50*
    calculating machines *118*, *120–1*, 121, 122, *123*
    chronometers *21*
    clocks 18
    coin-operated machines 142, *143*
    computers 124–5, *124–5*
    globes 46–7, 47, 48, *48*
    household technology *133*, *137–9*, 138–9, 140–1
    mechanical music 108–9, *109*, 111, 112, *112*, 113
    medicine *127*
    microscopes *61*, *62*, 68, 69
    moving pictures 104–5, *104–5*
    navigation instruments 37, 38, *38–9*, 41–3
    photography 92–3, 94, *95*, 96
    radios 89–90
    stereoscopic viewers 100–1, *100–1*
    sundials 16, 19, *19*
    surveying instruments 23, *23–7*, 24, *29*, 30–1, *30–1*
    telegraphy 84–5, *84*
    telephones 86–7
    telescopes 55, 58, *58*
    televisions 91
    typewriters 82, *82*, 83

weights and measures 70, 72, *72*, 74–7, *74–7*
Unitron 61
Univac *124*, 125
Universal *139*
US Bureau of Mines 77, *77*
US Patent Office 144, 145

vacuum cleaners 139, *139*
vacuum-pump outfits *6*
values **9**
Vassos, John *117*
vending machines 142, *142*
Vernier, Pierre 29
Victor 90, 115, 116, *116*, *117*
Victoria, Queen of England 100
Vidie, Lucien 51
viewers **98–101**, *98–101*
Vogl, Andreas 18
Voigtländer 59
Volta, Alessandro 134

Waltham Watch Co. *39*
washing machines 137, *137*
Washington, George 128
watches 14, 16
water clocks 14–15
Watkins *27*
Watkins, Carleton A. 101
Watkins, W. *17*
Watt copiers *80*, 81
weather forecasting 44–5, *45*, **50–3**, *50–3*
weights and measures **70–7**, *70–7*
Wells, S.R. & Co. *130*
Western Union *84*, 86
Westinghouse Electric 90, *133*
Weston Electrical Instrument Company *135*
wet-plate process, photography 95
Wheatstone, Sir Charles 84, 100
wheel barometers 50
White 101
Williams, Sir F.C. 124–5
Wilson, G.W. *24*
Wilson, James 63
Wilson, Woodrow 90
wireless **88–9**, *88–9*
Wireless Telegraph Co. *88*
Wiseman, Richard 126–7, *126*
Wollaston, William 64
wooden theodolites **31**, *31*
wool weights *70*
World War II 41, 124
wringers 137, *137*

Y-levels 27
yardsticks 77
yarn counters 71, *71*

Zeiss 68–9
zithers, automatic 109, *109*
zoetropes 102
Zuleger of Leipzig *108*

Acknowledgments

The author would like to thank Robert Maher for all his assistance and support throughout the project. The publishers would also like to give special thanks to Christopher Proudfoot for his expert assistance and advice, and to Yvonne and Norman Bain and Dr Brian J. Bain for their help with the book.

PHOTOGRAPHIC CREDITS

All photographs are reproduced courtesy of **Skinners, Auctioneers and Appraisers of Antiques and Fine Art, Bolton, Massachusetts,** with the exception of the following:

Auction Team Köln/Breker: 23 top, 73 right, 80 left, 87 left; **Christie's Images:** 17 right, 70, 85 left, 88 right, 89 bottom left, 92, 94 left, 94 right, 97 right, 102 left, 102 right, 104 right; **Jim Kreuzer:** 84 left; **Octopus Publishing Group Ltd:** 2, 34 left, 34 centre, 34 right, 35 left, 35 right, 36; **Octopus Publishing Group Ltd/Premier Photography:** 16 right, 33 top right, 65 left, 66 left, 71 top left, 148 bottom left; **Octopus Publishing Group Ltd/Antiquarian Scientist:** 22; **Octopus Publishing Group Ltd/Derek Howard:** 59 left, 63 left; **Octopus Publishing Group Ltd/John Millham:** 32 right, 33 bottom right; **Octopus Publishing Group Ltd/Peter Delehar:** 98 centre; **Octopus Publishing Group Ltd/Richard Twortt:** 45 right, 52 left, 52 top right; **Octopus Publishing Group Ltd/Wallis:** 98 left; **Sony United Kingdom Limited:** 83 right; **Sotheby's Picture Library:** 14, 15 left, 15 right, 95 right.